THE FIFTH AMENDMENT

**Recent Titles in
Contributions in Legal Studies**

THE FIFTH AMENDMENT

A COMPREHENSIVE APPROACH

ALFREDO GARCIA

CONTRIBUTIONS IN LEGAL STUDIES, NUMBER 103

GREENWOOD PRESS
WESTPORT, CONNECTICUT • LONDON

Library of Congress Cataloging-in-Publication Data

Garcia, Alfredo, 1952–
  The Fifth Amendment : a comprehensive approach / by Alfredo Garcia.
     p.   cm.—(Contributions in legal studies, ISSN 0147–1074 ; no. 103)
  Includes bibliographical references and index.
  ISBN 0–313–29685–5 (alk. paper)
  1. United States. Constitution. 5th Amendment.   2. Self-incrimination—United States.
  3. Grand jury—United States.   4. Double jeopardy—United States.   I. Title.   II. Series.
  KF45585th.G37   2002
  345.73′056—dc21   2002023253

British Library Cataloguing in Publication Data is available.

Library of Congress Catalog Card Number: 2002023253
ISBN: 0–313–29685–5
ISSN: 0147–1074

First published in 2002

Greenwood Press, 88 Post Road West, Westport, CT 06881
An imprint of Greenwood Publishing Group, Inc.
www.greenwood.com

Printed in the United States of America

∞™

The paper used in this book complies with the
Permanent Paper Standard issued by the National
Information Standards Organization (Z39.48–1984).

10 9 8 7 6 5 4 3 2 1

Copyright Acknowledgments

The author and publisher gratefully acknowledge permission to use the following material:

From Alfredo Garcia, "The Fifth Amendment: A Comprehensive and Historical Approach,"
29 *University of Toledo Law Review* 209 (1998). Reprinted by permission of *The University of Toledo
Law Review*, Volume 29 (1998).

From Alfredo Garcia, "Is Miranda Dead, Was It Overruled, or Is It Irrelevent?" *St. Thomas Law
Review* 10(3) (Spring, 1998). Reprinted by permission of *The St. Thomas Law Review*.

CONTENTS

PREFACE

Why should anyone attempt to write another book about the Fifth Amendment to the United States Constitution? The amendment conjures images of its most famous clause, which affords criminal defendants the right to invoke the privilege against self-incrimination. Sometimes we forget that the amendment contains two other critical clauses that impact the criminal process: the right to a grand jury indictment for "a capital, or otherwise infamous crime," and the protection from being placed in jeopardy twice for the same offense. I attempt to fill the void by examining, analyzing, and linking these three discrete yet related clauses of the Fifth Amendment. This endeavor attempts to correct the myopia that accompanies discussion of the amendment. This work, however, does not encompass the other two famous clauses in the Fifth Amendment: the due process clause, and the "takings" clause, which prohibits the appropriation of private property for public use "without just compensation."

I begin by looking at the history of the three criminally related clauses embodied in the Fifth Amendment. History informs the ideals behind the clauses, although it is merely a template against which the U.S. Supreme Court interprets and provides its own view of the meaning and scope of the safeguards. The history of the three clauses, however, provides a glimpse of how they are integrally related. In effect, the grand jury, self-incrimination, and double jeopardy clauses represent the beginning, middle, and end of the criminal justice system. This work is organized within the parameters of this framework. It is a work of synthesis and integration in that it attempts to distill commonality rather than disjunction from the three criminal provisions of the Fifth Amendment.

Although the privilege against self-incrimination is a trial-related safeguard, it has been held to apply to the pretrial stage; that is, the point at which the suspect is apprehended and the police seek to extract a confession from him or her. Therefore, after exploring the historical landscape, I examine the privilege against self-incrimination as it has been applied to pretrial confessions in the pre-*Miranda* era. Next, I critique and analyze the famous (or infamous, depending on one's perspective), *Miranda* case and doctrine that accompanied it. Concluding with the grand jury and double jeopardy clauses, the book takes a dim perspective of the interpretive gloss the Supreme Court has put on those provisions. In a brief epilogue, I trace the tortuous historical path the three criminal provisions of the Fifth Amendment have undergone as the Supreme Court has construed and interpreted their reach.

I have incurred numerous debts during the course of completing this work. Chapter 3 originally appeared in the *St. Thomas University Law Review*, and chapter 1 in the *University of Toledo Law Review*. I thank those publications for allowing me to include those articles, with modifications and additions, in this work. Deans Daniel Morrissey and John Makdisi furnished generous financial assistance and encouragement. Several former students provided generous research assistance: Cheryl Barnes, Pascale Chancy, Frank De Ciutiis, and Kathleen Phillips. Finally, this book would not have reached fruition without the emotional and motivational support of my wife, Cindy, and my deceased mother, Rosalina, who always prodded me to "keep on writing."

INTRODUCTION

The Fifth Amendment, as currently understood and interpreted, is largely a modern artifact. Identified with the right against self-incrimination, the amendment is viewed as a vital pretrial- and trial-related right that protects both the criminal suspect and the defendant. This conception represents an incomplete version of the amendment. Often forgotten are the other two criminal clauses embodied in the text: the right to a grand jury indictment for a serious crime and the freedom from double jeopardy for the same offense.[1] Remarkably, this partial view of the amendment is reflected not only in public discourse but also in scholarly works. Perhaps the most prominent example of this phenomenon is Leonard Levy's prize-winning work, *Origins of the Fifth Amendment*,[2] which is a historical examination of the privilege against self-incrimination.

Are the three criminal provisions of the Fifth Amendment distinct and analytically discrete, or do they have common threads binding them? This book seeks to answer that question and does so in the affirmative. Underlying these clauses is the axiom that the government must not overpower the individual in the criminal process. Not only must the government prove its case without necessarily relying on or extracting a confession from the accused (i.e., the privilege against self-incrimination), it must also develop its case independent of the accused's testimony by adducing proof to a body of independent citizens (i.e., the right to a grand jury indictment or presentment).

Finally, the government must afford the defendant finality with respect to his or her criminal liability (i.e., protection from double jeopardy).

Approaching the amendment from this perspective risks the objection of reading the Constitution by *hyper*-integration rather than *dis*-integration.[3] Although one must guard against these two "interpretive fallacies," the argument for reading the three criminal clauses of the Fifth Amendment's text as integrated parts rather than disjointed entities is compelling. From the starting point of the criminal process through its finality, the three provisions connect the three major phases of a criminal investigation and prosecution: the initial part (a grand jury), the trial phase (the right against self-incrimination), and the final stage (the protection from double jeopardy). The right to a grand jury review and the privilege against self-incrimination are intextricably linked; the double jeopardy clause attempts to bring closure to the process and, by implication, protects all the criminal provisions enumerated in the Bill of Rights.

The major theme of this book is the relationship among these criminal protections. Closely tied to this thesis is the effect of the interaction on the criminal process. If the three clauses serve to protect the defendant from the overwhelming power of the government through all phases of the process, then how well has the modern interpretation of the provisions adhered to this purpose? More important, is the link among the clauses supported by historical developments? Indeed, although history does not weigh conclusively toward connecting the seemingly disparate provisions, recent scholarship suggests that trial-related rights, including the right against self-incrimination, were part of a larger design to provide constitutional protection for "*all rights*."[4]

A historical perspective, therefore, is the starting point for the analysis. To what extent did history shape the development and interpretation of the three provisions outlined in the Fifth Amendment? History provides a framework within which to explore the amendment; the original vision and purpose that prompted the amendment must be set against the interpretive variations it has undergone. Moreover, the premise underlying the three provisions, the check upon the potential abuse of governmental power over the individual, permeated both the colonial and Revolutionary periods.

Beyond the historical record, the practical and conceptual links among the three clauses will be explored as a point of departure for a more detailed treatment of each separate provision. The doctrinal evolution of the self-incrimination clause, for example, provides a fascinating glimpse into the Supreme Court's attempt to give substance to a complex ideal. From the ambiguous due process–voluntariness doctrine to the more concrete rule set out in the *Miranda* case, the right against self-incrimination has bedeviled the Court with hard "value" choices.

Though less prominent than self-incrimination, the grand jury is a venerable institution that has direct ties to that right. Serving investigative and accusatory roles, the institution of a grand jury has undergone tremendous historical changes. The transformation has dramatically altered its role, turning the institution into a prosecution-dominated enterprise rather than an independent "watchdog" mechanism. One must question whether the new role comports with the historical origins and purpose of the institution.

If the grand jury is the starting point of a formal criminal prosecution, the protection from double jeopardy seeks to bring closure to that process. Tackling what has become an interpretive "Sargasso Sea"[5] for the Supreme Court is a formidable undertaking. Nevertheless, such a task is made possible by comparing that interpretation to the provision's history and philosophy. Is the underlying goal of double jeopardy finality for the accused? Or is the overarching theme protection from government oppression? My interpretation is that both theories are part of the same system: that is, both are conceptually linked. More important, double jeopardy is the obverse side of the coin of self-incrimination: it prevents the accused from being "incriminated" twice for the same offense.

The goal of this work is to stimulate thinking about the Fifth Amendment from a more comprehensive outlook than the reigning perspective allows. This approach should provide benefits not only for scholars but also for criminal practitioners engaged in the "rough and tumble" of the courtroom. Although Akhil Amar[6] has produced wonderful scholarship viewing the discrete provisions of the Bill of Rights in a coherent fashion, he has not conjoined the three clauses of the Fifth Amendment that deal with the criminal process. In the unlikely event that the public should encounter this book, it would at least alert them to the "other" two criminal clauses of the Fifth Amendment and the possible ties among the provisions in the amendment. Indeed, a panoramic sweep lends balance in a world marked by increasing microspecialization.

NOTES

1. The Fifth Amendment states: "No person shall be held to answer for a capital, or otherwise infamous crime, unless on a presentment or indictment of a grand jury, except in cases arising in the land or naval forces, or in the militia, when in actual service in time of war or public danger; nor shall any person be subject for the same offense to be twice put in jeopardy of life or limb; nor shall be compelled in any criminal case to be a witness against himself; nor be deprived of life, liberty, or property, without due process of law; nor shall private property be taken for public use, without just compensation."

2. Leonard Levy, ORIGINS OF THE FIFTH AMENDMENT: THE RIGHT AGAINST SELF-INCRIMINATION (2d ed. 1986). Professor Levy cites the text of the amendment in the book but italicizes the self-incrimination clause. *See id.* at 2.

3. LAURENCE H. TRIBE & MICHAEL C. DORF, ON READING THE CONSTITUTION 19–30 (1991).

4. Eben Moglan, *Taking the Fifth: Reconsidering the Origins of the Constitution Privilege against Self-Incrimination*, 92 MICH. L. REV. 1086, 1118 (1994).

5. This is the term used by Justice William Rehnquist in *Albernaz v. United States*, 450 U.S. 333, 343 (1981). He described the Court's double jeopardy decisions as "a veritable Sargasso Sea which could not fail to challenge the most intrepid judicial navigator." *Id.* at 343.

6. Akhil Reed Amar, THE BILL OF RIGHTS: CREATION AND RECONSTRUCTION (1986).

THE FIFTH AMENDMENT: A COMPREHENSIVE APPROACH

The historical roots of the American Bill of Rights derive from two fundamental concepts: liberty and republicanism. These two ideals distinguished eighteenth-century England from its continental national counterparts. Indeed, as Bernard Bailyn tells us, "England prided herself on her success . . . in having established, after the upheavals of the seventeenth century, liberty as the principal goal of a stable and secure constitution."[1] Yet what meaning did these concepts have for eighteenth-century Britons and, most important, for the revolutionary leaders of the American colonies? The answer to this question reveals much about the philosophical underpinnings of the Bill of Rights. More germane to the theme of this work, the reply uncovers how these ideas shaped the provisions of the Fifth Amendment.

To a large degree, both liberty and republicanism are integrally connected. At their root, they are normative constructs designed to achieve a common objective: a check upon unbridled and arbitrary governmental power. In eighteenth-century England, liberty was an "absolute" concept not "subject to political change or redefinition."[2] Britain's unwritten Constitution rested, above all, on the notion of liberty as the hallmark of freedom. Preservation of liberty depended on a balanced government, legitimated through consent by the body politic, who would control the purse strings. Besides these "institutional guarantees," British constitutional theorists listed few individual rights other than the right to be free from arbitrary police power. Arbitrary arrests and imprisonment were feared by eighteenth-century

Britons as the antithesis of liberty. Two specific protections were perceived as vital to liberty: the right to an indictment and a jury trial. Without these rights, liberty would vanish in Great Britain.[3]

If liberty defined the essence of the English constitutional order, republicanism both subsumed it and was its colonial American analogue. The colonists borrowed the concept from the English Commonwealthmen who employed it to stress the antinomy between liberty and authority. We are indebted to Bernard Baylin's path-breaking work, *The Ideological Origins of the American Revolution*,[4] for pointing out how colonial pamphleteers used this classical republican model to emphasize the corrosive effect of capricious power on liberty and to premise the common good "upon a delicate constitutional balance of the one, the few, and the many."[5] In effect, this prescription paralleled the institutional and individual conditions evident in the British conception of liberty as the indispensable element of the English Constitution.

Republican values implied, at root, a disinterested sacrifice of personal gain for the sake of the public weal. Republics, however, were vulnerable because they required supreme virtue. This "civic virtue" rendered such polities "extremely liable to corruption."[6] Consequently, a republic's success depended on the extent to which its leaders possessed the disinterested virtue that insulated them from the evils inherent in the exercise of power.

These contending paradigms of civic virtue and the need to preserve liberty by curbing power were manifested in the "Court" versus "Country" factions in England. The classic and liberal republican models were reflected in America by the opposing Federalist and Jeffersonian camps.[7] Ultimately, the libertarian model dominated the debate over whether a bill of rights had to be embedded in the United States Constitution. Individual rights, especially safeguards against arbitrary power in the criminal process, were part and parcel of both state constitutions and the federal Bill of Rights.

In the colonial "Whig" mind, however, liberty was collective and resided in and was possessed by the people, not the individual. Those who governed were subject to the evil, corrupting influences exerted by power; the governed, on the other hand, were the sole repositories of liberty.[8] The collective nature of liberty posed a potential conflict between the rights of the polity and those of the individual. This conflict was muted, at the time of the American Revolution, because the solution to the revolutionary crisis lay not in emphasizing individual rights as much "as it did in stressing the public rights of the collective people against the supposed privileged interests of their rulers."[9] A vigorous defense of individual rights was not necessary because it was illogical for the repositories of liberty to infringe upon their own possession.[10]

Perhaps this view of liberty helps to explain why a bill of rights was not appended to the federal Constitution in 1787. Ironically, the author of the Bill of Rights, James Madison, saw no need for a catalogue of individual rights. He did not see a bill of rights as being "essential to liberty."[11] Neither, for that matter, did Alexander Hamilton. In providing the most forceful argument against a bill of rights, Hamilton pointed out that because the Constitution placed powerful constraints upon governmental power, it was "in every rational sense and useful purpose, a Bill of Rights."[12] It was only in response to the strident attack of the Antifederalists upon the Constitution, largely premised on the absence of a bill of rights, that Madison yielded to the inevitable and proposed the amendments that became such an inestimable part of our heritage.

Another reason for the lack of a bill of rights in the new federal Constitution was that, by and large, these rights were preserved in state constitutions. Even before such constitutions were enacted, many rights embodied in the federal Bill of Rights were recognized, if imperfectly, in the English "customary" landscape.[13] Colonial charters more specifically enumerated these rights. Indeed, "[b]y the end of the colonial period many of the rights later guaranteed in the Federal Bill of Rights were already expressly safeguarded in charters and enactments."[14] Moreover, as reflected in its most comprehensive form in the Virginia Declaration of 1776, by the time of the Revolution, and in the period immediately following it, state constitutions prominently featured individual rights, thereby putting them on a firm constitutional footing.[15]

Even at the state level, individual rights protected only those members of the new American polity who were not subjugated by the yoke of slavery. As the historian Edmund Morgan has shown, a remarkable paradox existed between the libertarian notions underlying the new constitutional framework and the fact that the authors of the federal Constitution and, eventually, the Bill of Rights were prominent Virginia slaveholders.[16] Morgan offers a compelling explanation for this contradiction. Thomas Jefferson, George Mason, James Madison, George Washington, and James Monroe were zealous republicans precisely because of their status as slaveholders. They knew too well what it meant to be entirely subservient to a master and therefore had a "special appreciation" for freedom.[17] Indeed, "Virginians may have had a special appreciation of the freedom dear to republicans, because they saw every day what life without it could be like."[18]

A similar phenomenon may explain why criminal procedural rights became so vital to the new constitutional structure and particularly to the enactment of the Bill of Rights. Freedom from arbitrary punishment by the sovereign was precious, because the sanctions meted out could infringe seriously upon individual liberty. Rather than viewing the individual criminal protections embedded in state constitutions— and, eventually, in the federal Bill of Rights—from an anachronistic perspective, one must focus on the nature, extent, and scope of criminal punishment in the pre- and immediate post-Revolutionary era.

The link between the range and scope of criminal punishments and constitutional provisions protecting individual rights against encroachments by the sovereign is critical. For the severity of criminal punishments may have influenced the jealous guarding of freedom through constitutional procedural roadblocks on convictions. Given this crucial nexus, a brief excursion into the history of punishment in England and the colonies will yield fruitful dividends.

Punishment in England in the late sixteenth and early seventeenth centuries was swift and severe. It was inextricably tied to the power wielded by royal authority. Indeed, draconian torture was a commonplace remedy to sanction those guilty of crimes. Serious crimes merited death, which came in horrid guises: by decapitation or strangulation, burning or boiling alive, or through crushing the offender by gradually adding weights.[19] For those who committed lesser offenses, the retribution was not as harsh, although the sheer force applied was still severe; the whipping post, pillory, branding iron, stocks, and ducking stool were means employed to "correct wrongdoers."[20]

Power exerted by the sovereign in this fashion generated both a fear and a need for personal security. These conditions were exacerbated by the ability of the king to apply such brute force arbitrarily. Thus, as the historians Oscar and Mary Handlin remind us, every able-bodied man in sixteenth-century England "feared the threat of impressment." Such a prospect meant that the sovereign "could well dispatch anyone to distant regions with little likelihood of return."[21] Power and liberty were thus two sides of the same coin: liberty hinged upon the ability of the individual to shield himself from the power that would eviscerate liberty.[22]

Enforcing the power of the state to sanction individual offenders, moreover, was a public event. Both the deterrent and didactic value of punishment in England in the sixteenth and early seventeenth centuries was reinforced through public imposition of sanctions. Executions were public, and so were the physical devices leveled to sanction less serious crimes. In turn, the public nature of criminal sanctions differentiated this punishment, allegedly imposed justly by the sovereign, from that arbitrarily and capriciously applied by the individual.[23]

Law, of course, played an integral role in securing liberty and applying the force of the state. Justice, freedom, and liberty were mere concomitants of power; that is, a symbiotic relationship existed among the three.[24] To a great extent, law served to legitimate the brute force exercised by the sovereign. Because it reflected the precedent or legislation emanating from royal authority, law was a protection against the whim of the individual. This conception of law was transplanted by the colonists to the shores of America.[25] Thus, law served the function of affording personal security against the draconian criminal sanctions that were part of everyday life in sixteenth- and seventeenth-century England.

The conception of punishment prevailing in England at the turn of the century was carried over to the American colonies. Before the advent of the prison, the penalties imposed in the colonies paralleled those meted out in the mother country. Whippings, the stock, public cages, and banishment were routinely administered. The death penalty was enforced by means of the gallows.[26] As in Britain, punishment was inflicted principally to achieve specific deterrence; this objective benefited the community in which the offense occurred ostensibly by preventing the offender from repeating the crime.[27]

The problem with the colonial justice system, however, was the lack of uniformity in dispensing punishment. Law enforcement agencies were weak and underdeveloped in colonial America. Therefore, the "punitive and coercive aspects of the law bore an unusually heavy burden."[28] If the penalties inflicted failed to deter the criminal, the remaining alternative was execution. For example, in mid-eighteenth-century Massachusetts, a convicted thief received either a fine or a whipping for the first offense, was whipped and assessed triple damages as well as having to sit an hour on the gallows platform with a noose around his neck for the second offense, and was executed on the third offense.[29] In short, the colonial justice system was simultaneously "lenient and harsh."[30]

Other than the repeat offender, however, colonial justice seemed kinder to the criminal suspect than its English counterpart did. This was a function of the tempering effect of the jury in hesitating to convict if it meant that the offender would be executed. Furthermore, the colonies showed hostility to the death penalty by reducing the number of crimes subject to its irrevocable effect; meanwhile, Britain increased the number of crimes punishable by death.[31] A pragmatic reason underlay this trend: the death penalty, as well as other harsh penalties involving the infliction of serious physical harm (maiming, burning, loss of limbs), was costly.[32]

If justice was administered in such an erratic, haphazard, yet sometimes brutal manner, the right to safeguard against such punishment would become increasingly precious. Just as the Founding Fathers knew too well that freedom must be zealously preserved because they saw what pernicious effects slavery had on human beings, they must have subconsciously appreciated the price of liberty in light of the nature, extent, and application of criminal sanctions in colonial America. Although the architects of the federal Bill of Rights were not personally affected by the uneven application of punishment, they must have realized the consequences of being caught up in its dangerous yet erratic web. The preservation of life and liberty, then, was as important as the "pursuit of happiness."

Indeed, a decade before the Declaration of Independence, John Adams reinforced how vulnerable the "people" were to the capricious power exerted by the sovereign. Whether the arbitrary acts of Parliament in enacting onerous taxes or in creating vice-admiralty courts in order to circumvent jury trials, Adams described in graphic terms the utter susceptibility of the "people" to the sheer arbitrary power of the Crown. More important, he emphasized how individuals were defenseless against the coercive power of the state. He noted that the liberty and security of the people ultimately rested upon the legislative and judicial branches and declared the following:

They have no other fortification against wanton, cruel power: no other indemnification, against being ridden like horses, fleeced like sheep, worked like cattle, and fed and clothed like swine and hounds: *No other defence against fines, imprisonments, whipping posts, gibbets, bastinadoes and racks.* [Emphasis added][33]

To put this point in perspective, it is instructive to compare the scheme of criminal penalties in colonial and post-Revolutionary

America with present-day sanctions. Indeed, in common law the Supreme Court recognized that felonies were punishable by, at a minimum, "a total forfeiture of the offender's lands or goods or both."[34] The difference, in terms of punishment, between a felony and a misdemeanor in common law was considerable. Only serious crimes were classified as felonies in common law. In contrast, today the line of demarcation seems to be drawn at any offense punishable by death or imprisonment exceeding one year.[35] Therefore, many crimes classified as felonies today under either state or federal law were misdemeanors in common law.[36]

Liberty and freedom were thus concepts that shaped revolutionary ideology and contributed to the need to define constraints upon the monopoly of force wielded by the state. Not only did the potential excesses of government power warrant safeguarding individual rights; the severity of criminal penalties also magnified the awesome power of the state. Ideological and pragmatic considerations underscored the need for constitutional protections to preserve the individual's right to that most revered possession: freedom from unjust punishment.

The importance attached to these concepts was emphasized by their appearance in the new constitutions enacted by the various states. As Michael Perry observes, when specific rights are embedded in the constitutional framework rather than in statutory provisions, the choice signifies the polity's desire to render exceedingly difficult the disestablishment of those protections by future generations.[37] Consequently, the protections that eventually found their way into the Fifth Amendment of the Federal Bill of Rights must have been of such import as to warrant inclusion not only in state constitutions but also in the new amendments to the federal Constitution.

Indeed, the experience in drafting state bills of rights made the states, as well as Jefferson, acutely aware of the fragility behind constitutional provisions enacted by state legislatures. Because the first state constitutions were drafted and passed by state legislatures, such rights embodied in the documents were vulnerable to the legislature's whim. Jefferson recognized this problem in pointing out that Virginia's constitution was transitory because "the ordinary legislature may alter the constitution itself."[38] In response to this quandary, various state constitutions contained clauses prohibiting the legislatures from tampering with the protections. Ultimately, the problem was obviated through drafting the constitutions in constitutional conventions and by popular ratification. Massachusetts led the way in 1780, followed by New

Hampshire four years later.[39] The distinction was thus drawn between mere legislation and "entrenched rights."[40]

Why were these rights so critical to the new nation? In exploring this question, one must necessarily begin by focusing on the historical antecedents of the privilege against self-incrimination, the right to a grand jury indictment, and the proscription of double jeopardy. How did these safeguards, built into the criminal process, gain such prominence in the colonial mind? Given such an exalted nature, why did these amendments come to be grouped in the Fifth Amendment to the U.S. Constitution? These questions are useful points of departure for divining the extent, scope, and nature of the criminal protections embodied in the amendment.

THE PRIVILEGE AGAINST SELF-INCRIMINATION

We seem to take for granted today the well-known privilege of a person not to be compelled to incriminate him- or herself. Perhaps this stems from the pervasive influence the *Miranda* decision has exercised on television shows and in the media in general. However, the history of the privilege does not bespeak such certitude. Indeed, historians have diverged on the questions of the historical origins and the changing scope of the privilege's application in America. It is critical, therefore, to not only examine the lineage behind the privilege but also to delve into its interpretation and application in colonial and post-Revolutionary America.

Perhaps the best defense for examining the history of the privilege was put forth by Supreme Court Justice Felix Frankfurter, who said that in interpreting the privilege, "a page of history is worth a volume of logic.[41] Herein lies the problem: historians differ on whether the privilege was a product of the English common law or of Roman or canon law. In addition, historians dispute the precise point at which the privilege came to be applied in its modern form.

In his prize-winning book on the Fifth Amendment,[42] Leonard Levy traces the origins of the privilege to the contrasting systems of criminal procedure exemplified by the English common law and the continental system, which was rooted in both Roman civil law and the Inquisition. The common law placed emphasis on the rights and liberties of the individual; on the other hand, the inquisitorial, civil law system stressed "the rack and the *auto-da-fe*."[43] In turn, the continental approach was dominant in English ecclesiastical courts.

It was in the English ecclesiastical courts, Levy contends, that the privilege against self-incrimination was born. The use of the *ex officio* oath by such courts in the seventeenth century prompted the invocation of the privilege. The oath required the parties to swear to answer all questions truthfully. Such a condition confronted criminal defendants with what the modern U.S. Supreme Court has labeled a "cruel trilemma": testify truthfully and risk conviction, refuse to answer and face an inevitable contempt proceeding, or violate the oath by knowingly presenting perjured testimony.[44]

The weight of the *ex officio* oath fell heavily on religious dissenters, most forcefully on Puritans and Catholics, who strenuously objected to the religious orthodoxy imposed by Queen Elizabeth I. More important, the dissenters faced criminal sanctions and fines in the Court of High Commission, which was formed by the Tudors to deal with the most serious religious offenses. The High Commission assiduously enforced its power, employing the *ex officio* oath to obtain convictions, often out of the accused's "own mouth."[45]

Refusal to take the oath, moreover, was not a viable option; a failure to answer the questions fully and accurately was tantamount to a confession of guilt according to a special rule fashioned by the Commission. The so-called *pro confesso* rule was predicated on the principle that the innocent had no reason to refuse the oath—the "truth could not hurt him." Only the guilty would face the proper adverse consequences deriving from the oath.[46]

A legendary figure played a significant role in opposing the *ex officio* oath and ensuring its eventual demise. John Lilburne was a radical in every sense—political, religious, economic—who sorely tested the resolve of the Crown to squelch dissent. Indeed, his trial was the triggering event for the abolition of the *ex officio* oath in the ecclesiastical courts of the High Commission and in the common law as well. As Levy puts it, Lilburne was "the catalytic agent in the history of self-incrimination."[47]

An ardent Puritan, Lilburne was tried during the reign of Charles I for shipping seditious books into England from Holland. This was merely the first of many trials for Lilburne, whose staunch belief in civil liberties earned him the sobriquet "Freeborn John" among his contemporaries. Indeed, his martyrdom for these beliefs led to four trials, imprisonment for almost his entire adult life, and death while in banishment. However, it was his refusal to answer questions of the

High Commission during this first trial that, along with auspicious political circumstances, precipitated the abolition of the oath.[48]

Forced to reconvene Parliament after an eleven-year hiatus, Charles I did so in 1640 because he was in dire need of funds. The "Long Parliament," composed principally of Puritans, wrested significant concessions from the king in exchange for the badly needed funds. On July 5, 1641, "the king reluctantly assented to bills abolishing the Courts of High Commission and Star Chamber."[49] The end of the *ex officio* oath thus ushered in the beginning of the right against self-incrimination in the English ecclesiastical courts.

In the common law courts, however, the privilege against self-incrimination was still not recognized. In fact, the privilege was invoked and honored first in the common law when twelve "leading prelates" of England were tried for high treason. The bishops, excluded from the House of Lords by statute in 1642, protested their exclusion to the king through a petition. In that petition, the bishops argued that all laws, votes, and resolutions passed without their participation were null and void. Impeached for high treason by the House of Commons, the bishops refused at their trial to answer the prosecutor's question of whether they had signed the petition. Paradoxically, the former judges of the High Commission, who had rejected the privilege in principle and practice, asserted it vigorously when charged with such a serious offense. To their credit, the Puritans, who controlled Parliament, acknowledged the bishops' invocation of the privilege.[50]

Thus runs the traditional account of the origins of the privilege, as reflected in Professor Levy's influential book. Revisionist historical scholarship, however, has recently cast doubt upon Levy's version. In an article challenging Levy's theory, R.H. Hemholz argues that the privilege against self-incrimination traces its roots not to conflicting processes of criminal procedure—that is, adversarial versus inquisitorial—but rather to the European *ius commune*, a combination of sixteenth- and seventeenth-century Roman and canon laws.[51] Rather than emerging from the common law tradition, says Hemholz, the privilege is the continental heritage of the *ius commune*.[52] Hemholz's argument is bolstered by Michael McNair, who simultaneously reached the same conclusions.[53]

Indeed, Hemholz's account finds support in the common law tradition, which not only did not embrace the privilege but also forbade defendants from testifying under oath under any circumstances.[54] Paradoxically, the English ecclesiastical courts, as well as the advocates who practiced before them, accepted and invoked the rule against self-incrimination, justifying it on the basis of the letter of Roman canon law. The exact scope of the privilege, however, was another matter, raising difficult interpretational issues. Nevertheless, the assumption underlying the privilege was not subject to question.[55]

If the privilege emerged from the ecclesiastic and Roman tradition and not from the common law, one must probe the reasons for this apparent irony. The justification for the privilege was traced to a commentary on St. Paul's letter to the Hebrews by the fourth-century Church father St. John Chrysostom.[56] More important, twin rationales arose to support the privilege's existence. One rationale was pragmatic: to the extent that most citizens had committed a crime sometime in their lifetimes, the privilege would engender structural chaos in any society. The other reason mirrors the modern foundation for the rule: that is, compelling an answer from the accused would create the "cruel trilemma" of forcing the suspect to choose from perjury, contempt, or conviction.[57]

An individual's right to a modicum of personal dignity and privacy from the intrusion of organized authority therefore underlay the origins of the privilege against self-incrimination. This rationale, however, was not absolute; rather, it was qualified, when it was finally applied by common law judges, to encompass principally "a protection against intrusive questioning into one's private conduct and opinions by officious magistrates."[58] From a historical standpoint, therefore, the privilege against self-incrimination is rooted in a fundamental recognition that individuals have a certain zone of privacy beyond which the authorities must not pry. Although the precise reach of the privilege may have been open to question and may not have included an absolute right to refuse the oath, it did in its application acknowledge the primacy of individual autonomy as the focal point for its vitality.[59]

The historical question regarding the origins of the privilege should not detract from Levy's work. Whatever the source, the fact remains that the privilege was adopted and expanded by the common law. Indeed, Professor Hemholz concedes this much.[60] Legal principles are not hollow entities that exist in a vacuum. Instead, they represent inchoate concepts whose life depends on the degree to which the polity incorporates and applies them to the legal system. The privilege against self-incrimination illustrates the evolutionary path taken by a now commonplace precept whose origins reflect ambiguities regarding the proper place for confessions as vital instruments of social control and the countervailing norm that the individual citizen deserves a certain zone of privacy that the organized power of the state ought not abridge.

How this principle took shape and evolved in America illustrates the link between the principle and its application in a particular socio-political context.

To a large extent, the privilege's development is inextricably tied to the emergence and growth of the adversary process and the critical role played by defense counsel in that system. However noble and revolutionary the concept may have appeared, the right not to testify rang hollow if the accused had no counsel to invoke the privilege on his behalf. The common law nevertheless was slow in recognizing the right to counsel. Not until the Treason Act of 1696 did the British accept the necessity of counsel in serious criminal prosecutions, and such recognition had a limited impact because treason trials were not commonplace.[61] Counsel came to be an ordinary part of the process through the exercise of judicial discretion in the half century between 1730 and 1780.[62]

Who, then, represented the defendant's interest in the trial? Quite simply, "it was dogma that the court was meant to serve as counsel for the prisoner."[63] This practice placed the accused in an imponderable quandary. If the defendant did not speak, the likelihood of conviction loomed large. It forced the defendant to speak, for "[t]he right to remain silent when no one else can speak for you is simply the right to slit your throat."[64] Given the prominence of the death penalty as the punishment for criminal offenses, remaining silent during the trial was tantamount to suicide.[65]

The privilege assumed its modern character only when the criminal trial shifted from an emphasis on the accused speaking to the adversarial crucible it has come to stand for in the common law tradition. As John Langbein perceptively notes, the adversarial system is predicated upon six fundamental features. Partisan control of the trial defines the adversary process. The presumption of innocence places the burden of proof upon the prosecution. Evidentiary rules emerged, restricting the kinds of admissible proof and giving full rein to cross-examination as a means of testing the opponent's case. Increasing reliance on defense counsel produced an "ever greater use of prosecuting counsel." The emphasis on counsel shaping the course of the trial reduced the judge's influence and control over the trial. That diminished role in turn led to a segregation of the functions of the judge from the functions of the jury; this replaced an "older informal system of jury control that presupposed the causal intimacy of judge and jury."[66]

The transformation of the criminal trial in England from the "accused speaks" to the adversarial model intuitively confirms the modern view of the privilege against self-incrimination. Although Langbein deserves credit for the historical research underlying this conclusion, we must not forget an important insight. The right to remain silent may have reached full bloom when defense counsel assumed a prominent role in the criminal trial, but the bedrock principle must have been available for counsel to invoke its protections. Defense counsel may have "made the privilege against self-incrimination possible."[67] More important, however, is the fact that the principle was available for counsel's strategic purposes. Defense attorneys therefore relied upon a "centuries-old maxim" to radically transform the nature of the criminal trial. Without the existence of the maxim, this extraordinary feat would not have been possible.

THE PRIVILEGE IN THE COLONIES AND IN THE NEW NATION

If the privilege was slow to mature and develop in England, it likewise followed a similar course in the colonies and the United States. This development is not startling when viewed in historical perspective. Because legal traditions were transplanted to the colonies and thus constituted the framework of the law, it is logical that the right to remain silent should follow a similar path as it did in the mother country. Historical scholarship appears to substantiate the parallels in the tradition.[68]

Criminal procedure in the colonies was not uniform; it is difficult to discern a pattern in the enforcement and application of procedural rights. What can be illuminated is a tradition in which the right against self-incrimination was enforced in the breach; the elements of the "accused speaks" model, elucidated by Langbein, also predominated in the colonies. The criminal process was characterized by the absence of counsel, denial of compulsory process and discovery of the government's evidence, and a procedure lacking the now accepted burden of proof beyond a reasonable doubt.[69]

More critical to the defendant's fate was the influence exerted by the Justice of the Peace before the trial. A defendant was examined "unsworn" by the Justice, whose responsibility encompassed marshalling all evidence against the accused, including his or her own confession for admission at trial.[70] This practice left a defendant who was charged with a serious crime and who lacked counsel at trial with little choice but to attempt, however feebly, to counter such powerful evidence at trial.

How does this phenomenon relate to the appearance of the privilege in section 8 of the Virginia Declaration of Rights of 1776?[71] Of course, this first comprehensive Bill of Rights represented an attempt to codify the individual rights the colonist deemed essential to liberty. Drafted by Mason, this virtually exhaustive list of criminal procedural rights was the precursor to the federal Bill of Rights. As such, it was bound up with the rebellion against England and represented an attempt to shield Americans from arbitrary government power.

It is against this backdrop that one must judge the privilege against self-incrimination and other criminal provisions contained in the Bill of Rights. Power was the antithesis of liberty. Governmental power had to be checked, and curtailing the ability of the state to wield a coercive mechanism that meant the difference between life or death was critical. The specific protections embedded in the federal Bill of Rights took root and expanded as the new nation grappled with the proper constraints upon the coercive power wielded by the government.

As we have seen, counsel played a pivotal role in securing the benefits for the accused conferred by the privilege against self-incrimination. Replacing the judge as a neutral arbiter of the defendant's rights, the attorney was able to tap the principles that restricted government power on behalf of the accused. The shift in emphasis from a judge-dominated proceeding to one largely controlled by the lawyers exerted a powerful influence on the criminal justice process. The basis for the denial of counsel rested on the notion that if lawyers were given control over the process, they would use it to pervert the end result: justice. Judges occupied center stage because "[t]he potential threat to order was too great to allow the obfuscations of lawyers to delay or deny justice."[72]

Not only did the more prominent function assumed by counsel affect the course of the right against self-incrimination in America, so did the emergence of a body of law in England that limited the way in which the government obtained confessions. Physical torture and promises as means of securing confessions were denounced by an English court in 1783. *The King v. Warickshall*[73] held that "a confession forced from the mind by flattery of hope, or by the torture of fear, comes in so questionable a shape when it is to be considered as evidence of guilt, that no credit ought to be given it."[74]

Though seemingly far-reaching in scope, in fact the opinion, which was followed by most American courts, was circumscribed in its application. It limited the authorities from resorting to physical violence and promises; however, it did not preclude interrogation or the use of deception or trickery by family or friends to induce the accused's confession.[75] Moreover, the standard set forth in *Warickshall* was applied unevenly, leading courts to condone the use of "deceitful" behavior by officials. As long as physical torture or overt promises were avoided, the field was wide open for the police to resort to clever stratagems of interrogation as a means of getting the accused to confess.[76] Whatever its scope and application, however, this standard foreshadowed the evolution of the privilege against self-incrimination in the late nineteenth century and the early twentieth century.

Because *Warickshall* may be viewed as the prevailing archetype at the time of ratification of the self-incrimination clause in the federal Bill of Rights, it is important to examine the historical backdrop behind its emergence. Specifically, the question must be posed: what was the framers' understanding of the right against self-incrimination when they incorporated it into the Fifth Amendment? The answer lies in the state constitutional provisions that included the privilege, in its common law understanding as well as in the historical record surrounding the passage of the federal Constitution and the Bill of Rights.

The common law right against self-incrimination derived from the maxim *nemo tenetur seipsum accusare* (no one is bound to accuse himself). It was an open-ended safeguard that applied to and could be relied upon by all individuals, whether criminal defendants or witnesses. The precept, moreover, extended protection from both civil and criminal liability as well as from public embarrassment.[77] Although the axiom was construed in this wide-ranging fashion under common law, we must consider whether the colonists who broke from England's clutches adopted the same interpretation.

Seeking to bolster the weak national foundation established by the Articles of Confederation, the framers of the Constitution sought to erect a stronger federal framework. The Antifederalists attempted to retain state sovereignty by attacking the Constitution's failure to include specific individual guarantees: that is, a bill of rights. Ultimately, however, the opponents of the new framework won a Pyrrhic victory: the Federalists acceded to the demand for a bill of rights, although it was not appended to the Constitution but was accomplished through the amendment route. In the debate over ratification, however, several states made their claim for specific individual guarantees clear by recommending bill of rights as part of the ratification process. Massachusetts paved the way, suggesting several amendments, but the last four states to ratify the Constitution, "included comprehensive bills of rights in their recommendations."[78] Further, these recommendations contained provisions prohibiting self-incrimination.[79]

The tenacity of those who argued for a catalogue of individual rights convinced Madison, the most influential framer of the Constitution and architect of the Bill of Rights, that acceding to the demands was the inevitable price for a stronger union. Madison believed that such protections were mere "parchment barriers" in the face of tyrannical majorities. Rather than suggesting his contempt for individual rights, Madison's opposition and ultimate acquiescence to a federal bill of rights points to the contrary. Because Madison feared the power of state legislatures and communities in general, his primary interest at the time of the Constitutional Convention in 1787 was to protect individual rights against majoritarian excesses. As a prominent historian points out, "How to prevent majorities within both the community and the legislature from violating individual and minority rights was . . . Madison's overriding concern in 1787, and it was reflected in virtually every facet of his constitutional thought."[80]

Driving the desire to protect the right to remain silent was the fear that torture would be employed to secure confessions from criminal suspects. Indeed, Patrick Henry voiced serious concerns about the failure of the Constitution to explicitly prohibit this tactic. This omission could lead Congress to adopt "the practice of France, Spain, and Germany—of torturing to extort a confession of the crime."[81] Nevertheless, the historical record yields little evidence about the privilege in the ratification process of either the Constitution or the Bill of Rights. As Levy notes, other than recognizing the privilege as a shield against torture, the framers produced "nothing . . . of a theoretical nature expressing [an additional] rationale or underlying policy for the right in question or its reach."[82]

Ultimately, the question arises: What did the clause mean at the time of its ratification? Given the language of the clause, one could infer that the privilege against self-incrimination protected only witnesses who testified at trial. This interpretation is at odds with the practice at the time of ratification of the Fifth Amendment, which prohibited defendants from testifying at trial. Reality clashed with the putative safeguard, turning the privilege into a "meaningless gesture."[83] An important caveat accompanied this restriction: a criminal defendant was permitted to tell his story unsworn to the court.[84] As we have seen, the emphasis on the accused speaking at trial in practice meant that the defendant would be expected, or implicitly compelled, to testify, however informally, at his trial. Further, revisionist historians have convincingly argued that the privilege was an outgrowth of the emerging and prominent role played by defense counsel in the criminal trial.[85]

What can be discerned from the sparse historical record is that the framers and those who ratified the self-incrimination clause believed that torture was an unacceptable way of "extorting" a confession from a criminal suspect. Since the *Warickshall* case provided the standard, it stands to reason that the privilege extended beyond the trial stage, covering the investigative pretrial process through which a suspect might also confess. Apparently, this meant that torture was viewed as an unacceptable means of securing a confession, although other clever psychological stratagems were not.[86]

Apart from this conclusion, nothing else is definite about what the privilege may have meant at the time of ratification. Shifting definitions and applications betrayed uncertainty about the extent and scope of the right. The newly formed nation abhorred torture as a means to the end of obtaining a confession from the accused. Perhaps this reflected the antistatist bent of the citizens of the new nation, who desired to be left alone in order to pursue happiness and wealth.[87] To a lesser degree, privacy may have entered into the need to protect citizens from the coercive power wielded by the state. This interpretation, however, is undermined by the acceptance of psychological ploys to convince the suspect to confess. The mind was not so private a domain that it could not be subjected to psychological chicanery if such ruses would yield a confession.

Although the privilege against self-incrimination may not have been fully defined or articulated at the time of its adoption in either state constitutions or the federal Bill of Rights, it did in practice reveal a certain distrust of the police power exerted by the state. If physical punishment and torture were not acceptable means by which to extract a confession from a criminal suspect, then the colonists and now the new citizens must have feared the coercive power of the state in using these methods in an arbitrary fashion. This is what John Adams must have dreaded when he affirmed that in the hands of an imperious sovereign, the citizen would be defenseless against capricious imprisonment, fines, whippings, and the rack.[88]

Attempting to discern the meanings of specific constitutional guarantees carries great dangers. The legal academy has been mired in a debate over the correct way to interpret constitutional provisions.

From a historical standpoint, this exercise is futile; it is tantamount to writing a novel: mere fiction.[89] Such fiction, however, is a necessary concomitant of legal scholarship. Nevertheless, history reveals the trepidation with which one must approach the enterprise. Furthermore, the historical record belies Justice Frankfurter's facile conclusion that in analyzing the privilege against self-incrimination "a page of history is worth a volume of logic." At best, what we can glean from the historical record is a fluid and perhaps ambiguous perception of just what the privilege meant.

At this point in the narrative, I can be accused of succumbing to what some who preceded me suffered from: viewing the Fifth Amendment as coterminous with the right against self-incrimination. In order to correct the deficiency, therefore, I must explore the historical origins of the grand jury and the prohibition of double jeopardy. Although it would have made sense to deal with the grand jury first, the historical controversy surrounding the privilege against self-incrimination, coupled with the more spotty historical record on both the grand jury and double jeopardy, justify this ordinal preference. Finally, the theoretical and pragmatic ties among the three clauses must be emphasized to underscore my argument for treating the clauses as an entity rather than in piecemeal fashion.

THE GRAND JURY

As the starting point of the formal adjudicatory criminal process, the grand jury plays a pivotal role in the system. One commentator has noted, "It is the gateway to the heart of the criminal justice system—the trial and sentencing stages."[90] The grand jury is critical to the legal process because it presumably provides a double layer of protection from the potential abuse of governmental power. William Blackstone viewed the grand jury and the petit jury together as a "strong and two-fold barrier" to excesses by the Crown. Requiring one body of citizens to indict and a different body to convict created, in Blackstone's mind, a "sacred bulwark" between "the liberties of the people, and the prerogative of the crown."[91] Moreover, as we shall see later, the right to a grand jury indictment is intimately tied to the privilege against self-incrimination and the protection from double jeopardy.

Called "one of the greatest outworks of liberty,"[92] the grand jury reputedly was launched by Henry II in 1166 at the Assize of Clarendon. In fact, the grand jury arose before the Assize out of the feud between

Thomas Becket and Henry II over the Church's growing independence, power, and influence. This independence was reflected in the
clergy's immunity from the common law process. Claiming the "benefit of clergy," clerks and members of ecclesiastical orders were rendered immune from criminal liability for more than one hundred
murders during the first eight years of Henry's reign. Tried in ecclesiastical courts for their crimes, these clergy typically received a benign
punishment: loss of their orders.[93]

The ultimate slap at Henry II's authority occurred when a clergy-
man murdered one of Henry's knights, hid behind the "benefit of
clergy," and refused to answer for the crime in civil court, heaping
"abusive language" upon the king's justice in the process.[94] Asserting
the royal power, Henry II ultimately prevailed upon Thomas Becket
to sign the Constitutions of Clarendon in 1164, which recognized the
traditional rights of English kings. Furthermore, chapter 6 of the Constitutions provided for the use of a grand jury for laypersons who were
accused in ecclesiastical courts. Since these courts had broad jurisdiction over laypeople, this provision was aimed at preventing the practice of bringing a person before the bishop "ex officio upon private
suggestions."[95]

Henry II's other motive in creating the institution was far from pure;
he viewed the grand jury as a way to increase the crown's revenues.
The system in place before the Assize of Clarendon relied upon private complaints by individual citizens. The grand jury, composed of a
total of sixteen men from townships, was summoned to determine
which citizens were to be charged with criminal offenses. This was a
more efficient system of ferreting out crime, and it boosted revenues
because the offenders who were sentenced to death forfeited their
estates to the Crown.[96]

Traditionally, the grand jury performed two functions: accusatorial
and investigative. Initially, the grand jurors brought forth accusations
based on their own knowledge of criminal acts; eventually, however,
the jurors "came to consider accusations made by outsiders as well."[97]
The accusatory role resulted from hearing testimony against the
accused; the jurors then resolved to indict the accused, returning a
true bill, or returned a "no bill" if they found the charges to be unwarranted.[98] The investigative role of the jury came to be known as a
presentment, in which the jurors made an accusation (a presentment)
on their own initiative rather than reacting to the request for indictment by Crown prosecutors.[99]

Paradoxically, the origins of the grand jury belie the institution's role "as a barrier between the liberty of persons and the tyranny of the executive."[100] Indeed, the opposite is the truth: the grand jury began as an instrument with which the king subordinated the interests of the Church and the feudal barons to the royal power. The presentment did originate in the Assize of Clarendon as a means for Henry II to wrest jurisdiction from feudal barons of the right to confiscate the accused's "chattels."[101] Although acting from self-interest, Henry did create a more civilized accusatory system through the presentment. Previously, the accusation was initiated by the aggrieved party, followed by a trial through compurgation, in which the accused had to marshall the support of eleven "compurgators" to swear to his or her innocence. The alternative to this method was trial by ordeal or battle.[102]

If the new grand jury mitigated the harsh and primitive effects of the trial by compurgation or ordeal, it also, as administered by Henry II's minions, generated its own abuses. Indeed, the grand jury, we are told, was "oppressive and much feared by the common people."[103] The fear and oppression stemmed from the pressure and intimidation that royal officials exerted upon grand jurors to indict those suspected of crimes in order to boost Henry's coffers. Indeed, jurors were fined for failing to indict those suspected of crimes, a fate avoided by those barons sufficiently wealthy to buy their way out of grand jury service.[104]

Eventually, the grand jury came to resemble the modern-day institution for two reasons: its function became separate from that of the petit jury, and its role in the monarchy's securing of revenue dissipated as Parliament's power increased after the Restoration. Once Parliament recognized that it could assert dominance over the king through its ability to appropriate funds, the grand jury ceased to serve as an instrument to raise revenue for the king's coffers.[105]

Two cases are renowned for supposedly transforming the role of the grand jury from an instrument of the king's will to an independent bulwark of the people's liberty. It was five hundred years after the Assize of Clarendon "that this function made its significant appearance in the cases of Anthony, Earl of Shaftesbury, and Stephen Colledge."[106] Both men were fierce opponents of Charles II's desire to restore the primacy of the Catholic Church in England. Anthony was the leader in the movement aimed at preventing James, a Roman Catholic, from succeeding to the English throne and Colledge was his "humble, zealous follower."[107]

Seeking to quell this rebellion against the monarchy, Charles II unsuccessfully sought an indictment for treason against Colledge. The grand jury in London refused to return a true bill, thereby raising the king's ire. Charles II, however, did not give up the fight; he sought a more favorable venue in Oxford, where a second grand jury did return an indictment against Colledge. Unfortunately for Colledge, the independence asserted by the London grand jury did not protect him from the criminal charge, which led to his execution in August 1681.[108]

Anthony's fate followed a similar course, with a less macabre result because he fled to exile in Holland before he could be indicted for treason. In November 1681, a London grand jury refused to indict him for treason. Soon thereafter, Charles II ensured the Earl's demise when he masterminded the election of Tory sheriffs in London, whose responsibilities included summoning grand juries loyal to the Royalist cause.[109]

It is ironic that the independent judgment of the London grand juries was negated by the Crown's blatant manipulation of the process in these two cases. One wonders, therefore, why commentators single out these cases as the paradigm for the role of the grand jury as the "bulwark of liberty."[110] One might be tempted to agree with one scholar that these cases prove the opposite: the "extreme vulnerability of [the grand jury] to the cynical political machinations of the executive."[111] This analysis, however, misses the point. The grand jury served its purpose as a shield against government oppression quite well through its refusal to indict neither Colledge nor Anthony. The king managed to achieve his goal only by abusing the process. The precedent of grand jury independence from the executive had been established.

Paralleling its English analogue, the grand jury in colonial America exerted widespread influence over the government machinery. In fact, the foremost authority on the grand jury in the United States observes, "Colonial grand juries exercised greater independence of action than did their English counterparts."[112] Not subject to control by constables who would dictate who would be indicted, grand juries in America exercised greater autonomy than the grand jury in England. This was the pattern established by the first grand jury constituted in the colonies: Massachusetts Bay in September 1635.[113] The grand jurors in Massachusetts Bay were not selected by sheriffs; rather, they were elected in duly constituted town meetings.[114]

The role of the grand jury in colonial America took various shapes and forms. A more diffused power system in the colonies paved the way for the grand jury's greater influence over criminal matters and also contributed to its role as the pulse of the community. More important, the colonies gradually launched a tradition through which a criminal defendant could be charged with either a serious or capital crime only by a grand jury indictment.[115] The prominent exception to this trend was Connecticut. From the outset, that colony relied upon the information filed by the prosecutor rather than the indictment, which was reserved for capital cases only.[116]

It is not surprising, given the prominence and autonomy exerted by the colonial grand jury, that it would be a force in the struggle for independence. One case could be viewed as the harbinger of the role the grand jury would play in nudging the colonies toward freedom from the mother country. In 1734, John Peter Zenger, publisher of the *New York Weekly Journal*, began to criticize the governor of the colony, William Cosby. Chief Justice James DeLancey, a Cosby ally, attempted on two occasions to convince a grand jury to indict Zenger on a charge of seditious libel. Both juries refused to indict Zenger, thereby prompting Governor Cosby to circumvent the grand jury by filing an information. The petit jury acquitted Zenger, frustrating the governor as well as reflecting his diminished support among the New York populace.[117]

Juxtaposing the Zenger with the Earl of Shaftesbury and Colledge cases yields fascinating parallels. In both instances, the grand jury admirably performed its function by refusing to indict in the face of official executive pressure. Nevertheless, the executive in both situations abused the process by circumventing the grand jury: on the one hand by stacking the grand jury and on the other by evading the grand jury through the information. Again, the relevant lesson from these episodes is not that the grand jury cannot protect the citizen from governmental oppression; rather, the point is that an institution's aims can be perverted through the machinations of those wielding inordinate executive or legislative power.

It is precisely the danger posed by legislative or executive power that fueled the prominence of the grand jury in the late colonial period. To curb the influence and power of the royal prosecutor, colonies possessing a measure of self-rule required that a prosecution be initiated through an indictment rather than an information filed by a prosecutor. Indeed, the grand jury became the instrument through which the colonies resisted British authority. Thus, a Boston grand jury refused to indict the leaders of the Stamp Act riots in 1765. Similarly, other colonial grand juries leveled attacks against British "oppression." Throughout the Revolution, grand juries served as "patriotic organs and propaganda agencies," often exhorting the public to support the revolutionary struggle for freedom.[118]

Once the struggle for independence ended, the grand jury remained a fixture in the new American landscape. Not only did it find its way into state constitutions, it also played a role in the ratification of the Constitution. The Antifederalist opposition to the Constitution centered on the lack of a federal Bill of Rights, and the right to a grand jury indictment was one of the provisions recommended by four of eight states that proposed amendments to the Constitution.[119] Finally, the right to a grand jury indictment for a "capital or infamous crime" became part of Madison's proposal to Congress for a bill of rights and was included in the amendments passed by Congress on September 25, 1789. Ultimately, the right to a grand jury indictment for a serious crime was incorporated into the Fifth Amendment when the states ratified the congressional proposals, with the exception of the first two amendments, in 1791.[120]

In the new nation, the grand jury exercised divergent functions in the federal and state systems. Whereas the state grand juries played an active role not only in law enforcement but also in dealing with a variety of community issues, federal grand juries exercised limited authority because of the jurisdictional constraint placed on their powers. Consequenctly, the federal grand jury came to be viewed in the popular mind as an instrument of the federal courts and became embroiled in the political controversies of the 1790s. State grand juries tended to reflect the voice of the people while federal grand juries were seen as mere adjuncts to federal authority.[121]

Indeed, in an ironic twist of fate, federal grand juries in the 1790s were subject to the manipulation and influence redolent of the Earl of Shaftesbury and Colledge cases. Although some federal grand juries resisted attempts to influence their decision to indict, others succumbed to the pressures inherent in what turned out to be a partisan process. In the struggle for political control, the Federalists sought to curtail criticism of the government through the passage of the Sedition Act of 1798. In the process, federal judges placed considerable pressure on grand juries to indict those who dared to criticize the government. Perhaps the most glaring example of the abuse of the process occurred when a federal grand jury in Vermont indicted Congressman Matthew Lyon for describing President Adams as someone with "an unbounded thirst for ridiculous pomp, foolish adulation and selfish avarice."[122]

Much like the privilege against self-incrimination, the right to a grand jury indictment was firmly embedded in the legal landscape of the new nation. What the constitutional guarantee meant is difficult to discern from the record. A "bulwark of liberty," it presumably provided the necessary protection from the excesses of the executive or, to a lesser extent, the legislature. It also played a role as a pulse of the community, at least at the state level. Like any constitutional guarantee, however, it was vulnerable to abuse and manipulation for political purposes. This became evident early in the nation's history with the abuse of the grand jury to secure indictments under the Sedition Act.

Arising from political battles waged in England, the right to a grand jury indictment resembled, to a certain extent, the historical development of the privilege against self-incrimination. Moreover, the potential to achieve its purpose, much like the privilege against self-incrimination, was frustrated by the ability of the executive and the judiciary to thwart its fundamental objectives. The grand jury shared twin goals with the privilege against self-incrimination: an inherent distrust of authority, and the government's concomitant ability to abuse its police power.

More important, both protections have a common feature that distinguishes the adversarial from the inquisitorial system of criminal adjudication. In its mature form, the privilege against self-incrimination forces the state to prove its case without the accused's testimony. If the government is required to charge the accused formally through an indictment, it must do so without necessarily using the accused's testimony. As one scholar has noted, "The grand jury's action must be based on a *prima facie* against the accused, proved by the testimony of witnesses *other than* [emphasis added] himself."[123] When it is looked at from this perspective, there exists a conceptual and practical link between the privilege against self-incrimination and the right to a grand jury indictment.

Furthermore, this relationship is not undermined by the fact that the privilege against self-incrimination is a "fundamental trial right of criminal defendants,"[124] and that the right to a grand jury indictment is a pretrial right designed to protect the accused against malevolent prosecution. As the Supreme Court has observed, although the privilege may be jeopardized by police conduct prior to trial, a constitutional violation occurs when the statement is sought to be admitted at trial.[125] For practical purposes, however, it is the police conduct before trial that triggers the defendant's right to invoke the privilege in order to prevent the prosecution from introducing the statement at trial.

THE HISTORY OF DOUBLE JEOPARDY

Paralleling its counterparts, the protection from double jeopardy is a fundamental right designed to guard the individual against governmental oppression. One scholar has suggested, perhaps in exaggerated fashion, that the "history of the rule against double jeopardy is the history of criminal procedure." He goes on to explain, "No other procedural doctrine is more fundamental or all-pervasive."[126] The history of double jeopardy, however, is shrouded in mystery: it reflects bizarre twists and turns and shifting interpretations of its essential meaning.

The concept underlying double jeopardy has deep historical roots. Its origins may be traced to the Greeks and the Romans as well as to Jewish sources and early Christian doctrine. In formal terms, double jeopardy became part of the *Digest of Justinian*. The document embodied the notion that "the governor should not permit the same person to be accused of which he had been acquitted."[127] Despite this proscription, a defendant who was acquitted could be retried for the same offense as long as the government did so within thirty days.[128]

Like the privilege against self-incrimination, the ban on double jeopardy was embedded in the canon law. St. Jerome in the year 391 read the Bible (the prophet Nahum) to forbid a "double affliction," since God did not punish twice for the same offense.[129] Thus, the axiom that was to become a fixture in English and American jurisprudence had its origins in both Roman and canon law. It is ironic that these two precepts, the prohibition of double jeopardy and the privilege against self-incrimination, emerged from traditions that, in modern times, seem at odds with Anglo-American jurisprudence.

In England, the concept of double jeopardy shares a common historical root with the right to a grand jury indictment. Much like the grand jury, the principle barring double jeopardy arose out of the conflict between Thomas Becket and Henry II. Henry, as we saw in our discussion of the grand jury,[130] resented the privilege of the clergy to avoid prosecution in civil court by claiming that they had been already judged in ecclesiastical courts. Henry's ultimate challenge to Becket came in 1163 when he sought to retry a clerk who had been acquitted of the offense in the ecclesiastical court. Indeed, it is Henry's violation of the double jeopardy ban that supposedly triggered his feud with Becket, leading ultimately to Becket's murder.[131]

After the controversy between Becket and Henry II, the path of double jeopardy did not run smooth. One scholar concluded that the rule against double jeopardy was "neither clearly defined nor applied." In fact, even the Church backtracked on the principle. Becket's successor did not oppose multiple punishment, and neither did Pope Innocent III.[132]

In England, the double jeopardy ban was applied unevenly after Becket's death. To a large extent, this inconsistency reflected the amalgamation between civil and criminal law in England until very late in its legal history. Thus, prosecutions were initiated by private persons as well as by the authority of the king though indictment. In 1487, Henry VII issued an act that violated the double jeopardy principle in homicide cases. The act allowed the prosecution of a homicide through an "appeal" (i.e., a prosecution initiated by a private party) even though the accused was acquitted on the indictment. The only restriction on the reprosecution was that the "appeal" be brought within a year and a day.[133]

The trend of ignoring the double jeopardy principle continued through the sixteenth and early seventeenth centuries. One case serves as the paradigm for the cavalier treatment accorded double jeopardy. In *Vaux's Case*,[134] the court held that a dismissal of a defective indictment on the merits did not preclude reprosecution because the accused "was never in jeopardy when charged with an act which is not an offence according to the law."[135] Paradoxically, until the latter half of the seventeenth century, the double jeopardy principle in England had been observed mainly in the breach.

Indifference toward the double jeopardy bar underwent a metamorphosis during the latter half of the seventeenth century. This was due to a confluence of several factors. Lord Coke's—and, to a lesser extent, Blackstone's—influential writings served to heighten interest in and respect for the double jeopardy rule. Second, as the death penalty for criminal offenses proliferated, the need for the restraining influence of double jeopardy intensified. Finally, the distinction between the civil and the criminal spheres solidified, thereby bringing into focus the modern role of double jeopardy as a rule intended to curb governmental tyranny.[136]

Lord Coke's and Blackstone's formulation of the double jeopardy protection encompassed four discrete safeguards, prohibiting reprosecution for the same offense upon either a prior acquittal (*autrefois acquit*), a prior conviction (*autrefois convict*), a former pardon, and a previous conviction on a lesser-included offense (*autrefois attaint*).[137] These protections, however, were limited to those offenses that carried the potential of the death penalty.[138] Thus, the double jeopardy bar seemed reserved for the crimes that merited the ultimate sanction: death. This restriction was founded on English laws that decreed that upon a second conviction the defendant "be smitten so that his neck break." Thus, the phrase *life or limb*, which appears in the Fifth Amendment, "has a literal meaning in English history."[139]

DOUBLE JEOPARDY IN AMERICA

The double jeopardy bar appeared in this advanced stage in the American colonies. In the extensive catalogue of rights enumerated in the Massachusetts Body of Liberties of 1641, clause 42 stated, "No man shall be twise sentenced by Civill Justice for one the same Crime, offence, or Trespasse."[140] As this provision makes clear, the double jeopardy principle was considerably broadened in America: it was not limited to offenses punishable by death but included all criminal prosecutions and civil trespasses.

What is remarkably odd about the fate of double jeopardy in the American colonies and in the new nation is that the principle appears in no other instrument until it was incorporated in the New Hampshire Constitution of 1784.[141] Perhaps the most glaring omission occurs in article 8 of the Virginia Declaration of Rights, arguably the most comprehensive statement of criminal safeguards in the new nation.[142] None of the other Revolutionary constitutions incorporated the ban on double jeopardy. An attempt to explain this gap leads to pure conjecture. It is possible to surmise that the concept was so deeply embedded in the criminal tapestry that a written expression was superfluous. This explanation is supported, or belied, by sparse case law in colonial and Revolutionary times recognizing the protection in various hues.[143] A more probable reason is that although the right was not extensively recognized, it was viewed as "particularly dear" by James Madison, the architect of the federal Bill of Rights.[144]

Eventually, the clause embodied in the Fifth Amendment to the U.S. Constitution emerged from a tortuous path. First proposed as an amendment to the Constitution on June 8, 1789, to the House of Representatives, the double jeopardy principle was formulated in the following language: "No person shall be subject, except in cases of impeachment, to more than one punishment or trial for the same offense."[145]

This language prompted an objection by Representative Benson of New York because it was underinclusive. Benson accepted as fundamental the notion that a person's life should not be placed in jeopardy more than once. However, he opposed language that presumably excluded the accepted tenet permitting a defendant to appeal a conviction. The use of the word *trial* in the proposed amendment would preclude the defendant from appealing a conviction because a reversal would require a second trial for the same offense. Benson moved, therefore, to strike the words "or trial" from the amendment. Although Benson's proposal received some backing, it was defeated by a wide margin in the House.[146]

However imprecise and underinclusive, the amendment made its way to the Senate, ironically with the assent of Representative Benson and others who had objected to the reference to "trial" in the body of the amendment. The Senate tinkered with the language; after several alterations and a conference committee between the House and the Senate to settle differences, the double jeopardy clause was included in Article VII of the proposed amendments passed by the Senate on September 9, 1789. That amendment stated that "nor shall any person be subject for the same offense to be twice put in jeopardy of life or limb."[147] Ratified by Congress slightly more than two weeks later, the double jeopardy principle would be embedded in the Fifth Amendment and ultimately become a source of much interpretational controversy.

History does not yield definitive answers to the central meaning of the double jeopardy clause. The leading scholar affirms that the historical meaning behind the double jeopardy prohibition was, at best, "unclear," at worst unfathomable.[148] If anything can be derived from such a malleable concept, it is that it symbolized an inchoate antistatist sentiment. In effect, the sentiment recognizes the awesome power of the state; such power can be abused in order to harass, intimidate, oppress, and, ultimately, wear down the accused. From a broader perspective, the double jeopardy ban may be viewed "as a social policy limiting the power of the state to conduct criminal prosecutions."[149]

Characterized by indeterminacy, the double jeopardy principle would bedevil jurists and scholars in the twentieth century. History should have given them a clue about the difficulty of discerning just what double jeopardy means.

Although the historical record seems to confound rather than to illuminate, it is important to emphasize the historical ties among double jeopardy, the grand jury, and self-incrimination. The principles behind double jeopardy and the grand jury emerged from the political battles for power waged by Henry II and Thomas Becket. We have seen, moreover, that the privilege against self-incrimination grew out of the battle between Charles I and Parliament for political supremacy. The common thread running through all three protections is a libertarian, antistatist, individualistic tendency to curb the power of the dominant political authority.

HISTORICAL INTERPRETATION

What lessons can we derive from the history of the three criminal clauses of the Fifth Amendment? Furthermore, does history justify viewing these safeguards from a macro rather than a micro perspective? The answer to these questions lies in the approach one takes regarding the role of history in constitutional interpretation. History can yield definitive answers about the past in few, if any, cases. Some historians maintain that history can reveal the truth through a disinterested description of the past; nonetheless, they concede that the historian's account is "necessarily colored by the questions that he asks in the course of sifting through its record."[150]

A competing model of historical interpretation rejects a unilinear view of the past, emphasizing instead the complexity and multidimensional aspect of history. "Contextualists" recognize that the use of history in discerning the meaning of constitutional provisions is necessarily affected by moral, philosophical, and political preferences. As the noted legal historian William Nelson has aptly shown, reliance on history to decide constitutional questions produces few determinate answers and ultimately hinges on "value judgments." He observes, "Analysis of . . . historical questions that have come before the Supreme Court . . . illustrate[s] how most historical debates turn on value judgments about the desirability of looking at the past in a particular context, rather than on judgments about the probability that a particular rendition of the past is accurate."[151]

Given the controversy surrounding the interpretation of the amendments affording constitutional rights to criminal defendants, does history assist the Supreme Court in determining the appropriate scope of such protections? The previous discussion reveals that the "interpretivist," who seeks to distill the meaning of a particular constitutional provision from a specific historical moment in time, engages in "necessary fiction." On the other hand, the "antitheoretical realist" presupposes that political motives color all constitutional interpretation of historical data. Occupying the middle ground in the debate, the "neutralist" looks at the more recent past to find some kind of a societal consensus on the range of possible solutions to constitutional quandaries. Presumably, all three methods are useful, depending on the context and the particular constitutional question posed.[152]

We have seen that the history underlying the privilege against self-incrimination, the grand jury, and the principle of double jeopardy is far from definitive; in fact, one might conclude that it is riddled with ambiguities and varied interpretations. Despite this equivocal past, it is worthwhile to extract some tentative conclusions from such a nebulous record. Such conclusions will not necessarily furnish answers to questions about the scope of the constitutional protections. They will, however, inform the analysis and help point us toward both conceptual and pragmatic links among the clauses.

Although the Constitution failed to include a bill of rights within its provisions, the road for such protections had been paved by state constitutions, which had enumerated such rights.[153] At the most general level, the state bills of rights declared the American belief in the "overarching right to be free of arbitrary government."[154] Arbitrary government, in turn, could jeopardize the citizenry's sacred right to freedom from arbitrary and capricious punishments meted out by the sovereign. The severity of such sanctions, moreover, made procedural safeguards to secure individual freedom all the more compelling.

In the struggle over the ratification of the Constitution, the lack of a bill of rights became the focal point of the Antifederalist opposition. Foremost among the minds of the Antifederalists was the lack of specific provisions curbing the power of the state in the criminal justice process. Indeed, when Richard Henry Lee proposed amendments to Congress before it conveyed the Constitution to the states, he focused primarily on such protections as the right to a jury trial and to trial in the community in which the crime occurred. One historian has observed that this emphasis revealed the Antifederalist emphasis of criminal protections "as the crucial test of the security of rights."[155] Even though Madison was the architect of the federal Bill of Rights, he did not initially think such a catalogue of rights was necessary. He did not oppose such rights; rather, he viewed them as superfluous, given the limited powers conferred on the federal government by the Constitution. More important, he knew too well that "repeated violations of these parchment barriers ha[d] been committed by overbearing majorities in every state. In Virginia I have seen the bill of rights violated in every instance where it has been opposed to a popular current."[156]

Historians who have discerned Madison's about-face on the need for a bill of rights as a bow to political expediency perhaps offer too cynical a view. The consensus seems to be that Madison acceded to the federal Bill of Rights as a means of countering Antifederalist opposition to the Constitution.[157] As Lance Banning perceptively demonstrates, however, Madison ultimately saw that the benefits to a bill of rights outweighed the dangers. In fact, Madison preferred that the amendments be interwoven into the text of the Constitution rather than becoming appended to its body.[158]

Rather than belabor the obvious, it is important to point out the critical role that criminal provisions of the federal Bill of Rights play in the constitutional order. As one historian has observed, "The federal Bill of Rights devotes more attention to the requirements for a fair criminal process than it does to any other right or group of rights."[159] From a historical as well as a philosophical and pragmatic viewpoint, I have argued that criminal procedural rights enumerated in the federal Bill of Rights ought to be viewed from an integrated, rather than piecemeal, perspective.[160] Similarly, the Fifth Amendment has been associated almost exclusively with the privilege against self-incrimination, with the other two criminal clauses almost severed from the amendment.[161]

In the popular mind, this association is evident, given the prominent role the privilege against self-incrimination plays in the media. "Taking the Fifth" is a term more than a few members of the public would understand as symbolizing the ability of a criminal suspect or defendant to claim the shield against self-inculpation. How many laypersons— or lawyers, for that matter—would know that the prohibition against double jeopardy and the right to a grand jury indictment are included in the Fifth Amendment? One can understand such a gloss among laypersons or attorneys not specializing in criminal law, but is the gap excusable among scholars steeped in the nuances of the criminal justice process? I argue that it is not.

HISTORICAL AND PRAGMATIC BASES
FOR A COMPREHENSIVE APPROACH

We have seen how the history behind the three criminal clauses of the Fifth Amendment reveal their common bonds. Three themes unite the ideals embraced by the Fifth Amendment as well as the other amendments relating to the criminal process. What distinguishes the "American Creed" from the continental value system is an emphasis on individual rights. As the great political sociologist Seymour Martin Lipset asserts, "America began and continues as the most anti-statist, legalistic, and rights-oriented nation."[162] This tradition reflects the battle waged by Antifederalists for a bill of rights. Indeed, the "American revolutionary, libertarian tradition does not encourage obedience to the state and the law."[163]

Second, because draconian criminal sanctions were the norm at the time of the Revolution, the importance of checks upon the potentially unbridled power of the state emerges in bold relief. It is not mere coincidence that state constitutional provisions highlighted criminal due process protections. Nor is it mere happenstance that Antifederalists made criminal procedural safeguards the centerpiece of their insistence on a federal bill of rights. The criminal process was the example, *par excellence*, of the awesome power of the state vis-à-vis the individual.

Finally, the three criminal safeguards embedded in the Fifth Amendment are conceptually joined. The right against self-incrimination places the burden on the government to prove the accused's guilt with evidence other than his admissions. As the gateway to the criminal justice system, moreover, the grand jury must formally charge the defendant without necessarily relying on his or her testimony.[164] Furthermore, just as the state bears the burden of going forward without the defendant's testimony, it must not subject him or her to *double incrimination*. In effect, the proscription of double jeopardy stands for the broad principle that a defendant who has been incriminated through a formal charge cannot be placed through the process again for the same offense. Not only must the state seek to incriminate the defendant formally through a grand jury indictment without his or her testimony; once it does so and is unsuccessful, the government cannot attempt to incriminate the individual one more time.

An example of the practical tie between self-incrimination and double jeopardy produces a fascinating insight. Suppose the government initiates a prosecution of the defendant. The defendant testifies at trial and waives the privilege against self-incrimination regarding the crime charged. In spite of this waiver, the jury exercises its right to nullify the law in the case and acquits the defendant. Because the defendant is no longer in jeopardy—that is, the government cannot formally attempt to incriminate an individual twice, he or she can no longer invoke the privilege, especially in a civil proceeding.

The right to a grand jury proceeding is also integrally related to the prohibition of double jeopardy. A primary function of a grand jury indictment is to apprise the defendant specifically of the charges. To fulfill this purpose, the Federal Rules of Criminal Procedure provide that an indictment must be a "plain, concise, and definite written statement of the essential facts and elements of the alleged offense necessary to inform the accused of the charge."[165] This notice and specificity requirement also serves the goal of facilitating the preparation of a defense to the charge.

More important for our purposes, the defendant must be aware of the charges in order to seek a dismissal on double jeopardy grounds.[166] Although most courts liberally construe this specificity requirement against double jeopardy challenges,[167] the fact remains that the government cannot successfully initiate the grand jury proceeding against the accused if double jeopardy stands in the way. In short, the "gateway" to the criminal justice system must be clear of double jeopardy problems before it can be opened.

As we have already noted, the grand jury proceeding requires the government to offer sufficient proof to secure an indictment without relying on the accused's testimony. The Supreme Court has failed to answer the question of whether the target of a grand jury investigation must be warned of the right against self-incrimination if the grand jury issues a subpoena.[168] Perhaps to underscore the importance of the privilege, and because the grand jury is dominated by the prosecutor, some states have required warnings through statutes.[169] If the target of a grand jury subpoena is either shrewd and wealthy enough to retain an attorney, he or she will no doubt be advised of the privilege against self-incrimination and will invoke it, if necessary, in the absence of immunity.[170]

A further historical nexus exists between the grand jury's function and the prohibition of double jeopardy. Explaining the distinction between the accusatorial role of the grand jury and the adjudicatory purpose of the petit jury, the court in *Republica v. Shaffer*[171] illumined the link between the grand jury and double jeopardy. The grand jury, the court explained, could not be transformed into an adversarial proceeding because that would usurp the function of the petit jury. More important, if the grand jury became adversarial, the defendant would in effect be placed twice in jeopardy. Rejecting the proposed examination of grand jury witnesses by the defendant, the court reasoned that "this would involve us in another difficulty; for by the law, it is declared, that no man shall be put in jeopardy for the same offense."[172] The court went on to observe that such a proposal "would necessarily introduce the oppression of a second trial."[173]

CONCLUSION

At the outset of this endeavor, I argued that the three criminal clauses of the Fifth Amendment should be viewed as a whole rather than as discrete entities. Conceptually, the three clauses represent the beginning, the middle, and the end of the criminal process. To the extent that the self-incrimination clause comes into play before the trial begins, one can quarrel with this interpretation.[174] The Supreme Court, however, has defined the clause as a trial right that is violated when the prosecution seeks to introduce the defendant's statement at trial.[175] In contrast with the Sixth Amendment, whose protections relate solely to fair-trial rights, the Fifth Amendment symbolizes the three phases of the criminal justice adjudicative process.

History also yields parallels among the three clauses. Emerging from political battles waged between the Crown, the clergy, and Parliament, the three clauses exemplify an attempt to curb the power of the government vis-à-vis the individual. Transplanted to America's shores, the clauses underwent transformations and emendations, ultimately becoming enshrined in the federal Bill of Rights. The clauses were entwined with the political struggle over the ratification of the Constitution; they illustrated how important criminal protections from the overwhelming power of the sovereign were to the Antifederalists who opposed the Constitution.

Although historical ties bind the clauses, we must not misuse history by taking the approach that the meaning behind the clauses was readily ascertainable at the time of the framing. It is inherently ahistorical to take the position that the clauses "mean what they say and say what they mean."[176] As we have seen, the meaning of the criminal protections embedded in the Fifth Amendment was far from certain at the time of both the framing and the ratification of the Bill of Rights. Aside from making broad generalizations, it is impossible to ascribe a precise meaning to each of the clauses. Double jeopardy represents the most extreme example of the variegated, ambiguous, and uncertain meaning attached to a criminal protection at the time of the passage and ratification of the Bill of Rights.

We must not forget, moreover, that pragmatic bases underlie the three criminal safeguards incorporated in the Fifth Amendment. The right against self-incrimination and to a grand jury indictment are intimately linked to the extent that they require the government to shoulder the burden of prosecution without the accused's assistance. Further, the protection from double jeopardy is tied to this principle by preventing the government from seeking to incriminate the defendant formally more than one time. Furthermore, the grand jury cannot issue an indictment if the defendant has already been placed in jeopardy for the same offense.

As the noted social historian Theodore Zeldin points out, "The vast majority of scientists devote a large part of their efforts to writing articles which are never read."[177] Of course, the same observation applies to the legal academy. [178] I hope that by expanding the boundaries of the Fifth Amendment beyond the self-incrimination clause, at least a few people will be more informed about the criminal process. Although the fear arises that I have omitted much in this endeavor, I take shelter in the following adage: "It is only curiosity that knows no boundaries which can be effective against fear."[179]

NOTES

1. BERNARD BAILYN, THE ORIGINS OF AMERICAN POLITICS (1967) 16–17.

2. JOHN PHILLIP REID, THE CONCEPT OF LIBERTY IN THE AGE OF THE AMERICAN REVOLUTION 76 (1988).

3. *Id.* at 76–77.

4. BERNARD BAILYN, THE IDEOLOGICAL ORIGINS OF THE AMERICAN REVOLUTION (1967).

5. *Id.* at 34–93. The quote is from JOYCE APPLEBY, LIBERALISM AND REPUBLICANISM IN THE HISTORICAL IMAGINATION 322 (1992).

6. GORDON WOOD, THE RADICALISM OF THE AMERICAN REVOLUTION 103–5 (1992) .

7. Appleby, *supra* note 5 at 323–24.

8. Bailyn, *supra* note 4 at 59.

9. GORDON WOOD, THE CREATION OF THE AMERICAN REPUBLIC, 1776–1787 61 (1969).

10. *Id.* at 62–63.

11. JAMES MADISON, NOTES OF DEBATES IN THE FEDERAL CONVENTION OF 1787 (A. Koch ed.) 651 (1966).

12. ALEXANDER HAMILTON, JAMES MADISON AND JOHN JAY, THE FEDER-
ALIST PAPERS (Clinton Rossiter ed.) 515 (1961).

13. BERNARD SCHWARTZ, THE GREAT RIGHTS OF MANKIND: A HISTORY OF
THE AMERICAN BILL OF RIGHTS 24 (1977).

14. *Id.* at 51.

15. *Id.* at 53–91.

16. EDMUND S. MORGAN, AMERICAN SLAVERY, AMERICAN FREEDOM: THE
ORDEAL OF COLONIAL VIRGINIA (1975).

17. *Id.* at 375–76.

18. *Id.* at 376.

19. OSCAR AND LILIAN HANDLIN, LIBERTY AND POWER 1600 TO THE
PRESENT, LIBERTY AND POWER 1600–1760 4–5 (1986).

20. *Id.*

21. *Id.* at 6.

22. *Id.* at 7.

23. *Id.*

24. *Id.* at 9.

25. *Id.* at 12.

26. DAVID J. ROTHMAN, *Perfecting the Prison*, in THE OXFORD HISTORY OF
THE PRISON (Norval Morris & David J. Rothman ed.) 112 (1995).

27. *Id.*

28. *Id.* at 113.

29. *Id.*

30. *Id.*; Handlin, *supra* note 19 at 217.

31. Handlin, *supra* note 19 at 217.

32. *Id.*

33. *Clarendon*, BOSTON GAZETTE, January 27, 1766, quoted in JACK
RAKOVE, ORIGINAL MEANINGS: POLITICS AND IDEAS IN THE MAKING OF THE
CONSTITUTION (1996) at 302.

34. *Kurtz v. Moffit*, 115 U.S. at 499.

35. *See, e.g.*, 18 U.S.C. Sec. 1 (1).

36. *United States v. Watson*, 423 U.S. 411 (1976) (Marshall, J., dissenting).

37. MICHAEL J. PERRY, THE CONSTITUTION IN THE COURTS: LAW OR POLI-
TICS? 17 (1994).

38. THOMAS JEFFERSON, NOTES ON THE STATE OF VIRGINIA (1787), in
JEFFERSON WRITINGS, ed. Merril Petersen (1984) at 246–50.

39. *Id.* For example, Pennsylvania's constitution precluded the legislature
from having "the power to add to, alter, abolish, or infringe any part of the
constitution." Moreover, it included a procedure for amending the document
under the supervision of a "Council of Censors." Pennsylvania Constitution
of 1776, ART. 46 & 47, in BEN PERLEY MOORE ed., THE FEDERAL AND STATE

CONSTITUTIONS, COLONIAL CHARTERS, AND OTHER ORGANIC LAWS OF THE UNITED STATES 1414 (1877).

40. *Id.* at 31.

41. *Ullman v. United States*, 350 U.S. 422, 438 (1956) (quoting *New York Trust Co. v. Eisner*, 256 U.S. 345, 356 (1921) (Holmes, J.)).

42. LEONARD W. LEVY, ORIGINS OF THE FIFTH AMENDMENT: THE RIGHT AGAINST SELF–INCRIMINATION (2D ed. 1986).

43. *Id.* at 20.

44. *Murphy v. Waterfront Comm'n*, 378 U.S. 53, 55 (1964). Although the phrase "cruel trilemma" is attributable to Justice Goldberg's opinion in *Murphy*, its origins go much further back. *See* J. McNaughton, *The Privilege against Self–Incrimination: Its Constitutional Affectation, Raison d'Etre and Miscellaneous Implications*, 51 J. CRIM. L, CRIMINOLOGY & POLICE SCI. 138, 147 (1960).

45. Levy, *supra* note 42 at 145–46.

46. *Id.* at 269.

47. *Id.* at 271–73. John H. Langbein has challenged Lilburne's reputedly important role in promoting the right against self-incrimination. Langbein argues that Lilburne "was an insignificant figure in the development of the privilege." Rather than emphasizing the privilege against self-incrimination, Langbein writes that Lilburne stressed the necessity of counsel and the concept of the prosecution's burden of proof. John H. Langbein, *The Historical Origins of the Privilege against Self-Incrimination at Common Law*, 92 MICH. L. REV. 1047, 1076–77, n. 131 (1994).

48. *Id.* at 272–83.

49. *Id.* at 281.

50. *Id.* at 285.

51. R. H. Hemholz, *Origins of the Privilege against Self-Incrimination: The Role of the European ius Commune*, 65 N.Y.U. L. REV. 962 (1990). Hemholz's conclusions are echoed by Michael McNair, who maintains that the privilege "came into English law from the common family of European laws and particularly the canon law." Michael R.T. MacNair, *The Early Development of the Privilege against Self-Incrimination*, 10 OXFORD J. LEGAL STUD. 67 (1990).

52. *Id.* at 964.

53. MacNair, *supra* note 51.

54. *Id.* at 968 (citing J.H. WIGMORE, EVIDENCE IN TRIALS AT COMMON LAW Section 2250, 284–89 (McNaughton rev. 1961).

55. *Id.* at 965–74.

56. *Id.* at 982.

57. *Id.* at 982–93. On the "cruel trilemma," see note 44, *supra*.

58. *Id.* at 988.

59. *Id.* at 988–89.

60. *Id.* at 989–90.

61. Langbein, *supra* note 47 at 1067–68.

62. *Id.* at 1068. Langbein first articulated this notion in his pathbreaking article published in 1978. John H. Langbein, *The Criminal Trial before the Lawyers*, 45 U. CHI. L. REV. 263, 307–11 (1978).

63. Langbein, *supra* note 50 at 1050.

64. *Id.* at 1054.

65. *Id.* at 1084.

66. *Id.* at 1070–71.

67. *Id.* at 1071.

68. *See* Eban Moglan, *Taking the Fifth: Reconsidering the Origins of the Constitutional Privilege against Self-Incrimination*, 92 MICH. L. REV. 1086 (1994).

69. *Id.* at 1092.

70. *Id.*

71. VA. CONST. art. I, 8.

72. DAVID J. BODENHAMER, FAIR TRIAL: RIGHTS OF THE ACCUSED IN AMERICAN HISTORY 40 (1992).

73. 168 ENG. REP. 234 (1783).

74. *Id.*

75. *Id.*

76. *Id.* at 53–54. Bodenhamer mentions an Indianapolis case in which the suspect confessed to counterfeiting when officers posed as accomplices.

77. *See, e.g.*, *Ullman v. United States*, 350 U.S. 422, 445–46 (1956) (Douglas, J., dissenting) (discussing history and subscribing to this expansive interpretation).

78. Ralph Rossum, *"Self-Incrimination": The Original Intent*, in THE BILL OF RIGHTS: ORIGINAL MEANING AND CURRENT UNDERSTANDING (Eugene W. Hickok, Jr. ed) 274 (1991).

79. *Id.* at 274–75.

80. Jack N. Rakove, *Mr. Meese, Meet Mr. Madison*, in JACK N. RAKOVE ed., INTERPRETING THE CONSTITUTION: THE DEBATE OVER ORIGINAL INTENT 187 (1990).

81. 3 THE DEBATES IN THE SEVERAL STATE CONVENTIONS ON THE ADOPTION OF THE FEDERAL CONSTITUTION 447–48 (Jonathan Elliot ed., 1886), quoted in Akhil Reed Amar & Renee B. Lettow, *Fifth Amendment First Principles: The Self-Incrimination Clause*, 93 MICH. L. REV. 857, 865 n.20 (1995).

82. Levy, *supra* note 42 at 430.

83. Leonard Levy, *The Right against Self-Incrimination*, in 3 L. LEVY, K. KARST, & D. MAHONEY, ENCYCLOPEDIA OF THE AMERICAN CONSTITUTION, 1570 (1986).

84. *Id.*

85. See notes 61–67 *supra* and accompanying text.

86. *See* notes 75–76 *supra* and accompanying text.

87. *See* Wood, *supra* note 6 at 336.

88. *See* note 33 *supra* and accompanying text.

89. The historian Gordon Wood contends, "While it must be a necessary fiction for lawyers and jurists to believe in a "correct" or "true" interpretation of the Constitution in order to carry on their business . . . we historians have different obligations and aims." The principal goal of the historian, according to Wood, is to distill the "contrasting meanings" assigned to the Constitution from the time of its ratification. *See* Gordon S. Wood, *Ideology and the Origins of Liberal America*, 44 WILLIAM & MARY QUARTERLY 632–33 (1987). Wood, in turn, relies on the pathbreaking article by William E. Nelson, *History and Neutrality in Constitutional Adjudication*, 72 U. VA. L. REV. 1237 (1986).

90. Walter W. Steele, Jr., *Right to Counsel at the Grand Jury Stage of Criminal Proceedings*, 36 MISSOURI L. REV. 193, 194 (1971).

91. PHILIP KURLAND & RALPH LERNER eds., 5 THE FOUNDERS' CONSTITUTION 255 (1987).

92. Bishop Gilbert Burnett coined this term in a book he authored, published in 1900. Gilbert Burnett, 2 History of My Own Time 301–2 (1900), cited in RICHARD D. YOUNGER, THE PEOPLE'S PANEL: THE GRAND JURY IN THE UNITED STATES, 1934–1941 (1963).

93. Helene E. Schwartz, *Demythologizing the Historic Role of the Grand Jury*, 10 AM. CRIM. L. REV. 701, 704 (1972).

94. *Id.* at 705. The defendant was Philip of Broi, the canon of Bedford. Henry sought to have Philip answer in the royal court for his brazen defiance of royal authority but was rebuffed by Becket. Becket refused Henry's order by claiming that a layman could not judge the clergy.

95. *Id.* at 707, quoting 1 F. POLLOCK & F. MAITLAND, THE HISTORY OF THE ENGLISH LAW 151 (2d. ed. 1898).

96. *Id.* at 704, 708–10.

97. Younger, *supra* note 92 at 1.

98. *Id.*

99. *Id.*

100. *People v. Galarotti*, 46 Misc. 2d 871, 872, 261 N.Y.S. 2d 218, 220 (Westchester Ct. 1965), citing *People v. Harris*, 182 Misc. 787, 799, 50 N.Y.S. 2d 745, 757 (Sup. Ct. 1944).

101. Chapter 5 of the Assize of Clarendon stated: "In the cause of those who have been arrested through the aforesaid oath of this assize, no one shall have court, or judgment, or chattels, except the lord king in his court before his justices, and the lord king shall have all their chattels." G. ADDAMS & H. STEPHENS, SELECT DOCUMENTS OF ENGLISH CONSTITUTIONAL HISTORY 14–18 (1926), quoted in Schwartz, *supra* note 93 at 708.

102. *Id.* at 707–8.

103. *Id.* at 709.

104. *Id.* at 709–10.

105. *Id.* at 711.

106. MARVIN E. FRANKEL & GARY P. NAFTALIS, THE GRAND JURY: AN INSTITUTION ON TRial 9 (1977); Schwartz, *supra* note 93 at 710–21.

107. Schwartz, *supra* note 93 at 713–14.

108. *Id.* at 714–16; Frankel & Naftalis, *supra* note 106 at 9.

109. Schwartz, *supra* note 93 at 716–19.

110. *See, e.g.*, Younger *supra* note 92 at 2; Frankel & Naftalis, *supra* note 106 at 9–10.

111. Schwartz, *supra* note 93 at 719.

112. Younger, *supra* note 92 at 5.

113. *Id.* at 6–7; *see also* LEROY D. CLARK, THE GRAND JURY 13 (1975).

114. *Id.*

115. *Id.* at 6–19.

116. *Id.* at 8.

117. *See*, e.g., Eben Moglan, *Considering Zenger: Partisan Politics and the Legal Profession in Provincial New York*, 94 Colum. L. Rev. 1495 (1994); STANLEY N. KATZ, INTRODUCTION TO JAMES ALEXANDER, A BRIEF NARRATIVE OF THE CASE AND TRIAL OF JOHN PETER ZENGER (Stanley N. Katz ed., 2d ed. 1972).

118. Younger, *supra* note 93 at 27–40; Frankel & Naftalis, *supra* note 106 at 11–12; LEROY D. CLARK, THE GRAND JURY 17 (1975).

119. The states were Pennsylvania, New York, New Hampshire, and Maryland. *See* Schwartz, *supra* note 13 at 157.

120. The first two amendments related to the proportion of representatives to Congress per population and to the restriction of Congress's ability to "vary compensation for their services." *See* generally Schwartz, *supra* note 13 at 119–91.

121. *Id.* at 46–55. The controversies surrounding the federal grand juries in the 1790s focused upon enforcement of President Washington's Neutrality Proclamation of 1793 and the Sedition Act of 1798.

122. *Id.* at 51.

123. EDWARD DUMBAULD, THE BILL OF RIGHTS AND WHAT IT MEANS TODAY 78, n. 2 (1957).

124. *Malloy v. Hogan*, 378 U.S. 1 (1964).

125. *Kastigar v. United States*, 406 U.S. 441, 453 (1972).

126. MARTIN L. FRIEDLAND, DOUBLE JEOPARDY 3 (1969).

127. *Digest of Justinian*, Bk. 48, Title 2, n.7, trans. S.P. Scott (1932), Vol. XVII: The Civil Law, cited in JAY A. SIGLER, DOUBLE JEOPARDY: THE DEVELOPMENT OF A LEGAL AND SOCIAL POLicy 2 (1969).

128. *Id.*

129. *Id.* at 3; Friedland, *supra* note 126 at 5.

130. *See supra* notes 91–92 and accompanying text.

131. Friedland, *supra* note 126 at 6.

132. *Id.*

133. *Id.* at 9–10; Sigler, *supra* note 127 at 7–9.

134. 4 Co. Rep. 44a, 76 E.R. 992 (1591), cited in Friedland, *supra* note 126 at 11, n.3.

135. *Id.*

136. Sigler, *supra* note 127 at 15–19; Friedland, *supra* note 126 at 11–13. Even Coke's formulation of the double jeopardy principle did not parallel our modern American understanding because it permitted a subsequent reprosecution upon a former acquittal for a homicide, the critical factor being the quality of the previous acquittal. Sigler, *supra* note 127 at 17–18.

137. Lord COKE, THE THIRD PART OF THE INSTITUTES OF THE LAWS OF ENGLAND 212–14 (4th ed. 1669); BLACKSTONE, 4 COMMENTARIES ON THE LAWS OF ENGLAND 335 (1790); HALE, 2 THE HISTORY OF THE PLEAS OF THE CROWN 240 (1847), cited in Sigler, *supra* note 127 at 18–19.

138. *Id.* at 18.

139. *Id.* at 5. The quote on breaking the neck refers to Ethelred's laws. Cnuts laws also refer to the mutilation of hand, noses, ears, and the maiming of other "extremities." *Id.*

140. Massachusetts Body of Liberties (1641), excerpted in BERNARD SCHWARTZ, 1 THE BILL OF RIGHTS: A DOCUMENTARY HISTORY 76 (1971).

141. New Hampshire Bill of Rights XVI (1784), excerpted in Schwartz, *supra* note 140 at 377.

142. Schwartz, *supra* note 13 at 71.

143. Sigler, *supra* note 127 at 24–25.

144. Schwartz, *supra* note 13 at 90.

145. Annals of Congress at 434 (1st Cong.).

146. Sigler, *supra* note 127 at 30.

147. *Id.* at 31, citing 1 Senate Journal at 119, 130 (1789).

148. *Id.* at 35. Sigler notes that "the historical development of double jeopardy is so complex that its genesis provides no sure indication of its meaning." He also observes, "At the time of its adoption into the federal constitution, the meaning of the double jeopardy concept was unclear." *Id.*

149. *Id.* at 36.

150. Nelson, *supra* note 89 at 1247. The most prominent and sophisticated historians subscribing to this historiographical perspective are R.G. Collingwood, Oscar Handlin, and J.H. Hexter. *See* R.G. COLLINGWOOD, THE IDEA OF HISTORY (1946); OSCAR HANDLIN, TRUTH IN HISTORY (1979); J.H. HEXTER, THE HISTORY PRIMER. *See* Nelson, *supra* note 89 at 1246–49.

151. *Id.* at 1252. *See* also Lawrence Lessig, *Understanding Changed Readings: Fidelity and Theory*, 47 STAN. L. REV. 395 (1995) (arguing that fidelity in constitutional interpretation encompasses changed readings of the text and that such contextual changes are inevitable).

152. *Id.* at 1291–96 (summarizing three models of constitutional analysis and how history plays a role in each model).

153. *See supra*, part 1.

154. Rakove, *supra* note 33 at 306–7.

155. *Id*. at 318–19.

156. Letter from James Madison to Thomas Jefferson, October 17, 1788, 9 PAPERS OF JAMES MADISON (William T. Hutchison et al. eds.) 297–98 (1962–91). Madison reiterated the point in the Federalist Papers, number 48, in which he stressed that the danger of tyrannical rule in a republic emanates from the legislature, not the executive. He also pointed to repeated violations of constitutional guarantees in Virginia and Pennsylvania. He specifically highlighted the violation of the right to trial by jury. ALEXANDER HAMILTON, JAMES MADISON & JOHN JAY, THE FEDERALIST PAPERS (Clinton Rossiter ed., 1961), no. 48, at 309–13. *See* also *supra* note 80 and accompanying text.

157. LANCE BANNING, THE SACRED FIRE OF LIBERTY: JAMES MADISON AND THE FOUNDING OF THE FEDERAL REPUBLIC 280 (1995).

158. *Id*. at 281–88.

159. Bodenhamer, *supra* note 72 at 5.

160. Alfredo Garcia, *Toward an Integrated Vision of Criminal Procedural Rights: A Counter to Judicial and Academic Nihilism*, 77 MARQ. L. REV. 1 (1993).

161. *See supra* Introduction.

162. SEYMOUR MARTIN LIPSET, AMERICAN EXCEPTIONALISM: A DOUBLE-EDGED SWORD 20 (1996).

163. *Id*. at 21.

164. *See supra* note 123 and accompanying text.

165. FED. R. CRIM. P. 7 (c) (1).

166. *Hamling v. United States*, 418 U.S. 87, 117 (1974).

167. *See, e.g., United States v. Jawal*, 47 F.3d 539, 542–43 (2d Cir. 1995) (permitting omission of year in which narcotics transaction took place in the indictment, because trial transcript filled the gap, thus enabling double jeopardy challenge).

168. *United States v. Mandujano*, 425 U.S. 564 (1976); *United States v. Wong*, 431 U.S. 174 (1977); *United States v. Washington*, 431 U.S. 181 (1977). The Court has expressed reluctance to require such a warning on the ground that the grand jury proceeding does not possess the inherently coercive attributes of custodial interrogation. *United States v. Mandujano*, 425 U.S. at 564. Most courts that have confronted the issue conclude that such warnings are not constitutionally compelled. *See, e.g., Gollaher v. United States*, 419 F.2d 520 (9th Cir. 1969), cert. denied 369 U.S. 960 (1969).

169. *See, e.g.*, New Mex. Stat. Ann., Section 31-6-12; Idaho Code Section 19-1121. New Mexico requires the warnings only for targets; Idaho requires them for all witnesses subpoenaed by the grand jury.

170. The U.S. Supreme Court has held that use immunity is coextensive with the self-incrimination privilege. *Kastigar v. United States*, 406 U.S. 665 (1972). The federal immunity statute confers use immunity. 18 U.S.C.A. Sec. 6003.

171. *Republica v. Shaffer*, 1 Dall. 236 (Pa. 1788), in 5 THE FOUNDERS CONSTITUTION 261 (Phillip B. Kurland & Ralph Lerner, eds., 1987).

172. *Id.*
173. *Id.*
174. *See, e.g.*, Christopher Wolfe, *The Original Meaning of the Due Process Clause in* THE BILL OF RIGHTS: ORIGINAL MEANING AND CURRENT UNDERSTANDing 213, 218 (Eugene W. Hickok, Jr., ed., 1991).
175. *See* notes 124 and 125 *supra* and accompanying text.
176. *See, e.g.*, Amar & Lettow, *supra* note 81.
177. THEODORE ZELDIN, AN INTIMATE HISTORY OF HUMANITY, 197 (1994).
178. John Hart Ely made the following observation about his much-cited 1970 article, "Legislative and Administrative Motivation in Constitutional Law": "Unfortunately, no evidence exists that anyone has read it." Ely attributes the citations to the title of the piece, "which makes it sound like the sort of thing that should be cited." Paul M. Barrett, *'Citology,' the Study of Footnotes, Sweeps the Law Schools*, WALL STREET JOURNAL, January 22, 1997, at A8.
179. *Id.*

CHAPTER 2

WHAT IS A "VOLUNTARY"
CONFESSION?

INTRODUCTION

Americans have experienced a love-hate relationship with confessions. This dichotomy should not startle us; rather, it should help us define the fundamental social, cultural, and legal roots of confessions in the American landscape. Simply put, "we want confessions, yet we are suspicious of them."[1] Because confessions lie deep within our social fabric yet evoke such ambivalence, it is not surprising that the criminal justice system has encountered a similar reaction. The inherent paradox of desiring confessions while rejecting the baggage that produces them has yielded a jurisprudence beset with inconsistencies, contradictions, and vagueness. In a vain attempt to solve the inevitable confessional paradox, the Supreme Court delineated the *Miranda* warnings as the answer to the conundrum. Yet, the *Miranda* opinion was destined for failure from its genesis. Indeed, *Miranda* only generated more confusion and uncertainty than the "voluntariness" standard that it supplanted.

We should not, however, castigate the Supreme Court for not providing a solution to an intractable problem. Instead, we ought to place the confessional paradox in its proper historical, social, and cultural context. Although the subject lies beyond the scope of this work and has been the subject of Peter Brooks' perceptive book,[2] I believe that the cultural, societal, historical, and religious dimensions of confessions must inform the legal analysis. From a societal and religious perspective, for example, confessions might be good for the soul. On the other hand, to the extent that confessions represent "the queen of proofs in the law,"[3] they are instruments of the alleged offender's ultimate undoing. Therein lies the answer to our riddle: we want confessions because we want to hear from the person who has the answers we desperately seek. However, we do not know how far the police ought to go in obtaining the offender's confession, and we intuitively discern that the offender gets nothing in return for the confession but our most solemn form of punishment. Confessions might offend Americans' sense of fair play because the method of extracting them seems so one-sided.

How do we reconcile the American thirst for confessions with our simultaneous hostility toward them? More important, how do we explain the irony of the privilege against self-incrimination coexisting with our professed desire for confessions as the "queen of proofs?" As we saw in our historical overview of the privilege in America, it was circumscribed in its application, permitting officials to rely on psychological tactics to induce confessions while prohibiting them from using physical violence or overt promises.[4] More important, the privilege against self-incrimination was ignored in formal adjudication of guilt because the "accused speaks" model prevailed. The accused was not represented by counsel and thus was forced to speak, or otherwise expect a certain conviction, because he did not have a lawyer to speak on his behalf. Only when lawyers assumed an influential role in the trial did the privilege attain a meaningful role in the new nation.[5] The right to remain silent, therefore, was not integral to the established norms from the outset of the American experience.

Americans' conflicting attitudes regarding confessions parallel to some extent their mixed emotions about the death penalty. Although support for or opposition to the death penalty has oscillated, we seem to approve the penalty for egregious cases while also seeking to avoid its draconian effect by affording safeguards against its arbitrary or erroneous application. Indeed, the administration of the death penalty is similar in many ways to the securing of a confession by law enforcement agents. In both instances, governmental agents are alone in a room with either a suspect or a defendant. In the case of confessions, the isolation and control by law enforcement agents serve to induce a confession from the suspect; this is the act of shame, opprobrium, guilt, and expiation by the offender. Similarly, the death chamber is a study in ultimate control and isolation: the defendant is alone in the room with the law enforcement agents entrusted with administering state-sanctioned death. The defendant is asked whether he wishes to say anything before he dies. We expect the ultimate act of contrition and expiation from the defendant. When we instead encounter defiance and denial of guilt, it reaffirms our sense that the defendant was beyond redemption. This emotion approximates the reaction to the suspect who fails to confess despite the detectives' efforts to obtain the ultimate proof of the crime.

In this chapter and the next, I will review the attempt by American courts to deal with the conundrum of reconciling our contradictory opinions about confessions. In this chapter, I will examine the genesis, development, and decline of the "voluntariness" standard as a means of determining the legality of confessions. The next chapter will delve into the historical, social, and legal roots of the *Miranda* opinion as the failed symbol of the Supreme Court's attempt to forge a simple solution to an implacable quandary: how to decide when law enforcement has crossed the threshold into "coercing" a suspect rather than securing a "voluntary" confession. I employ quotation marks in the preceding sentences to convey my sense that these legal terms are feeble endeavors to fashion what are essentially unworkable criteria. Our legal system is incapable of providing certitude where philosophical, moral, and societal ambivalence reign supreme.

It is counterintuitive to imagine such a phenomenon as a "voluntary" confession in a setting where detectives or law enforcement agents seek to obtain an admission of guilt from a suspect. A perceptive observer has noted that "by any standards of human discourse, a criminal confession can never truly be called voluntary."[6] In modern America, the detective in an interrogation room is "trained in a genuinely deceitful art" and seeks to secure a confession from a suspect by either compelling, provoking, or manipulating the person into confessing.[7] How does this reality square with the tenets ascribed to the privilege against self-incrimination, which embodies, according to the Supreme Court, "many of our fundamental values and most noble aspirations?"[8] Quite simply, even though we chafe at the tactics necessary to extract a confession from a suspect, we simultaneously recognize the need for the interrogation process. The question that the legal system has unsuccessfully tackled involves this fundamental antinomy.

The Anglo-American legal process attempted to delineate, through the amorphous voluntariness criterion, the factors that triggered our sense of justice to exclude a confession in spite of how much we longed for its benefits. During the 1960s and the liberal transformation wrought by the Warren Court in the criminal justice system, we erected a "symbol" with the *Miranda* opinion. *Miranda* is still part of our legal landscape, despite the best efforts of those who sought to discard it, because it satisfies our "collective conscience." As David Simon has aptly put it, *Miranda* "is a slave for a collective conscience that cannot reconcile libertarian ideas with what must necessarily occur in an interrogation room."[9] The historical progression reflected in the law of confessions is a prism refracting our profound neurosis about a subject that has confounded even the most brilliant legal minds.

Before embarking upon the Supreme Court's desultory journey to define what constitutes a "voluntary" confession, I should emphasize the obvious: no such thing exists. Rather, the Court has spun a fictional tale in determining on a case-by-case basis whether the police have gone too far in their interrogation of the suspect to warrant exclusion of the confession. The distinguished legal scholar Yale Kamisar placed the issue in proper context by remarking that "involuntariness" is "little more than a fiction intended to vilify certain 'effective' interrogation methods."[10] Its counterpart, a "voluntary" confession, is similarly "little more than a fiction designed to beautify certain other interrogation techniques."[11]

Stressing the causal nexus between the police's conduct and the suspect's confession, Joseph Grano has underlined the distinction between placing the blame on the police for the confession or, alternatively, making the accused "accountable" for it.[12] In turn, Grano acknowledges that "coercion" and "voluntariness" are normative concepts dependent upon our beliefs about police interrogations, confessions, or the role of the criminal justice system in remedying police abuse.[13] In short, Grano recognizes that the proper role of confessions in determining guilt in the criminal justice system ultimately hinges upon our subjective notions. Although he labors valiantly by grounding his conclusions in philosophical, moral, and legal variables, Grano acknowledges the obvious in the introduction to his book: that he is unlikely to persuade the bulk of the legal academy or the judiciary to adopt his thesis. Grano maintains that the law "governing police interrogation" is overly rigid, "restrictive," and "formalistic."[14]

Indeed, our overarching values, attitudes, and emotions about police interrogations and confessions in the criminal process yield disparate and conflicting views. It should not surprise Grano that a subject evoking such passion and subjective opinions yields contrasting perspectives. It is very difficult, therefore, to persuade others to change their deep-seated and visceral reactions to such a volatile issue. The ambivalent attitudes we tend to harbor toward confessions and police interrogation techniques compound the problem. I do not pretend to have a solution to this impenetrable quandary. Nor, for that matter, do I harbor illusions about persuading the reader to adopt my point of view. Rather, the public's perception is shaped to a large degree, over an extended period of time, by cultural, societal, and political trends. These changes, moreover, are also a function of the influence exerted by the media. For example, when the media choose to focus on the injustices resulting from convictions based upon false confessions, the public may alter its views on the extent to which the police ought to rely on deceptive interrogation tactics to induce confessions.

To some extent, however, the public's conflicting attitudes toward the role of confessions in proving a crime are explicable by reference to our adversarial system of adjudication. The adversarial criminal process places the burden of proof exclusively on the prosecution. That burden, moreover, is a heavy one: the government must establish the defendant's guilt beyond a reasonable doubt.[15] Quoting from Dean McCormick, Justice William Brennan refers to the powerful impact of confessions on the adversarial system. In effect, the admission of a confession into evidence renders the trial superfluous, repudiating the tenet under which the prosecution is required to shoulder a "heavy burden of proof." [16] We can attribute our distaste for confessions, therefore, to the powerful influence exerted by the "queen of proofs" on a system that is supposed to give the defendant a fair chance to be aquitted.

HOW DOES THE LEGAL SYSTEM DEFINE A "VOLUNTARY" CONFESSION?

How does the legal system arrive at a solution to the conundrum raised by confessions in an adversarial process of adjudication? It seems that the American system of adjudication has been struggling with the problem since the colonies broke from British control. In its starkest form, the dichotomy posed by the role of confessions in our criminal process was outlined in radically different perspectives offered by two of our most eminent jurists: Felix Frankfurter and Robert Jackson. In the most cited and scholarly attempt to delineate the ethical and legal bases for determining what constitutes a voluntary confession, Justice Frankfurter delivered a tour de force in the *Columbe v. Connecticut*[17] opinion. Reducing a voluntary confession to its essence, Frankfurter defined it as "the product of an essentially free and unrestrained choice by its maker."[18] This required the accused, reputedly under the domination and control of the police and in custody, to speak in the unfettered exercise of a free will. If not, then "his will has been over-borne and his capacity for self-determination critically impaired," thereby rendering the confession inadmissible because it was secured in violation of the due process clause of the Fourteenth Amendment.[19]

Contrasting sharply with that famous and oft-cited standard for judging the voluntariness of a confession is Justice Jackson's sardonic yet trenchant analysis in his *Ashcraft v. Tennessee*[20] dissent. *Ashcraft* involved the continuous thirty-six-hour interrogation of a suspect by successive relays of detectives. Disagreeing with his colleagues that such an interrogation was "inherently coercive," Jackson probed the utter irrationality of deeming a suspect's confession "voluntary." Custody and interrogation of a suspect for thirty-six hours, he conceded, is "inherently coercive." So, for that matter, is custody and interrogation "for one hour." Furthermore, "arrest itself is inherently coercive, and so is detention."[21] The proper inquiry, according to Jackson, was whether the suspect had the fortitude to "withstand for days pressures that would destroy the will of another in hours."[22] In short, the peculiar vulnerabilities or characteristics of the suspect, as they relate to his ability to either withstand or succumb to the pressures of police custody and interrogation, should determine the legal validity of the confession.

Who has the more compelling argument in this inescapable debate? A prominent scholar provides the best answer to the question. Peter Brooks observes that "even the most indisputably 'voluntary' confession may arise from a state of dependency, shame, and the need for punishment, a condition that casts some doubt on the law's language of autonomy and free choice."[23] Nevertheless, the law must "promote" the fiction erected by Justice Frankfurter that "autonomy" or "free choice" is compatible with confessions wrought by police custody and interrogation.[24] In fact, Justice Jackson's more individualistic definition of a "voluntary" confession also relies upon the notion of "free choice." It is just a different, more realistic, version that takes into account the invariable pressures that accompany police custody and questioning of a criminal suspect.

With this caveat as our fundamental premise, we must proceed to examine the manner in which the U.S. Supreme Court has employed constitutional clauses to delineate the factors and criteria for determining whether a confession is "voluntary." The origins of the doctrine that a confession must be voluntary to be admissible against a defendant derive from the common law; in essence, the doctrine rested on the law of evidence, not the Constitution.[25] Eventually, as we shall see, the Court gave the "voluntariness" doctrine a constitutional dimension by relying on the Fifth Amendment's self-incrimination clause in federal cases and on the Fourteenth Amendment's due process clause in state cases.

The evolution of the law of confessions is inextricably linked to the rise of police departments in large metropolitan areas.[26] Before the mid-nineteenth century, law enforcement was a haphazard activity, performed by different individuals and organizations, primarily sheriffs, constables, and night watchmen. A series of riots—provoked in large part by social and economic transformations such as urbanization, industrialization, and immigration—brought about the creation of what ultimately would become the professional police department.[27] Further, the shift toward police investigation of crimes transformed the locale of questions about the legality of confessions from preliminary judicial proceedings to police interrogation rooms.[28] The extent to which the police would be constrained in the interrogation of suspects by constitutional restrictions embodied in the Fifth Amendment privilege against self-incrimination and the due process clause of the Fourteenth Amendment would take center stage.

Two cases decided by the Court in the late nineteenth century have assumed a prominent role in the history of the law of confessions. Invariably, any article or book that relates the story of the Supreme Court's jurisprudence on confessions, analyzes and dissects both *Hopt v. Utah*[29] and *Bram v. United States*.[30] Both cases constitute the first halting attempts by the Court to fashion a doctrine by which to gauge whether a confession was the "voluntary" product of a suspect's free will or the result of improper inducements by the police. *Hopt* offers little assistance and is rather prosaic; *Bram*, however, presages the conceptual and analytical problems the Court would encounter in assessing the threshold at which police behavior would render a confession "involuntary."

It is unremarkable that both *Hopt* and *Bram* involved murders; confessions are most coveted in a murder case, where the stakes for solving the crime are compelling. Confessions seem to satisfy our craving for punishment and expiation when the life of a human being has been taken without justification. Compared with, for example, an ordinary burglary, murder seems to call for the immediate and solemn condemnation of the offender. If the burglary goes unsolved, or the suspect does not confess, our collective sense of disdain for the offender is not compounded. On the other hand, an unsolved murder, or an unrepentant murderer, seems to evoke our deepest passions. When the suspect is apprehended in a murder case, the visceral reaction by those closest to the victim may be radical. This is what occurred in *Hopt*: the victim's father appeared to have drawn a revolver on the suspect at the time the offender was apprehended.[31] The detective who made the arrest, however, may have dissuaded the victim's father from exacting revenge. Circumstances in the western territories at the turn of the nineteenth century called for extraordinary measures. Detective Carr, therefore, wisely had a policeman take the suspect away from the scene of the arrest, and a "large crowd," into the local jail, where the suspect promptly confessed to the murder.[32]

A three-minute gap existed from the time that the suspect was whisked away from the crowd by a policeman to the time that he confessed when the detective arrived at the jail. Although Carr could not vouch for what transpired during that three-minute interval, he avowed that the confession was voluntary and that "he held out no inducement, and did not know of any inducement being held out to [the] defendant to confess."[33] Rejecting the possibility that the policeman might have improperly "induced" the defendant to confess in that three-minute gap, and in the absence of evidence of collusion by Detective Carr and the policeman, the Court concluded that the confession was "voluntary."[34]

At the outset, the Court acknowledges the difficulty of drawing clear lines of demarcation for determining when a confession is "voluntary." Indeed, Justice John Harlan concedes that "it is difficult, if not impossible, to formulate a rule that will comprehend all cases."[35] Recognizing that some English case law manifests extreme distrust of confessions generated by police interrogation, Harlan nevertheless rejects the notion that only confessions before judicial officers should be deemed voluntary.[36] Rather, he formulates the criterion that would ultimately guide the Court for decades: a confession is "evidence of the most satisfactory character"[37] if the police do not deprive the suspect "of that freedom of will or self-control essential to make his confession voluntary."[38] Completing the tautological syllogism, Harlan explains that as long as the police do not "induce" the suspect to confess through promises or threats, then they have not deprived him of the free will or "self-control" necessary to render the confession "voluntary within the meaning of the law."[39]

The stipulation employed by Harlan in the preceding quote is telling. It is as if he is recognizing the obvious: confessions rendered by suspects in police custody are "voluntary" only by reference to arbitrary legal definitions. Contemplating the nebulous and uncertain nature of the definition of a voluntary confession, and its case-by-case adjudication, one is left with a vacuum that will be filled by the Court as it sees fit under the circumstances. Whose word, moreover, will be credited by the Court when it assesses the voluntariness of a confession? *Hopt* is revealing in this respect. Justice Harlan uncritically accepts the testimony of the detective who obtained the confession, even though the self-serving testimony was the only evidence adduced to establish that the confession was voluntary and not the product of unseemly "threats," "promises," or "inducements."[40]

Although I may have denigrated *Hopt*'s judicial worth, I do not wish to undermine its fundamental value. What *Hopt* teaches is the dichotomy inherent in an extrajudicial confession elicited by police authorities engaged in the "often competitive enterprise of ferreting out crime."[41] One senses Justice Harlan's ambivalence toward police-generated confessions when he refers to an English precedent that casts doubt on extrajudicial admissions. Ultimately, however, he is swayed by the powerful nature of confessions as proof of a crime, especially a crime as grave as murder. Quoting Eyre, Justice Harlan points to the "highest credit" which confessions are accorded, since presumably they "flow from the strongest sense of guilt."[42] Harlan's opinion expresses the basic conflict that attends our need for confessions as well as our distrust of the means by which they may be obtained. In the final analysis, the Supreme Court in *Hopt* resolves the issue by accepting confessions, when voluntarily "made," as the "queen of proofs." It would have taken a "supreme" act of forbearance for the Court to have gone the other way and rejected the legal validity of police-induced confessions.

Hopt's bookend, *Bram v. United States*[43] provides insight into the Court's dilemma in forging a coherent law of confessions. Not only does the opinion link the Fifth Amendment's privilege against self-incrimination to confessions, it also holds that the circumstances under which the confession was given justified its exclusion as evidence. In the process, Justice Byron White, writing for the majority, exposes the clash of values and inconsistent application that would bedevil the Court's jurisprudence in future cases. Prompting a spirited dissent, *Bram* propelled the Court into a division over how much pressure can be brought to bear on a suspect before it calls for the exclusion of the confession. Although the *Bram* majority opinion is not a model of clarity, it does expound a troubling distrust of police-induced confessions lacking in the *Hopt* opinion.

Like *Hopt, Bram* involved the investigation of a murder, this time on the ocean rather than on land. The crime occurred while an American ship was bound from Boston to South America. The suspect was the first officer, and the victim was the captain.[44] Held in custody and questioned when the ship reached land at Halifax, Nova Scotia, Bram was subjected to the typical incommunicado interrogation that has become the stock-in-trade of police questioning of criminal suspects. He was questioned in the detective's office about the crime. Going beyond mere interrogation, however, the detective stripped the suspect, searched him, and examined his clothing.[45] The detective confronted the suspect by revealing that a crewmate had implicated him in the murder; the suspect replied that the witness could not have seen him commit the crime.[46] Buttressing the detective's questioning was his categorical belief in the suspect's guilt and his assumption that the suspect had an accomplice. Both of these premises, moreover, were conveyed to the suspect.[47]

In accord with the facts in *Hopt*, the detective told the examining court that he exerted no undue influence or pressure on the suspect.[48] Therefore, the Supreme Court again faced the usual circumstance associated with police-induced confessions: the testimony of the police officer who conducted the interrogation to the effect that, in his estimation, the suspect spoke of his own free will. How does one explain a different outcome in the *Bram* case? The *Bram* Court stressed the detective's clever interrogation stratagem as weakening the suspect's resistance. By simultaneously emphasizing the suspect's guilt while minimizing its effect through the suggestion of an accomplice's participation, the detective rendered the confession involuntary.[49]

Underlying the *Bram* majority opinion is a deep-seated antipathy toward extrajudicial confessions. Expressing this hostility in sweeping fashion, Justice White observes that, because it is impossible to discern either the extent or impact of the police influence on the suspect, it is better to suppress the confession "if any degree of influence has been exerted."[50] In effect, *Bram* is remarkable for its acknowledgment of the truism that it is impossible to determine when the threshold of coercion is crossed in police-dominated interrogations. It is more revolutionary, moreover, to the degree that it errs on the side of the suspect rather than the police.

The contrast between *Bram* and *Hopt* could not be starker. One opinion perceives police interrogation as a positive weapon in law enforcement's crime-fighting repertoire. The *Hopt* Court accepts the police version of what transpired in the interrogation room at face value. On the other hand, the *Bram* majority not only distrusts the techniques and methods employed by law enforcement to induce the suspect to confess; it also decides that when the least bit of evidence is adduced to suggest that any influence has been exerted on the suspect, the confession ought to be excluded as a matter of law. This explains Justice Brewer's dissenting opinion in *Bram*, joined by two other members of the Court. He questions the majority's rejection of the interrogating officer's testimony that the confession was voluntary. Furthermore, Justice Brewer saw nothing legally amiss in the fact that the suspect was both shackled and in custody at the time he confessed to the murder.[51]

Indeed, Justice White's majority opinion foreshadows the distrust of police-dominated interrogation that would underlie the famous *Miranda* decision. Justice White cited a nineteenth-century English statute that required a magistrate, before interrogating a suspect, to warn him of the right to remain silent and that any statements he made would be used against him at trial.[52] The precept underlying this statute was the probability that, without the warning, the suspect might feel compelled to speak.[53] One derives a sense of the *Bram* majority's unease about the process of interrogation and its mental effect on the suspect. If a suspect might feel compelled to give a statement to a magistrate, then it followed that he would feel more pressure from questioning by a police officer within the confines of an isolated room.

It is this sense of confinement that the Court emphasizes in *Bram*. In a graphic passage, Justice White, writing for the majority, stresses the factors that the *Miranda* opinion would underscore in determining that custodial interrogation is inherently coercive. In Justice White's words, "Bram had been brought from confinement to the office of the detective . . ., was interrogated by the officer, who was thus, while putting the questions and receiving answers thereto, exercising complete authority and control over the person he was interrogating."[54] Although the majority based its conclusion on the totality of the circumstances, the opinion is noteworthy because it underscored the difficulty of determining the voluntariness of a confession secured by police-dominated interrogation.

Bram is also remarkable for the emphasis it places on the free will of the suspect. Treating the suspect as an independent actor in the confessional drama, Justice White describes Bram's declarations as not "made by one who in law could be considered a free agent."[55] Bram was not a "free agent" when he denied complicity in the murder because the detective had impaired his mental freedom. In particular, the detective had employed psychological tactics that operated to negate Bram's mental freedom. According to the *Bram* majority, the detective's statement to Bram that someone else had implicated him in the murder "perturbed the mind" and "engendered confusion."[56] Bram's reply denying participation in the murder was, in effect, a confession. In the totality of the circumstances, the confession "could not have been a result of a purely voluntary mental action."[57] In its totality, the circumstances under which the confession was given evinced a plain violation of the "spirit and purpose" of the constitutional privilege against self-incrimination.[58]

Taken at face value, *Bram* stands for the proposition that any influence exerted by the police on a suspect's cognitive autonomy invalidates a confession. Employing such terms as "free agent," "purely voluntary mental action," and "perturbed mind," the *Bram* case emphasizes the causal link between police interrogation and a suspect's impaired mental freedom. Implicitly, the majority opinion discerns the irreconcilable conflict between a suspect's volition and the intimidating and coercive influence attending police custodial interrogations. Free choice and autonomy are inherently at odds with police questioning of a suspect in closed quarters. As Justice Jackson artfully put it in his *Ashcraft* dissent, custody and interrogation are "inherently coercive." Whether this tenet would legally invalidate the confession is another matter. The *Bram* majority seemed to imply that any mental or physical pressure on the suspect, however slight, violated the privilege against self-incrimination. That view was diametrically opposed to the notion espoused by the *Hopt* dissent as well as its opinion. The Supreme Court would have to grapple with the conflict in the ensuing century; it was a dichotomy, moreover, that by its nature would have an unsatisfactory resolution unless confessions were to be banished from the police investigative repertoire.

VOLUNTARINESS, "FREE WILL," PSYCHOLOGICAL AND PHYSICAL COERCION, AND RELIABILITY

In 1897, the *Bram* opinion had stated that a confession must be given by a "free agent," stem from "purely voluntary mental action," and reflect an "unperturbed mind." Imagine, then, a situation in which the police do nothing improper but receive a confession from a suspect who is technically not a "free agent" because he is suffering from paranoid schizophrenia at the time he confesses to a murder. That improbable scenario materialized in a celebrated case, *Colorado v. Connelly*,[59] the Supreme Court decided in 1986. *Connelly* is significant because it clearly defines the conundrum posed by the law of confessions: the criteria marking the boundaries beyond which the law will not permit a confession to play a critical evidentiary role in a criminal prosecution. It is also noteworthy for delineating the extent to which the suspect's "free will," or volitional autonomy, is a variable in the admissibility of confessions. Finally, *Connelly* represents a milestone in the Court's deviation from the spirit and letter of the *Miranda* opinion. It provides a lens through which we may view the development of the law of confessions in the twentieth century.

In the nearly a century that elapsed between *Bram* and *Connelly*, the Supreme Court fashioned the "voluntariness" doctrine to evaluate what burdens the Constitution places upon police interrogation of criminal suspects. We have seen how the Court employed the Fifth Amendment privilege against self-incrimination to constrain federal police interrogation tactics. Beginning in 1936, the Court relied on the Fourteenth Amendment's due process clause[60] to limit state police interrogation practices. Sweeping broadly, the Court seized upon a nebulous constitutional clause to regulate the states' ability to determine the admissibility of confessions. In doing so, it developed an amorphous standard as a regulatory device to deter physical and psychological techniques utilized by the police to obtain confessions. Until the Court handed down the *Connelly* opinion, it also placed an individual's "free will" or "volition" as the centerpiece of a "voluntary" confession.

Scholars have criticized the Court's "voluntariness" doctrine, describing it as inconsistent and lacking coherence.[61] As we shall see in the next chapter, the *Miranda* "bright-line" presumptive standard, as modified and diluted by the Court, became more muddled than the fuzzy voluntariness standard it modified. Although the voluntariness doctrine was principally fact-specific, the cases do fall into coherent and explicable categories. It is plausible, moreover, to argue that *Miranda* was the logical "outgrowth" of the due process doctrines.[62] With these qualifications in mind, one can begin to probe how the Court waded through possibly the most recondite area of its richly varied criminal justice jurisprudence. We will conclude this exercise by taking a close look at the *Connelly* opinion, which stands in marked contrast to the *Bram*'s Court solicitude for "free agency" and "voluntary mental action" as a prerequisite for a constitutionally "voluntary" confession.

Wayne LaFave, Jerold Israel, and Nancy King categorize the jumble of confession cases the Court decided under the voluntariness standard into three discrete areas: (1) confessions deemed unreliable because they were the product of offensive police practices, typically marked by the threat or use of physical violence; (2) confessions that, though reliable, were obtained as a result of police coercion, typically psychological ploys designed to break the suspect's will to resist; and (3) confessions secured under circumstances in which the defendant's free will was "significantly impaired," despite the absence of police wrongdoing.[63]

VIOLENCE, RELIABILITY, AND DUE PROCESS

The landmark case launching the Supreme Court's development and refinement of the voluntariness test is *Brown v. Mississippi.*[64] In emphatic terms, the *Brown* opinion states in the first sentence that the confessions upon which the defendants' convictions rested were "extorted" by the police through "brutality and violence."[65] Indeed, one can scarcely imagine more egregious and abhorrent methods of securing a confession. The police hung one defendant several times, inflicted brutal whippings, and demanded that the defendants confess to a murder. Compounding these fundamental violations of human dignity and freedom were transgressions of essential trial rights. The defendants were arraigned on murder charges and promptly tried on the indictment the following day. They were found guilty and sentenced to death. The convictions were based exclusively on the questionable confessions.[66]

Brown broke new legal ground on several fronts. It represented the Supreme Court's exercise of constitutional supervision over state confession cases under the Fourteenth Amendment's due process clause. Second, it put the Court on record as unequivocally opposing the use of violence as a means of securing a confession. Third, *Brown* stands for the proposition that a sham trial, based solely on a confession, violates fair trial norms embedded in the Constitution. Writing for the Court, Justice Charles Hughes declared that a "trial equally is a mere pretense where state authorities have contrived a conviction resting solely on confessions obtained by violence."[67]

Historically, *Brown* is significant because the Court encroached upon state jurisdiction "to enforce rudimentary norms of racial equality on the southern justice system."[68] The defendants in *Brown* were black men accused of murdering a white man and were subjected to the specter of mob violence and lynching characteristic of the South in the 1930s. In addition, the Court sought to regulate abusive police interrogation methods visited especially upon the poor and minorities.[69] Five years before the Court handed down the *Brown* opinion, the Wickersham Commission had issued a report documenting police reliance on third-degree tactics in securing confessions.[70]

Third-degree methods create a grave risk that a confession will be unreliable; the will to resist physical violence varies according to individual characteristics and susceptibilities. It is unusual, however, to find an individual who can withstand sustained brutality and violence and yet not confess to a crime that he or she has not committed. Therein lies the danger of the use of violence as a means of "extorting" a confession from a suspect. At some point, the will to resist a false confession will erode; the result will, in all likelihood, be a grave miscarriage of justice. This is precisely what transpired in the *Brown* case. Coupled with a sham trial designed to arrive at a quick guilty verdict, the tactics that produced the confession in *Brown* were reminiscent of "the crowning infamy of the Star Chamber, and the Inquisition, and other similar institutions."[71]

There is another way one may analyze *Brown*. It may be that the Court was not concerned with reliability, or the risk of false confessions created by third-degree tactics, but rather with the "fairness of the process through which a [confession] was obtained."[72] The traditional analysis, however, diverges from this perspective, viewing the "fairness" rationale as collateral to the Court's emphasis on reliability and reducing the potential for false confessions.[73]

These competing rationales are not mutually exclusive. As the foremost authority on the law of confessions noted in 1963, the due process cases condemned interrogation techniques that created a "substantial risk" of false confessions regardless of the reliability of a particular confession.[74] To the extent that interrogation tactics employed by the police are designed to extract a confession from the suspect, it follows that certain interrogation practices will create the risk of a false confession. Although it is equally, if not more, likely that these methods will lead to true confessions,[75] the fact remains that such methods must be repudiated to the extent that they will lead to unreliable or false confessions. Indeed, the *Bram* case, decided by the Court in the 1890s, may be viewed as an extreme example of such an axiom. Because the police exploited the suspect's vulnerable position, they undermined his mental freedom and created the risk that his confession might be untrustworthy.

Violence as a tactic designed to extort a confession from a suspect not only creates a substantial risk of an unreliable confession, it also represents an unfair method of securing a suspect's admission. The police need not, however, rely on violence to accomplish their goal; the mere threat of violence may bring about the same result. This is what a bare majority of the Court concluded in one of the few cases decided under the voluntariness standard since the advent of *Miranda*. In *Arizona v. Fulminante*,[76] the Court held that a confession induced through a "credible threat of physical violence" was involuntary. Justice White, speaking for the majority on that particular issue, concluded that the suspect's "will was overborne in such a way as to render his confession the product of coercion."[77] It is noteworthy that Justice White felt compelled to note that "the question [of the voluntariness of the confession] is a close one."[78]

The facts in *Fulminante* betray the shifting sand upon which the voluntariness doctrine, and confession law in general, is predicated. An FBI informant in that case befriended the defendant, who was incarcerated on a weapons charge. Because the defendant was suspected of having sexually assaulted and murdered his stepchild, and the inmate population targets for special abuse those who have committed such a crime, the FBI informant offered "protection" to Fulminante if he confessed. Posing as an organized crime figure, the informant presumably offered credible protection to Fulminante in exchange for a confession.[79] In addition to such a "creditable threat of physical violence," the *Fulminante* majority emphasized the defendant's physical attributes (he was short and "slight in build"), his low intelligence, and his unease with the vagaries of prison life.[80]

By contrast, the dissent saw the facts from a different perspective. Stressing the defendant's admission that he did not fear other inmates or seek the FBI informant's protection, Justice William Rehnquist construed the majority's conclusion as not "warranted by any of our decided cases."[81] According to the dissent, the defendant felt no pressure to confess from the FBI man, a conclusion buttressed by the defendant's familiarity with the prison system and his ignorance of the FBI informant's status as a governmental agent.[82]

The split in the Court reflects the imponderable and insuperable issues raised by the law of confessions. In 1991, the Court was no closer to deciding just how much pressure inflicted on the suspect by the police was required to render a confession involuntary. On the one hand, Justice White classified the case as a "close one," reflecting the majority's ambivalence on the coercion issue. On the other hand, Chief Justice Rehnquist expressed frustration at the majority's supposed distortion of the facts, which pointed to a free and voluntary confession by a savvy suspect. Whether the majority or the dissent has the correct version of the facts in *Fulminante* is irrelevant. Rather, the case reveals the vicissitudes the Court must confront in the futile path of creating the fiction that a confession by a criminal suspect can ever be a product of a free will and intellect. The facts are always murky and two-sided, the law is always subjective, and the conclusions reached by the Court are questionable, depending upon the reader's outlook.

PSYCHOLOGICAL STRATAGEMS, TRUTH, AND CONFESSIONS

The threat of physical violence constitutes a form of psychological coercion. Once the Supreme Court decreed and reinforced the notion that "violence is an outlaw," it forced law enforcement to rely on a different stratagem: psychological games designed to coax a confession from a suspect. As we have seen at the outset of this endeavor, the effective interrogator relies on guilt, shame, minimization of culpability, and atonement as his fundamental psychological tools. The "overbearing of the will"—terminology employed by the Court to mark an involuntary confession—makes the point. Although the government agent in *Fulminante* did not resort to the abominable violence pervading *Brown v. Mississippi*, he preyed, at least in the view of the majority, on the psychological vulnerability of the suspect to obtain the confession. Indeed, a successful interrogator combines both physical and psychological pressures to induce a suspect to confess. This explains Justice White's emphasis in *Fulminante* not only on the threat of physical violence but also on the suspect's physical limitations. What induced Fulminante to confess was not only the psychological threat of violence but also his short stature, slight build, and the stresses of prison life. If the case was "close," then the suspect's physical limitations, as well as the characteristics of prison life, must have played a role in Fulminante's decision to confess.

The *Fulminante* case straddles the divide between sheer physical torture and subtle as well as overt psychological ploys designed to induce the suspect to confess. Speaking for a unanimous Court in 1960, Chief Justice Earl Warren observed that, from early in its modern confession-law jurisprudence, the "Court has recognized that coercion can be mental as well as physical."[83] Perhaps the Court realized at an early stage of its voluntariness jurisprudence that once it outlawed physical coercion, psychological inducements would quickly supplant sheer physical force as the stock-in-trade of police interrogation. Implicitly recognizing the transformation, Warren noted that "the thumbscrew can be matched, given the proper subject, by more sophisticated modes of 'persuasion.'"[84]

That the Court acknowledged the mental element inherent in securing a confession from a criminal suspect confirms the truism that no confession is truly "voluntary." Whether the methods employed are physical or mental, the "game," as we have seen, is ultimately psychological rather than physical. After all, the physical torture is a means to the end of breaking down the suspect's mental resistance. If shame, guilt, and self-hate cannot be induced through psychological ploys, then physical violence must either complement mental pressure or induce the amoral suspect to confess. The extent to which such methods offend either our sense of justice or the Court's notion of what the Constitution prohibits is a different matter. From the legal perspective, the Court acknowledged in *Bram* that psychological stratagems, combined with police domination, were tactics most likely to succeed in bringing about a confession. Then the Court shifted the focus to physical violence in *Brown*, questioning the reliability of a confession extorted through physical violence.

Reliability, however, is not the sole concern manifested by the Court in construing the due process clause of the Fourteenth Amendment. Not only is physical violence or mental coercion apt to produce false confessions; both may also offend a sense of fairness implied in the elastic, due process clause of the Constitution. However trustworthy a confession may turn out to be, it may nonetheless transgress constitutional principles if it was secured in a fashion that offends the right of the suspect to due process of law.

Applying this axiom to a concrete example, Justice Frankfurter decried the cruel psychological pressure police interrogators used to obtain a confession in the oft-cited *Rogers v. Richmond*[85] case. In that case the police had incontrovertible evidence linking the suspect to the murder for which he was convicted. At the time he was arrested, the suspect was in possession of the revolver that subsequent ballistic tests verified was used in the fatal shooting.[86] If the police in effect possessed the "smoking gun" to convict the defendant, one wonders why they sought additional evidence against him. When the stakes to solve a crime are high, and the need to secure a conviction compelling, there is nothing better than to obtain the "queen of proofs," the suspect's confession. I doubt that the police would have sought a confession with such fervor had the crime been an ordinary burglary, for example, rather than a murder stemming from a liquor store robbery.

After a six-hour interrogation session yielded no results, the chief of police was brought in. He resorted to a most clever artifice: he pretended that he was going to arrest the suspect's wife, who was suffering from arthritis, unless the suspect confessed.[87] Although he was interrogated for six hours, the suspect "was at no time subjected to violence or the threat of violence."[88] Furthermore, even though there was conflicting testimony, the suspect indicated that he sought the assistance of a lawyer "shortly after" the beginning of the interrogation.[89] It is also noteworthy that Chief Eagan joined the interrogation six hours after it commenced, after a team of three interrogators had failed to obtain an admission.[90]

Emphatically affirming that reliability was not the relevant constitutional measure of a voluntary confession, Justice Frankfurter wrote that a confession brought about by psychological or physical coercion "cannot stand." He elaborated on the underlying rationale of a voluntary confession: regardless of its truth, a confession secured through either of those means is diametrically at odds with our accusatorial system of adjudication. Justice Frankfurter took pains to note that the Court had reversed convictions involving confessions obtained through psychological or physical coercion, despite the incontrovertible truth "of what the defendant had confessed."[91] Indeed, one scholar has suggested that the Court's confession "due process" cases "have always focused on the propriety of the officer's interrogation methods rather than the resulting confessions."[92]

Rogers is replete with lessons about the Court's modern analytical and normative approach toward the law of confessions. It is instructive that the opinion, in the second paragraph, notes the lack of physical violence attending the interrogation. Indeed, the Court notes that the suspect was allowed to smoke and eat during the time he was subjected to questioning. Yet what Frankfurter misses is the physical stamina necessary to withstand sustained interrogation within the confines of a police station. Isn't a prolonged interrogation session a physical contest in which the suspect is subjected to questioning in close quarters by experienced interrogators? Is physical stamina not relevant to the ability to fend off the psychological pressure? Although the main instrument employed by law enforcement is psychological, the police also rely upon the physical toll inflicted on the suspect who must withstand the interrogator's mental gymnastics.

Prolonged interrogation, combined with the mental torture the police inflicted upon Rogers, achieved the desired effect: a full-fledged confession. Would Rogers have confessed had the interrogation continued? Obviously, the police made a determination that prolonged interrogation alone would not have produced a confession. Relying on a compelling psychological stratagem, Chief Eagan shamed the suspect into confessing. Although Eagan denied it, the suspect testified that Eagan suggested he would be "less than a man" if he did not confess and thus caused his own wife to be taken into custody.[93] The lesson one draws from *Rogers* is that the police altered their strategy to fit the peculiar vulnerability of the suspect. When sustained interrogation did not change the suspect's determination not to confess, the interrogators successfully exploited the mental factor that would break Rogers' will: arousing sympathy for his ill spouse. The art of interrogation relies both on police domination and control as well as exploitation of a suspect's particular frailty.

Spano v. New York[94] provides intriguing parallels to both the facts as well as the rationale of *Rogers*. In *Spano*, a number of detectives and a skillful prosecutor questioned a twenty-five-year-old murder suspect for nearly eight hours.[95] Spano had an eighth-grade education and a history of emotional instability.[96] He repeatedly but unsuccessfully requested an attorney during the interrogation session. When the police could not wear him down, they relied on a childhood friend, who was a "fledging" policeman, to elicit Spano's sympathy in order to obtain a confession.[97] Again, although the Court did not stress the point, it was the method of interrogation rather than the reliability of the confession that rendered it "involuntary."[98] The prolonged interrogation, conducted at night, coupled with Spano's particular susceptibility to a false friend's importuning, produced the confession. When the questioning and the denial of the services of an attorney proved futile, the police used the ultimate emotional trump card: a friend who implored Spano to confess because his job as a policeman and his family's well-being would be jeopardized unless Spano confessed.

In both *Rogers* and *Spano*, the interrogation techniques employed by the police elicited the Supreme Court's condemnation. Although the Court focused on the questioning techniques and not on the confession's reliability, we should ask whether specific interrogation methods are more likely to generate false confessions. The likelihood that an interrogation technique will produce a false confession should lead the Court to ban that method, regardless of the truth of the confession or the effectiveness of the practice. Thanks to the efforts of two prominent social psychologists, Richard Leo and Richard Ofshe, it is now plausible to draw some assumptions on the perilous nature of certain interrogation methods. Two interrogation practices appear to play a prominent role in false confession cases: prolonged questioning and the use of standard interrogation methods on mentally impaired suspects.[99]

It should not be surprising that these circumstances are more apt to produce false confessions. As I have argued, prolonged interrogation exerts mental and physical pressure on a suspect confined to the unfriendly and constrained ambience pervading the interrogation room. To relieve the coercive effects of continuous, incommunicado interrogation, the "normal suspect" might falsely confess.[100] As we have seen in Justice Jackson's thoughtful *Ashcraft v. Tennessee* concurrence, a suspect could bear as much as thirty-six hours of continuing interrogation without breaking down. Conversely, a suspect who suffers from extreme claustrophobia could reach the breaking point within minutes. Ultimately, Justice Jackson is correct in presuming that any type of interrogation is "inherently coercive" and that drawing an arbitrary line is futile. If that is the case, and if the Court's goal is to eliminate questioning likely to generate false confessions, then logically the only way to eliminate unreliable confessions is to ban custodial interrogation. As we shall see in the next chapter, this is something the Court has failed to do, even in the famous *Miranda* opinion.

Questioning a mentally impaired suspect presents a different quandary. As an initial matter, one has to probe whether a civilized society should tolerate the interrogation of a suspect suffering from mental illness or retardation. To the extent that we approve of the interrogation of children suspected of serious crimes, and even their convictions as if they were adults, then it logically follows that we should permit the questioning of mentally impaired suspects. How reliable the confession of a mentally infirm suspect may be is a separate matter. Intuitively, we may question the reliability of such an admission of guilt, but beyond reliability concerns lies the intractable question whether the admission of guilt by a mentally disturbed suspect should play a role in the criminal investigative process. The Court confronted these issues in two landmark confession cases: *Blackburn v. Alabama*[101] and *Townsend v. Sain*.[102]

Blackburn was a paranoid schizophrenic who had spent the bulk of his adult life in and out of mental hospitals.[103] He committed an armed robbery after escaping from a mental ward. The psychiatric diagnosis reflected that Blackburn was insane and incompetent at the time he confessed to the armed robbery.[104] Questioning the suspect for approximately eight to nine hours in a small room, a team of three officers succeeded in obtaining Blackburn's confession. Significantly, Blackburn advised the officers that he had been a patient in a mental institution, so the chief interrogator, rather than the suspect, composed the confession.[105]

Blackburn is a remarkable opinion for several reasons. First, the Court acknowledged that a "complex of values" governed the doctrine against a state's reliance on involuntary confessions. Second, the Court recognized that the voluntariness standard was fact-specific, varying "according to the particular circumstances of the case."[106] Finally, the Court emphatically renounced the legal admissibility of a confession given when a suspect is "insane."[107]

Systemically, *Blackburn* broke new ground because the Court emphatically rejected the notion that a confession of an insane person should play a role in our adversarial criminal process. In unmistakable terms, Chief Justice Warren, speaking for the Court, observed that "in the present stage of our civilization a most basic sense of justice is affronted by the spectacle of incarcerating a human being on the basis of a statement he made while insane."[108] Chief Justice Warren elucidated three bases for this conclusion. The confession of an insane person might be less than reliable; it reflects a lack of rational choice by the offender; and it undermines the fairness built into the adversarial system of adjudication to the extent that the police take advantage of the suspect's mental impairment.[109]

The concept of volitional freedom underlies the *Blackburn* opinion. Simply put, the suspect's confession was not "the product of a rational intellect and a free will."[110] Indeed, the Court compared Blackburn's lack of volition in confessing with the *Brown v. Mississippi* defendants being coerced into admitting guilt through sheer physical torture.[111] In short, Blackburn's admission of guilt was no more freely "willed" than the *Brown* suspects' confession. In rather stark language, Chief Justice Warren compares lack of volition induced by mental illness with lack of a choice provoked by physical violence.

One may quarrel with my thesis by pointing to other factors that the *Blackburn* opinion stressed: the lengthy interrogation; the isolation of the suspect from friends, family, and counsel; and the composition of the confession by the chief interrogator. As I have argued, however, "It is in the form of an afterthought that the Court delineates the conduct of the police as a factor in its holding."[112] Preceding the allusion to the police tactics, Chief Justice Warren maintained that "civilized society" could not countenance the "spectacle" of a conviction based upon a confession given by a suspect who was insane. He then adds, "when the other pertinent circumstances are considered . . . the chances of the confession's having been the product of a rational intellect and free will become *even more remote*."[113] In essence, the police conduct aggravated the lack of volition underlying Blackburn's confession, rendering the "denial of due process *even more egregious*."[114] A close reading of the Court's language underscores my conclusion that the suspect's mental illness, impairing his volitional freedom, and not the police interrogative practices, is the foundation of *Blackburn*.

An even more telling example of the Court's solicitude for mental freedom as a precondition of a voluntary confession is *Townsend v. Sain*.[115] In that case, the suspect confessed after a police physician administered a drug that supposedly had the qualities of a truth serum. The physician administered the drug to alleviate the withdrawal symptoms, since the suspect was a heroin addict. Not relying on claims of physical coercion, Townsend instead contended that "his confession was inadmissible simply because it was caused by the injection of hyoscine."[116]

Elaborating on *Blackburn*'s requirement that a confession must be the "product of a rational intellect and a free will," *Townsend* unequivocally affirmed the Court's insistence on volitional freedom as a minimum condition for a voluntary confession. The causal nexus that rendered the confession involuntary was not police wrongdoing; rather, it was the link between police questioning and the resulting confession "which is not the product of a free intellect."[117] Quoting from *Blackburn*, the *Townsend* majority stressed that police overreaching was "irrelevant" to their holding in *Blackburn*.[118] In effect, *Townsend* accepted at face value the suspect's argument that his confession was involuntary because it was triggered by the administration of a drug. After dismissing the relevance of police knowledge of the drug's qualities, Chief Justice Warren observed, "Any questioning by police officers which in fact produces a confession which is not the product of a free intellect renders that confession inadmissible."

With both *Blackburn* and *Townsend*, the Supreme Court reaffirmed the suspect's mental freedom as a core value in its confession law jurisprudence. As one prominent scholar noted in 1979, "Beginning with its very first confession case, decided under evidentiary rather than constitutional standards, the Supreme Court has premised the voluntariness doctrine on a postulate of free will."[119] Grano acknowledged that even though most confession cases decided by the Court since 1884 contained elements of police coercion or misconduct, it was impossible to ignore "the cases in which mental freedom alone was crucial."[120]

As we discovered in our discussion of the first case in which the Supreme Court conferred constitutional status on the voluntariness doctrine, *Bram v. United States*, the law of confessions had put great emphasis on mental freedom as the hallmark of a voluntary confession. Any mental pressure exerted by the police on the suspect made him or her less than a "free agent." Taken to its logical conclusion, *Bram* would exclude any confession induced by police tactics designed to impair the suspect's free will. Of course, the Supreme Court never took the *Bram* doctrine to its extreme. It seemed, however, that *Blackburn* and *Townsend* took the notion of "free will," or "free agency," to previously uncharted territory. To the extent that those cases minimized, if not altogether eliminated, police misconduct or coercion as a minimum and necessary requirement for an "involuntary" confession, they placed mental and volitional freedom as twin predicates for a constitutionally valid confession.

Decided by the Warren Court on the eve of its monumental *Miranda* opinion, both *Blackburn* and *Townsend* foreshadowed a different investigative regime, under which the police would be severely hamstrung in their ability to question suspects and obtain confessions. As we shall see in the next chapter, however, *Miranda* proved to be a paper tiger. Indeed, rather than hampering law enforcement, *Miranda* provided the police with a weapon to sanitize otherwise "involuntary" confessions. Substantially diluted by the post-Warren Court, *Miranda* became the relic of a bygone era. One may postulate that *Blackburn* and *Townsend* were the "last hurrah" for an expansive dimension to the voluntariness doctrine. Free will, or free agency, would take a back seat to the need to afford the police sufficient leeway to extract confessions from all but the most hardened criminal suspects.

THE END OF "FREE WILL" AND RELIABILITY

Imagine the following improbable, yet true, scenario: Francis Connelly approached an off-duty, uniformed police officer in downtown Denver, Colorado, on August 18, 1983. Connelly told the officer, without any prompting, that he had murdered someone and wanted to discuss the crime. The officer promptly read Connelly his *Miranda* rights, and the suspect indicated that he understood those rights but still desired to speak about the murder. Bewildered by the suspect's behavior, the off-duty officer asked Connelly whether he was under the influence of alcohol or drugs. Although Connelly denied this allegation, he admitted that he had previously been a patient in a mental hospital. Jealously safeguarding Connelly's legal rights, the officer told the suspect that he was under "no obligation to say anything." Nevertheless, Connelly insisted on speaking to the officer about the murder, stating that his conscience "had been bothering him."[121]

A homicide detective became involved in the case upon being summoned by the off-duty officer for assistance. The detective once more administered the *Miranda* warnings to the suspect and asked him "what he had on his mind." Connelly told the detective that he had come to Denver from Boston to confess to the murder of a young woman he had killed in Denver the previous year. The suspect was then taken to police headquarters. Police records authenticated that a body of an unidentified female had been found the previous year. Connelly subsequently volunteered to take police officers to the scene of the murder, where he accurately pinpointed the site of the murder.[122]

The next day, Connelly became confused and disoriented when he met with public defenders for an interview. He was sent to a hospital for a psychiatric evaluation and was deemed incompetent to stand trial.[123] After six months of being hospitalized and treated with antipsychotic and sedative medications, Connelly was found competent to stand trial.[124]

Connelly sought to suppress his confession, relying principally on the evaluating psychiatrist's testimony that he was suffering from paranoid schizophrenia as of the day before he confessed. This illness, according to the psychiatrist, "motivated his confession." Further, the "condition interfered with [Connelly's] 'volitional abilities;' that is his abilities to make *free* and *rational* choices"[125] (emphasis added). By contrast, the doctor conceded that Connelly's illness did not impair his cognitive ability—in essence, his ability to understand the *Miranda* rights.[126]

Connelly is a unique case that tested the Court's ability to deal with an unfathomable and intractable subject: to what extent any confession by a suspect to law enforcement authorities is "voluntary." Noticeably absent from the case is any evidence of police misconduct. Although the police were aware that Connelly had been a patient in a mental hospital, they neither sought to exploit his condition nor endeavored to coax a confession from him. Yet the spectacle of securing a confession from an insane person who lacked the capacity to control his behavior and not confess is strange in the extreme.

If free will, or volitional freedom, plays a fundamental role in the law of confessions, then admitting the confession of an insane suspect runs contrary to that principle. *Blackburn* and *Townsend* ratified the Court's acceptance of mental freedom as a precondition to a voluntary confession. Rejecting the notion that our legal system should indulge the confession of an insane person, Chief Justice Warren noted in stark terms: "Surely in the present stage of our civilization a most basic sense of justice is affronted by the spectacle of incarcerating a human being upon the basis of a statement he made while insane."[127] As this language reflects, the notion that free will is indispensable to the finding of "voluntariness" pervaded both *Blackburn* and *Townsend*.

Construing that precedent in a different light, Chief Justice Rehnquist, writing for the majority, held in *Connelly* that "coercive police activity is a predicate to the finding that a confession is not 'voluntary' within the meaning of the Due Process Clause."[128] Although the holding seems to fit within the parameters established by the Court in assessing "voluntariness," it flies in the face of *Blackburn* and *Townsend*. Chief Justice Rehnquist's task, therefore, was to explain away, or somehow distinguish, both cases. In the process, the Supreme Court rejected "free will," "free agency," or "volitional freedom" as a requirement of due process. Confessions, in short, need not be the product of a free will or intellect, as long as they are not triggered by "police coercive activity."

How did Chief Justice Rehnquist reconcile the Court's holding in *Connelly* with the strong free will rationale underlying *Townsend* and *Blackburn*? Rather simply, he emphasized police conduct in both cases. Rehnquist argued that the police "exploited" Blackburn's mental illness and coupled that misconduct with typical police tactics: isolation and lengthy interrogation of the suspect. Similarly, Rehnquist dwelled on the fact that the police knew that Townsend "had been given" drugs before he confessed.[129] Acknowledging that a suspect's mental condition plays a role in determining whether the suspect's confession is voluntary, Rehnquist nevertheless invoked the precept that state action is a predicate for a finding of a violation of the Fourteenth Amendment's due process clause.[130]

Even if we take Rehnquist's reading of *Blackburn* and *Townsend* at face value, we are still left with a conundrum: how can our legal system admit into evidence the confession of a suspect whose defective mental condition impairs his volitional freedom? The answer to the riddle, according to the *Connelly* majority, is that requiring a confession to be the product of a suspect's free will would place the Court in the unseemly position of attempting to discern his motivation in "speaking or acting as he did" despite the absence of police coercion. Ultimately, this explanation begs the question: should the confession of a mentally ill suspect play a role in our criminal justice system? Flowing from this query is the collateral issue of whether the confession of a mentally ill suspect comports with the values underlying the Court's due process jurisprudence.

The first hurdle the *Connelly* majority had to surmount was to square its holding with the tenet the Court enunciated in *Brown*: that reliability was a mainstay in the law of confessions. Although the confessions in *Brown* were less than reliable because they were extorted through physical violence, the confession of a mentally ill suspect is equally unreliable. Chief Justice Rehnquist recognized this truism but readily dismissed it by shifting responsibility to the state evidentiary laws to exclude such presumptively unreliable confessions. What is remarkable about *Connelly* is Rehnquist's concession that a statement made by someone suffering from mental illness "might prove to be quite unreliable."[131]

As I have argued, *Connelly* marks a watershed transformation in the law of confessions. By discarding reliability as a critical component of a voluntary confession, the *Connelly* Court rewrote a "new version" of the old voluntariness standard.[132] Although the Court had noted in *Rogers v. Richmond* that a confession induced by psychological or physical coercion violated the due process class despite its reliability, it did not reject the principle that reliability was an element of the due process clause. Given the compelling proof that a confession provides in a criminal trial, it goes against the grain of the adversary system of adjudication to base a conviction on the confession of a paranoid schizophrenic.[133] Leaving the task of excluding such confessions from a criminal trial to the states in effect represented an abdication of the Supreme Court's duty to ensure fairness in the criminal process.

Indeed, it seems that the Court took a step backward into the pre-*Brown* era when it dispensed with reliability as a standard for determining whether a confession is voluntary. By deferring to state evidentiary laws, it seems that the *Connelly* majority saw no need to apply a uniform, constitutional standard to the admission of confessions at the state level. Without the predicate of police coercion, therefore, states are free to admit less than reliable confessions in criminal trials. As Justice Brennan's dissent demonstrated, Connelly could conceivably have been convicted solely on the basis of his uncorroborated confession. The record did not reveal physical evidence linking the defendant to the murder, the police did not identify the victim's body, and no independent evidence pointed to either a crime or the victim's body being found at the location Connelly documented for the police.[134]

To a lesser degree, *Connelly* departs from the second pillar of the voluntariness standard. Although the police did not exert physical or psychological pressure on the suspect, they were aware that Connelly suffered from mental illness in the past. The bewildered off-duty officer to whom the suspect first confessed believed that Connelly was a "crackpot."[135] Connelly confirmed his history when he told the officer he had previously been hospitalized for mental illness on five occasions. In turn, the off-duty officer relayed this information to Detective Antuna when he became part of the investigation.[136]

Interpreting the police's knowledge of Connelly's mental history as evidence of "wrongdoing," Justice Brennan maintained in dissent that this fact rendered Connelly's confession involuntary, even under the old test.[137] Perhaps Justice Brennan's conclusion stretches the limits of the old voluntariness standard. Nevertheless, the *Connelly* opinion implicitly condones police exploitation of a suspect's mental illness. Let us assume that the police saw the need to administer antipsychotic medication to Connelly for therapeutic purposes before he confessed. Would Chief Justice Rehnquist follow *Townsend* and suppress the confession under those circumstances? It would seem so, given the *Connelly* majority's gloss on *Townsend*. Yet the only distinction between *Townsend* and *Connelly* is the fortuitous circumstance that the confession preceded the treatment in *Connelly*. The police in *Townsend* were not apparently motivated by the potential of a confession when they administered the injection designed to alleviate the suspect's withdrawal symptoms. In both cases, therefore, the police were aware of the suspect's condition prior to the confession. The police knew that Townsend was a drug addict; they also knew that Connelly was, or at least had been, mentally ill.

Although the evidence of police misconduct was stronger in *Blackburn*, it was evident that the Court was condemning the police taking advantage of a suspect suffering from mental illness. As I have argued, the *Blackburn* holding rests on the notion that it offends the adversarial system's basic values to convict a person who confesses while suffering from mental illness. Yet the *Connelly* majority conveniently glosses over this elemental point. Mental freedom is relevant only to the extent that it is further impaired by the police's psychological or physical stratagems. At that point, the notion of a "voluntary" confession becomes absurd.

Ultimately, the *Connelly* opinion betrays the modern Court's ethos: a "voluntary" confession is a euphemism for the degree of psychological and physical pressure the police may exert on a suspect in order to obtain an admission of guilt. The Court has provided law enforcement with convenient guideposts for determining the extent to which the police may influence, cajole, or subtly coerce a suspect's will but not "overbear" it. *Connelly* evokes Justice Jackson's prescient *Ashcraft* dissent; there exists no such beast as a "voluntary" confession. Even the confession of a madman accords with the Constitution despite the fact that the police are aware of the suspect's condition. Furthermore, the reliability of such a confession is not a matter of constitutional moment; rather, it is an issue best left to the "evidentiary laws of the forum."

If reliability is no longer a prerequisite of a voluntary confession, then the logical corollary of this novel shift is that false confessions may not necessarily breach the due process clause of the Fourteenth Amendment. Grano has argued that the voluntariness doctrine guards against the "unnecessary" risk of a false confession.[138] Yet if the confession of a paranoid schizophrenic may be admissible because it does not contravene constitutional imperatives, then the risk of a false confession becomes quite real. That prospect did not seem to trouble the *Connelly* majority, despite the unfairness and injustice attending the admission of false confession into evidence.

Two other facets of *Connelly* ease the police's burden when they seek to obtain a confession that will withstand constitutional scrutiny. Those factors also undermine the principle that a confession should be the product of a suspect's free will and intellect. The first issue deals with a suspect's waiver of *Miranda* rights. When Connelly inexplicably confessed to a murder, the off-duty police officer, and later the lead detective, read him the *Miranda* warnings. He waived his rights and proceeded to speak about the murder. The *Miranda* rights, among other things, inform a suspect of the right to remain silent and not to speak with police without a lawyer's assistance. Further, *Miranda* held that a waiver of those rights must be "voluntary" and intelligent.[139]

How, then, is it possible for a suspect who is suffering from severe mental illness to "voluntarily" waive his *Miranda* rights? Indeed, the court-appointed psychiatrist who had examined Connelly concluded that the suspect was "not capable of making a 'free decision with respect to his constitutional right of silence . . . and his constitutional right to confer with a lawyer before talking to the police.'"[140] Citing a string of precedents construing *Miranda*, the *Connelly* majority interpreted a waiver of the Fifth Amendment privilege against self-incrimination as depending on the critical variable of police coercion, and "not on 'free choice' in any broader sense of the word."[141] In sum, volitional impairment that might impinge upon a suspect's "voluntary" waiver of the *Miranda* rights is irrelevant.

It borders on the illogical to maintain that a waiver of constitutional rights is voluntary even though it is not "the product of a free and deliberate choice." This was Justice Stevens's quarrel with the waiver part of the *Connelly* holding. The preceding quote was excerpted by Justice John Stevens from the Court's opinion in *Moran v. Burbine*.[142] As he pointed out, the absence of police misconduct does not render a waiver "free and deliberate," which is a precondition to the relinquishment of a constitutional right.[143] This part of the *Connelly* holding is at odds with the due process safeguards prohibiting the trial of an incompetent defendant.[144] By definition, an incompetent defendant lacks either a factual or rational understanding of the proceedings or is unable to assist an attorney in forging a defense.[145] Connelly was found incompetent to stand trial and had to receive treatment, including medication, for six months before regaining competency. How he could have made the deliberate, free, and intelligent choice to waive his *Miranda* rights in light of his incompetence and mental illness defies logic.

Completing its task, the *Connelly* Court held that a suspect's waiver of *Miranda* rights need only be established by a preponderance of the evidence. The majority relied on *Lego v. Toomey*,[146] in which the Court held that the government may prove the voluntariness of a confession by a preponderance of the evidence. The irony behind this ruling is that a suspect who suffers from paranoid schizophrenia may waive his *Miranda* rights, and the state need only establish that it is more likely than not that he waived those rights knowingly and voluntarily. By setting a minimal threshold of proof, the *Connelly* opinion makes a waiver of the vaunted, and overvalued, *Miranda* rights a relatively easy burden for the prosecution to satisfy.

Connelly poses the ultimate legal conundrum by advancing the illogical proposition that a "voluntary" confession need not be the product of a free will or intellect. To that extent, the opinion divorces a confession from the question of mental freedom. As one prominent scholar has observed, the law of confessions is inextricably tied to the question of mental freedom. The notion espoused in *Connelly* that a confession comports with the Constitution even though it is not freely willed is counterintuitive. The Court has fashioned the hackneyed, yet ill defined, "overborne will" as the hallmark of an involuntary confession. Logically, the obverse of an overborne will is a free one. Nevertheless, *Connelly* dispenses with a free will as long as the impaired will is not provoked by police misconduct.

Not only does *Connelly* radically alter the law of confessions, it also significantly erodes the protections afforded by *Miranda*. Given a weak standard of proof to establish a *Miranda* waiver, the prosecution may gain the upper hand. Because, as we shall see, many *Miranda* issues boil down to a swearing match between the defendant and the police, the preponderance of the evidence standard ensures that the police will have a strategic advantage in contested waiver hearings. Similarly, the prosecution has an edge in establishing a *Miranda* waiver in circumstances where the suspect suffers from a mental disease, the police are aware of the mental impairment, but they are careful to avoid overt coercion in securing a confession.

CONFESSIONS AND "HARMLESS ERROR"

A scant five years after deciding *Connelly*, the Court stripped the voluntariness doctrine from its firm constitutional moorings by applying the harmless error doctrine to the admission of involuntary confessions. In *Chapman v. California*,[147] the Court held that constitutional error during a trial does not necessarily require the reversal of a conviction. Certain types of errors, however, do infect the trial so as to render it meaningless. For example, a trial in which the defendant is deprived of counsel or in which the judge is not impartial constitutes an example of a fundamental constitutional violation not subject to the harmless error doctrine. As Chief Justice Rehnquist has remarked, these types of errors "are structural defects in the constitution of the trial mechanism, which defy analysis by 'harmless error' standards."[148]

In *Arizona v. Fulminante*, however, a majority of the Court distinguished the admission of an involuntary confession into evidence from the structural defect that invalidates the fairness of a trial. Under *Chapman*, if a constitutional error occurs during a trial, the prosecution may avoid a retrial if it can establish that the error was "harmless beyond a reasonable doubt." In effect, this means that if the evidence apart from the constitutional error strongly pointed toward guilt, then the conviction is affirmed despite the constitutional defect. The *Fulminante* majority held that the admission of an involuntary confession is a "classic trial error" rather than a "structural defect," and thus it is subject to harmless error analysis. In short, the prosecution may avoid a retrial in a case in which an involuntary confession was admitted into evidence if it proves "beyond a reasonable doubt" that the confession did not affect the outcome.

Ignoring the powerful weight that a jury attaches to a confession, the *Fulminante* majority indulges the ultimate legal fiction: a confession will not affect the jury's perception of the defendant's guilt. No matter how compelling other evidence pointing to the defendant's guilt may be, a confession as we have seen, is the "queen of proofs." Indeed, the Court has acknowledged this elemental fact. Quoting from *Cruz v. New York*,[149] the dissenters from that part of the *Fulminante* holding noted that a "defendant's confession is 'probably the most probative and damaging evidence that can be admitted against him.'"[150] Indeed, the *Fulminante* majority's application of the harmless error doctrine to coerced confessions contradicts the *Chapman* harmless error doctrine. In dicta, the *Chapman* opinion classifies coerced confessions as a type of error not subject to harmless error analysis. *Chapman* acknowledges that some constitutional rights are so integral to a fair trial that their "infraction can never be treated as harmless error,"[151] and it places coerced confessions into that category.

The rationale supporting the application of the harmless error doctrine to confessions is telling. Chief Justice Rehnquist, the author of that part of the *Fulminante* opinion, relies on an intriguing syllogism. He explains that because governmental violations of the Fourth and Sixth Amendments are susceptible to harmless error analysis and may be "as reprehensible as conduct that results in an involuntary confession," it follows that involuntary confessions should be accorded the same treatment.[152] He then remarks that Fourth and Sixth Amendment violations "can involve conduct as egregious as police conduct used to elicit statements in violation of the Fourteenth Amendment."[153] The final part of the syllogism concludes that "it is thus impossible to create a meaningful distinction between confessions elicited in violation of the Sixth Amendment and those in violation of the Fourteenth Amendment."[154]

What this syllogism conveys is cynicism toward constitutional rights designed to protect criminal defendants. Beyond that skepticism lies an unmistakable attitude toward involuntary confessions: they are mere stumbling blocks to the end game of getting at the putative factual truth of a criminal case. Further, this philosophy clashes with the axiom embodied in the *Rogers v. Richmond* opinion; that is, an involuntary confession is a by-product of the police conduct that produced it rather than the truth underlying the suspect's admission. The admission of an involuntary confession, moreover, detracts from the core of the adversarial process. By admitting the most powerful evidence against a criminal defendant, secured through methods antithetical to a democratic polity, the message conveyed is that constitutional rights are mere symbols obscuring reality.

To a certain extent, the *Fulminante* opinion might tempt police officers to secure confessions from suspects through either psychological or physical coercion. After all, the erroneous admission of such a confession might not result in a reversal of the conviction if the error is deemed "harmless." Although such a prospect might seem remote, particularly because the prosecution will have to establish that such a compelling piece of evidence did not affect the outcome, *Fulminante* carries potent symbolic weight. The notion that the introduction of an involuntary confession will not automatically render a trial fundamentally unfair goes against the grain of our adversarial system.

Fulminante is also emblematic of the Court's transformation of the voluntariness standard. We saw that metamorphosis in *Connelly*, as the Court jettisoned mental freedom as a cornerstone of a voluntary confession. Repudiating the core holding of *Bram v. United States*, Justice White notes that a confession may be voluntary even though obtained by promises or the exertion of improper influences.[155] Emphatically, Justice White rejects the *Bram* dictum that a confession may not be obtained through either direct or implied promises or "the exertion of any improper influence." In sum, the police may employ psychological pressure when interrogating a suspect without violating his or her constitutional rights. The modern Court seems more comfortable with Justice Harlan's opinion in *Hopt v. Utah*. If we desire confessions from criminal suspects, then the Court believes that we ought to allow law enforcement to exert a certain amount of psychological, and even physical, pressure to induce the suspect to admit guilt. Mental freedom is a luxury, according to the modern Supreme Court, that the criminal justice system can ill afford to indulge.

CONCLUSION

We began this endeavor by challenging the theory that a confession can, in the true sense of the word, ever be voluntary. Although this tenet might reflect reality, our legal system has chosen, for pragmatic reasons, not to embrace it. Therefore, the U.S. Supreme Court has

been embroiled in the tangled web of defining the meaning of a coerced versus a voluntary confession. Even though the privilege against
self-incrimination embodied in the Fifth Amendment and the due process clause of the Fourteenth Amendment provide a vague and nebulous threshold, the Court has dealt with an intractable problem.
Deciding just how much physical, psychological, and emotional pressure the police may employ to secure a confession is a quagmire from
which the most intrepid victim will not emerge.

Despite this caveat, the Supreme Court has rendered the concept
of a voluntary confession meaningless. By divorcing mental freedom
from the notion of voluntariness, and by establishing an easy evidentiary burden for the prosecution, the Court has set a course in which
a "voluntary" confession becomes a cruel absurdity. Symbolically,
moreover, the modern Court has set a path in which the specter of an
involuntary confession infecting a trial may be a possibility, however
remote. Paradoxically, this trend has coincided with the schizophrenic
creation of the *Miranda* doctrine, which is supposed to guard the criminal suspect against his or her own folly: giving a confession to the police. As we shall see in the next chapter, *Miranda* has also become a
dead letter, a doctrine that has served to sanitize otherwise involuntary confessions in the guise of protecting the suspect. Perhaps *Miranda*
helped to assuage the modern Court's conscience while simultaneously
ensuring that most confessions would be admissible against a criminal suspect. A "voluntary" confession is voluntary in the eyes of the
legal beholder.

NOTES

1. PETER BROOKS, TROUBLING CONFESSIONS: SPEAKING GUILT IN LAW
AND LITERATURE 3 (2000).

2. *Id.*

3. *Id.* at 9.

4. *King v. Warickshall*, 168 Eng. Rep. 234 (1783); DAVID BODENHAMER,
FAIR TRIAL: RIGHTS OF THE ACCUSED IN AMERICAN HISTORY 53 (1992).

5. John H. Langbein, *The Criminal Trial before the Lawyers*, 45 U. CHI.
L. REV. 263, 307–11 (1978); John H. Langbein, *The Historical Origins of the
Privilege against Self-Incrimination at Common Law*, 92 MICH. L. REV. 1047,
1050–54 (1994); Eben Moglan, *Taking the Fifth: Reconsidering the Origins of
the Constitutional Privilege against Self-Incrimination*, 92 MICH. L. REV. 1086,
1091–94 (1994).

6. DAVID SIMON, HOMICIDE: A YEAR ON THE KILLING STREETS 211 (1991).

7. *Id.*

8. *Murphy v. Waterfront Comm'n*, 378 U.S. 52, 55 (1964).

9. Simon, *supra* note 6 at 212.

10. Yale Kamisar, *What Is an Involuntary Confession: Some Comments on Inbau and Reid's Criminal Interrogation and Confessions*, 17 RUTGERS L. REV. 728, 745–46 (1963).

11. *Id.*

12. JOSEPH D. GRANO, CONFESSIONS, TRUTH, AND THE LAW 78 (1993).

13. *Id.* at 79.

14. *Id.* at 3.

15. *In re Winship*, 397 U.S. 358 (1970).

16. *Colorado v. Connelly*, 479 U.S. 157, 182 (Brennan, J., dissenting) (citations omitted).

17. 367 U.S. 568 (1961).

18. *Id.* at 602.

19. *Id.*

20. 322 U.S. 143 (1944).

21. *Id.* at 161.

22. *Id.* at 162.

23. Brooks, *supra* note 1 at 74.

24. *Id.*

25. JOHN W. STRONG ET AL., MCCORMICK ON EVIDENCE SECTION 146 (4th ed. 1992).

26. Steven Penney, *Theories of Confession Admissibility: A Historical View*, 25 AM. J. CRIM. L. 309, 323–24 (1998).

27. *See, e.g.,* SAMUEL WALKER, THE POLICE IN AMERICA: AN INTRODUCTION, 6–19 (1983); on the movement toward police reform, *see* ROBERT. M. FOGELSON, BIG CITY POLICE (1977).

28. Penney, *supra* note 26 at 322.

29. 110 U.S. 574 (1884).

30. 168 U.S. 532 (1897).

31. *Hopt v. Utah*, 110 U.S. at 584.

32. *Id.*

33. *Id.*

34. *Id.* at 584–87.

35. *Id.* at 583.

36. *Id.* at 584.

37. *Id.*

38. *Id.* at 585.

39. *Id.*

40. *Id.* at 584.

41. This is the phrase employed by the Supreme Court in *Johnson v. United States*, 333 U.S. 10 (1948).

42. *Hopt v. Utah*, 110 U.S. at 584 (citations omitted).

43. 168 U.S. 532 (1897).

44. *Id.* at 534.

45. *Id.* at 538.

46. *Id.* at 539.

47. *Id.*

48. *Id.* at 538–39.

49. *Id.* at 565.

50. *Id.* (Justice White quotes approvingly from William Oldham Russell *Russell on Crimes* to underscore this broad-based principle.)

51. *Id.* at 569–71 (Brewer, J., dissenting).

52. *Id* at 550. Justice White observed that the statute embodied a traditional judicial rule reflecting solicitude for the suspect's right to speak of his own will and accord.

53. *Id.*

54. *Id.* at 563.

55. *Id.* at 564.

56. *Id.*

57. *Id.* at 562.

58. *Id.* at 564.

59. 479 U.S. 157 (1986).

60. The Fourteenth Amendment declares that states shall not "deprive any person of life, liberty, or property, without due process of law." U.S. CONST. Amend. XIV, Section 1.

61. See, for example, Penney, *supra* note 26 at 313; Catherine Hancock, *Due Process before Miranda*, 70 TUL. L. REV. 2195 (1996).

62. Hancock, *supra* note 61 at 2232–36.

63. WAYNE R. LAFAVE, JEROLD H. ISRAEL, NANCY J. KING, CRIMINAL PROCEDURE, 312–13 (3rd ed. 2000).

64. 297 U.S. 278 (1936).

65. *Id.* at 279.

66. *Id.* at 279–86.

67. *Id.* at 286.

68. Penney, *supra* note 26 at 335.

69. *Id.* at 335–36.

70. THE WICKERSHAM COMM'N, NATIONAL COMM'N ON LAW OBSERVANCE AND ENFORCEMENT, PUB. NO. 11, REPORT ON LAWLESSNESS IN LAW ENFORCEMENT (1931).

71. *Brown v. Mississippi*, 297 U.S. at 287.

72. Charles J. Ogletree, *Are Confessions Really Good for the Soul?* 100 HARV. L. REV. 1826, 1832 (1987).

73. Penney, *supra* note 26 at 334, n. 134.

74. Yale Kamisar, *What Is an Involuntary Confession: Some Comments on Inbau and Reid's Criminal Interrogation and Confessions*, 17 RUTGERS L. REV. 728, 753 (1963).

75. Welsh S. White, *What Is an Involuntary Confession Now*, 50 RUTGERS L. REV. 2001, 2036 (1998). Professor White states, "In the normal course of things, most interrogation methods—whether they are likely to induce untrustworthy confessions or not—will produce many more true confessions than false ones." *Id.*

76. 499 U.S. 279 (1991).

77. *Id.* at 288.

78. *Id.* at 287.

79. *Id.* at 282–83.

80. *Id.* at 286.

81. *Id.* at 305–6.

82. *Id.* at 306.

83. *Blackburn v. Alabama*, 361 U.S. 199, 206 (1960). Chief Justice Warren cited *Chambers v. Florida*, 309 U.S. 227 (1940), to support his conclusion.

84. *Id.*

85. 365 U.S. 534 (1961).

86. *Id.* at 535.

87. *Id.* at 535–37.

88. *Id.* at 535.

89. *Id.* at 536–37. Chief Egan testified that the suspect never requested a lawyer during the course of the interrogation. The Court noted that the suspect testified that he sought an attorney's services at the outset of the interrogation, which was not inconsistent with Chief Egan's testimony; he became involved in the investigation six hours after it began.

90. *Id.* at 535.

91. *Id.* at 541.

92. White, *supra* note 75 at 2022.

93. *Rogers v. Richmond*, 365 U.S. at 536–37.

94. 360 U.S. 315 (1959).

95. *Id.* at 317–19.

96. *Id.*

97. *Id.* at 318–19, 322.

98. *Id.*

99. Richard A. Leo & Richard J. Ofshe, *The Consequences of False Confessions: Deprivations of Liberty and Miscarriages of Justice in the Age of Psychological Interrogation*, 88 J. CRIM. L. & CRIMINOLOGY, 429 (1998); Richard J. Ofshe & Richard A. Leo, *The Social Psychology of Police Interrogation: The Theory and Classification of True and False Confessions*, 16 STUDIES IN LAW, POLITICS AND SOCIETY 189 (1997).

100. George C. Thomas III, *Justice O'Connor's Pragmatic View of Coerced Self-Incrimination*, 13 WOMEN'S RTS. L. REP. 117, 124 (1991). Thomas argues that a person not suffering from psychological infirmity would not falsely admit guilt "unless she found the pressure to confess overwhelming."

101. 361 U.S. 199 (1960).

102. 372 U.S. 293 (1963).

103. *Blackburn v. Alabama*, 361 U.S. at 200–02.

104. *Id.* at 203–4.

105. *Id.* at 204–8.

106. *Id.* at 207.

107. *Id.*

108. *Id.*

109. *Id.*

110. *Id.* at 208.

111. *Id.* at 211. Chief Justice Warren stated: "Just as in *Brown*, the evidence here establishes that the confession most probably was not the product of any meaningful act of volition."

112. Alfredo Garcia, *Mental Sanity and Confessions: The Supreme Court's New Version of the Old "Voluntariness" Standard*, 21 AKRON L. REV. 275, 278 (1988).

113. *Blackburn v. Alabama*, 361 U.S. at 207–8.

114. *Id.*

115. 372 U.S. 293 (1963).

116. *Id.* at 307.

117. *Id.* at 308.

118. *Id.* at 309.

119. Joseph Grano, *Voluntariness, Free Will, and the Law of Confessions*, 65 VA. L. REV. 859, 868 (1979).

120. *Id.* at 869. Professor Grano cited *Blackburn* and *Townsend* as the two prominent examples.

121. *Colorado v. Connelly*, 479 U.S. at 160.

122. *Id.* at 160–61.

123. *Id.* at 161.

124. *Id.* at 175 (Brennan, J., dissenting). The majority did not point this out. Justice Brennan cited to the record in emphasizing this fact in his dissent.

125. *Id.* at 161.

126. *Id.* at 161–62.

127. *Blackburn v. Alabama*, 361 U.S. at 207.

128. *Colorado v. Connelly*, 479 U.S. at 167.

129. *Id.* at 164–65.

130. *Id.* at 165.

131. *Id.* at 167.

132. Garcia, *supra* note 112 at 280–81.

133. As Justice Brennan noted in his *Connelly* dissent, "Our distrust for reliance on confessions is due, in part, to their decisive impact upon the adversarial process." *Colorado v. Connelly*, 479 U.S. at 182 (Brennan, J., dissenting).

134. *Id.* at 183.

135. *Id.* at 180.

136. *Id.*

137. *Id.*

138. Grano, *supra* note 119 at 944.

139. *Miranda v. Arizona*, 384 U.S. at 444, 476; *North Carolina v. Butler*, 441 U.S. 369, 373 (1979).

140. *Colorado v. Connelly*, 479 U.S. at 169 (citations omitted).

141. *Id.* at 170.

142. *Moran v. Burbine*, 475 U.S. 412, 421 (1986).

143. *Colorado v. Connelly*, 479 U.S. at 173 (Stevens, J., dissenting in part).

144. *Pate v. Robinson*, 383 U.S. 375 (1966).

145. *Dusky v. United States*, 362 U.S. 402 (1960).

146. 404 U.S. 477 (1972).

147. 368 U.S. 18 (1991).

148. *Arizona v. Fulminante*, 499 U.S. 279, 309 (1991).

149. *Cruz v. New York*, 481 U.S. 186, 195 (1987) (White, J., dissenting).

150. *Arizona v. Fulminante*, 499 U.S. 292 (White, J. dissenting in part).

151. *Chapman v. California*, 368 U.S. at 23 and n. 8.

152. *Arizona v. Fulminante*, 499 U.S. at 311–12.

153. *Id.* at 311.

154. *Id.* at 311–12.

155. *Id.* at 285.

CHAPTER 3

MIRANDA REDUX, OR HOW THE COURT ATTEMPTED TO REVIVE A DEAD PATIENT

INTRODUCTION

The voluntariness standard came under scrutiny by the Warren Court in the 1960s. The result of that evaluation was perhaps the most famous case in modern jurisprudence: *Miranda v. Arizona*. *Miranda* did not, however, live up to its promise. Indeed, as we shall see, it became the symbol of how the change in the makeup of the U.S. Supreme Court transformed *Miranda* into a doctrine that was, at best, a dead letter; and, at worst, a boon to law enforcement. Rather than protecting criminal suspects from the inherent compulsion of custodial interrogation, *Miranda* wound up allowing the police, in some circumstances, to sanitize otherwise "involuntary" confessions. When a majority of the Court upheld the constitutional basis for *Miranda* in *United States v. Dickerson*,[1] it ratified the continuation of a doctrine that had long ceased to exert any meaningful impact on the interrogation of suspects.

The Fourth Circuit Court of Appeals recognized this proposition when it ruled that *Miranda* was not a constitutional holding and that it was therefore superseded by Congress when that institution enacted the Omnibus Crime Control and Safe Streets Act of 1968.[2] Although the Supreme Court would overrule that holding, such a momentous undertaking serves as a point of departure to evaluate the renewed academic debate that has emerged over the relative merits or costs of the opinion. What this scholarly joust and the attempt to overrule *Miranda* obscures is a fundamental premise: in the more than three and a half decades since its genesis, the opinion has been transformed into a relic of a bygone era. Contrary to what scholars and Justice Antonin Scalia believe, *Miranda* has been rendered meaningless through a series of contradictory and baffling interpretations by the very Supreme Court that handed down the opinion. This bizarre exegesis has not only damaged the Court's credibility; it has stripped the decision of its allure as the symbol of an attempt to strengthen individual rights against potential law enforcement abuse. Indeed, a return to the much-maligned voluntariness test would have presented the Court with a way to save face from its folly. Although I hesitantly endorse such a remedy, the realities underlying the Court's jurisprudence dictate this result.

This chapter does not enter into the debate over *Miranda*'s reputed costs to law enforcement objectives. That controversy has been resurrected, with the same inconclusive and contradictory results that marked the previous one.[3] Rather, my argument is that such a polemic is irrelevant. *Miranda* was overruled by congressional fiat, despite what the majority opinion in *Dickerson* contends; it has been decimated by judicially crafted qualifications and the public safety exception; and it no longer serves as the brake upon overzealous law enforcement that its progenitors intended. Furthermore, through its efforts to circumscribe the impact of the opinion, the Court has invited law enforcement to evade and openly defy *Miranda* normative prescriptions. There is not much left to *Miranda*: the patient is either on life-support or clinically dead. However much its supporters or detractors may wish to invoke its seductive appeal or pragmatic influence, they fall short when one critically analyzes the evolution of the *Miranda* doctrine. *Miranda* has been rendered an abject failure, even when viewed from the limited perspective of providing a "bright-line" rule for police interrogation practices. To a large extent, *Miranda* has produced paradoxes that the Warren Court would never have imagined: circumstances in which the "old" voluntariness approach affords more protection to criminal suspects than the putative safeguards outlined in the decision.[4] In short, *Miranda* is dead and has been rendered largely irrelevant. To the extent it survives, *Miranda* is merely a useful adjunct to law enforcement.

Although my conclusion appears at first glance to be radical, the evidence suggests otherwise. Indeed, the Court has stripped Miranda of its constitutional status, has implicitly ratified the overruling of the opinion in U.S.C. section 3501, and has cabined the thrust of its reach by narrowly construing the definition of custody and interrogation.

Indeed, the revival of a shopworn debate over *Miranda*'s reputed costs to law enforcement is attributable to the opinion's "symbolic status as the epitome of Warren Court activism in the criminal law area."[5] Indeed, the limitations upon *Miranda*'s scope, in conjunction with the public safety exception, have divorced the opinion from its doctrinal moorings.

Three recent opinions militate against the force of my conclusion. In *Withrow v. Williams*,[6] the majority seemed to revive and "endorse" *Miranda*'s "underlying principles."[7] Within a year, however, the Supreme Court quickly reminded us that Miranda was merely a "prophylactic" remedy intended to protect the privilege against self-incrimination.[8] Another opinion that flies in the face of the decimation of Miranda is *Minnick v. Mississippi*,[9] in which the Court extended the effect of the Edwards doctrine. Again, the Court receded from this seeming expansion by requiring an unequivocal assertion by the suspect of the right to the presence of counsel as a precondition to Edwards' protection. Indeed, the slavish adherence to Edwards in Minnick seems to be the anomaly to the Court's attempt to restrict Miranda's reach. However, even Edwards is no longer sacrosanct: I will argue that the public safety exception, taken to its logical conclusion, trumps an Edwards violation. Indeed, two federal appellate courts and a state appellate court concur with this assessment.[10] Furthermore, there is precedent allowing the prosecution to use statements taken in violation of Edwards to impeach the defendant's testimony at trial.[11] Finally, the fruit-of-the-poisonous-tree doctrine, which excludes evidence derived from a constitutional violation, is not applicable to Edwards or any of Miranda's progeny because Miranda has been upheld with all of its attendant qualifications and the public safety exception. Finally, despite upholding the constitutional status of *Miranda* in *Dickerson*, the Supreme Court left *Miranda* in its denuded form by legitimizing its manifold qualifications and exception.

This chapter will proceed in three stages. In the first section, I will provide the historical, social, and political backdrop to the *Miranda* opinion. I will also discuss the pragmatic basis for the path the Court chose to follow in *Miranda*. In the second section, I will underscore the attempts to overrule *Miranda* and the Court's almost instant departure from its doctrinal foundation. In doing so, my argument is that the Court's retreat can in large measure be viewed as a reaction to the negative response the opinion engendered both politically and socially. It can also be viewed as the logical outcome of the Court's need to respond to sociopolitical realities in fashioning the doctrine. In the third section, I will show that *Miranda* is no longer viable, even as a symbol or as a bright-line alternative to the much-maligned voluntariness test. I will also analyze the *Dickerson* opinion, in which the Supreme Court ratified Miranda's constitutional status. I will argue that *Dickerson* merely acknowledged my point: that *Miranda*, with its myriad qualifications and exception, is no longer an obstacle to law enforcement. Finally, in examining potential alternatives to Miranda, I will demonstrate that neither videotaping of confessions nor truncated warnings provide satisfactory antidotes to *Miranda*'s current flaws. Given the current political climate, as well as the Supreme Court's reluctance to expand the rights of criminal suspects, a return to the voluntariness standard is the only way out of the doctrinal morass the Court has created. Indeed, the state of confession law today is not much different from the prevailing climate prior to *Miranda*. To a large extent, most law enforcement organizations would chafe at the overruling of *Miranda*: the doctrine provides the means to render admissible an otherwise involuntary confession. The doctrine also serves to deflect attention from the voluntariness issue through focus on its "prophylactic" character. That is why a return to the voluntariness standard would, in many cases, especially "high-profile" ones, afford criminal defendants a greater degree of protection than *Miranda* currently does.

THE HISTORICAL, SOCIAL, AND POLITICAL BACKGROUND OF *MIRANDA*

Let us not be guilty of maudlin sympathy for the criminal who, roaming the street with switchblade knife and illegal firearms seeking a helpless prey, suddenly becomes upon apprehension a poor, underprivileged person who counts upon the compassion of our society and the laxness or weakness of too many courts to forgive his offense.[12]

These words reflected former president Dwight Eisenhower's assessment of the problem with crime in America as he spoke to the Republican National Convention in 1964 on the eve of Senator Barry Goldwater's nomination for president. The speech captured the social conflict engendered by the perception and reality of rising crime rates in the late 1950s and early 1960s. The Federal Bureau of Investigation, through its vast resources and control, had reported in the Uniform Crime Reports that from 1958 to 1964, "the incidence of crime had been growing six times faster than the American population."[13] In the midst of this "crime wave," the U.S. Supreme Court had set out on a course designed to expand the individual rights of criminal defendants. It was an issue seized upon by Senator Goldwater in his failed campaign for the presidency and successfully exploited by Richard Nixon in his successful quest for the position in 1968. Indeed, Goldwater coined the term "violence in the streets" in his 1964 acceptance speech for the Republican nomination. It was a phrase that would "serve candidates for some years."[14]

It is against this sociopolitical backdrop that the *Miranda* opinion must be viewed. Legal commentators often ignore, or briefly gloss over, this important phenomenon. It is, unfortunately, a commonplace that criminal procedure scholarship seems divorced from the realities of social life.[15] It is impossible to dispassionately analyze *Miranda* without the benefit of the sociopolitical realities that underlay it. The majority of Justices who crafted *Miranda* had several alternatives to consider in deciding the scope of the right against self-incrimination. In effect, the "compromise" struck by the majority reflected the sociopolitical conditions that must have either subtly or consciously affected the majority's reasoning. A more radical approach than the majority crafted could have spelled the end for confessions as a vital tool for law enforcement. A weaker alternative to *Miranda* could have run against the countervailing current of protection for the poor, the underprivileged, the disempowered against the overwhelming power of the government. Indeed, the Warren Court majority was cognizant that *Miranda* was an evolutionary rather than a revolutionary doctrine and openly acknowledged this fact[16] within one week of rendering its opinion.

This motif was accentuated by social conditions, in which race riots played a prominent role, prompted in large part by the conflict between the police and the black community in northern ghettos. The civil rights movement had projected in bold relief the abuse of power by police as a means of stifling the demand for equal rights. As a prominent historian aptly put it, "The criminal justice crisis of the 1960s focused on the cops in the ghetto."[17] Rioting erupted in New York City in 1964 when a white police officer shot and killed a black teenager, and it proliferated throughout forty-three American cities from 1964 to 1968.[18] Ultimately, the Kerner Commission, appointed by President Lyndon Johnson to investigate these civil disorders, concluded that the root cause of the problem was racism. Significantly, as the first riot in New York City reflected, the police were the primary instigators of the riots. Blacks in northern ghettos, in turn, viewed the all-white police as a virtual "army of occupation" in their communities.[19]

It is within this context that one must view former president Eisenhower's speech to the Republican National Convention in 1964 and Senator Goldwater's political exploitation of this grave crisis in the 1964 presidential election. The "conservative" solution to "violence in the streets" was to "get tough" on crime by meting out swift and severe punishment for criminal offenses. This "solution" emerged amid the rapid rise in the incidence of violent crimes and property crimes. The increase in violent crimes from 1963 to 1974 far outpaced the increase in property offenses. For example, robbery increased by 310 percent during that period.[20]

As a conception of "rough justice," the clarion call for a more stringent, punitive approach to crime no doubt influenced police actions, attitudes, and mores. The tension between adhering to the rule of law and enforcing order is the fundamental dichotomy confronted by police officers. Sociopolitical factors in turn affect police reactions to this tension. As Jerome Skolnick aptly observed, "When prominent members of the community become far more aroused over an apparent rise in criminality than over the fact that Blacks are frequently subjected to unwarranted police interrogation, detention, and invasions of privacy, the police will continue to engage in such practices."[21] The Republican platform in both the 1964 and 1968 presidential elections made the rule of order, and the apprehension and punishment of the guilty, the centerpiece of the party's campaign. As a counterweight to this trend, the U.S. Supreme Court, led by Chief Justice Warren, emphasized the need to temper police zeal and afford a measure of justice and equality to the disempowered.

If 1963 was a watershed year marking the dramatic rise in crime, it was also an exceptional year for the Court's attempt to balance the need for order with protection of a criminal defendant's constitutional rights. The Court's decision in *Gideon v. Wainwright*[22] affirmed the "fundamental nature" of the Sixth Amendment's right to counsel. Holding that in all state felony prosecutions indigent defendants were entitled to counsel, the *Gideon* Court recognized the obvious: without counsel a defendant would be pitted against powerful governmental forces, leading necessarily to an unequal contest and, fundamentally, an unfair trial.[23] Because lawyers were correctly perceived by the Court as being necessities and not luxuries, *Gideon* was well-received in public opinion. Indeed, Yale Kamisar has characterized *Gideon* as "one of the most popular decisions ever handed down by the Supreme Court."[24]

The personal attributes of Clarence Earl Gideon typified the traits of most criminal defendants whose fate wound up in the hands of the U.S. Supreme Court in the 1960s. Gideon was a classic "poor defendant." He was a "loner," "constantly in trouble," and "without resources or attachments."[25] Ernesto Miranda, a Mexican American, was the quintessential "poor" defendant whose fate with the law was unfavorable from the outset of his life. He had an eighth-grade education and had had six arrests and four imprisonments between the ages of fourteen and eighteen. Miranda not only had an extensive criminal record at age twenty-three, when he was arrested for the crimes that would bring him fame and notoriety, but he also had a spotty employment record in which he held menial jobs for short periods of time.[26] Similarly, Danny Escobedo was a "laborer" of Mexican heritage, although he differed from both Gideon and Miranda in that he had no prior encounters with law enforcement before his case came to the Supreme Court.

In selecting cases with these individual defendants as the fulcrum by which to "revolutionalize" criminal procedure, the Supreme Court did not act in a vacuum. Rather, the legal community had identified the issue of the indigent defendant facing the powerful interests of the state without the resources to combat it. Attorney General Robert F. Kennedy, shortly after taking office in 1961, announced the formation of the Committee on Poverty and the Administration of Criminal Justice, headed by the eminent legal scholar Francis Allen of the University of Michigan Law School. The mission of the committee was "to evaluate the quality of justice being offered the poor in the courts."[27] Among the recommendations of the Allen Committee was the appointment of counsel for defendants no later than at arraignment. More important, the Committee failed to urge the appointment of counsel at an earlier stage because it would be "vigorously opposed by those who fear its consequences on law enforcement."[28] Aptly enough, the Allen Committee handed down its recommendations in the fateful year of 1963.

THE PRECURSORS: *ESCOBEDO* AND *MASSIAH*

However momentous the year of 1963 may have been from a social perspective, it was eclipsed by 1964 in terms of legal developments. Two decisions handed down by the Supreme Court that year foreshadowed the issue that *Miranda* would ultimately resolve: What are the proper ground rules for the police in conducting the interrogation of a criminal suspect? Although the third-degree tactics condemned in the 1930s by the Wickersham Commission had fallen into disrepute, the so-called nebulous aspect of the voluntariness standard augured a new approach to how confessions could be obtained. Both *Massiah v. United States*[29] and *Escobedo v. Illinois*[30] promised a new frontier in the law governing confessions. What is remarkable about these cases is that, taken to their logical conclusion, they portend the end of confessions as a vital adjunct to law enforcement.

Bottomed upon the Sixth Amendment right to counsel, *Massiah* can be construed as the natural outgrowth of the Court's pathbreaking approach in *Gideon*. If the right to counsel was critical to a defense, regardless of a defendant's financial resources, then the time during which the right became operative was also significant. In *Massiah*, the government surreptitiously elicited incriminating statements from a defendant who had been indicted and had retained an attorney. This feat was accomplished through the use of a codefendant who had decided to cooperate with the authorities. The prosecution introduced Massiah's inculpatory statements at trial, despite the strenuous objections of defense counsel.[31]

The *Massiah* Court cited the concurring opinion in *Spano v. New York*,[32] which furnished the doctrinal rationale for its decision. In *Spano*, four Justices subscribed to the notion that an indicted defendant could not be interrogated by the police without the presence of counsel.[33] Allowing such a practice, reasoned those four Justices, might deny a defendant "effective representation by counsel at the only stage when legal aid and advice might help him."[34] Accordingly, the majority in *Massiah* held that "the petitioner was denied the basic protections of that guarantee [the right to counsel] when there was used against him at his trial evidence of his own incriminating words, which federal agents had elicited from him after he had been indicted and in the absence of counsel."[35]

Extending the reasoning in *Massiah*, the Warren Court held in *Escobedo v. Illinois*[36] that the right to counsel as a condition precedent to interrogation of a suspect did not hinge on the initiation of formal adversarial proceedings. Rather, when an investigation focuses on a "particular suspect" instead of being a "general inquiry into an unsolved crime," the right to counsel is as necessary as at any formal stage. Arguing for the State of Illinois at the Supreme Court, James Thompson observed that if the Court found the right to counsel applicable at the time of arrest, it would spell "the end of confessions as a tool of law enforcement." Furthermore, the logical outgrowth of this extension would be to furnish counsel to indigent defendants and to ensure that the waiver of such a right be intelligent, knowing, and not dependent on the suspect making a request.[37]

The problem with *Massiah* and *Escobedo* was that both rested on the Sixth Amendment right to counsel and that *Escobedo* was an ambiguous opinion subject to divergent interpretations. Leaving more questions open than answered, *Escobedo*'s precedential impact was limited. Referring to a suspect's "absolute constitutional right to remain silent," yet resting on Sixth Amendment right-to-counsel grounds, *Escobedo* was indeed enigmatic. As Justice White pointed out in dissent, "It is incongruous to assume that the provision for counsel in the Sixth Amendment was meant to amend or supersede the self-incrimination provision of the Fifth Amendment, which is now applicable to the States." What the focus of an investigation meant was also susceptible to interpretation.

Miranda: The Evolution of a Doctrine

It is given in American popular culture that the privilege against self-incrimination is engrained in our jurisprudence. Indeed, this prompted current Chief Justice Rehnquist to remark in 1974, "At this point in our history virtually every schoolboy is familiar with the concept, if not the language, of the provision that reads: 'No person shall be compelled in any criminal case to be a witness against himself.'"[38] The vacuum and ambiguities created by both *Massiah* and *Escobedo* demanded resolution. If the guiding rationale behind these decisions was to shift the manner in which police-controlled interrogations occurred, then the self-incrimination clause seemed a more logical vehicle than the Sixth Amendment right-to-counsel provision. Furthermore, if lawyers were present at the arrest stage, then confessions would surely vanish, as Thompson noted in his *Escobedo* oral argument. Arguing the *Miranda* case on behalf of the National District Attorneys Association, Duane R. Nedrud echoed Thompson's sentiments. He noted, "If defense counsel comes in at the arrest stage, he will, as he should, prevent the defendant from confessing to his crime, and you will have fewer convictions."[39]

The issue before the Supreme Court was joined: To what extent were confessions a vital adjunct to law enforcement? Were confessions compatible with the criminal adversarial process, or did they subvert its goals? The majority in *Escobedo* had come close to rejecting confessions in an accusatory system. Drawing on history, the Court stated that "a system of criminal law enforcement which comes to depend on 'confession' will, in the long run, be less reliable and more subject to abuses than a system which depends on extrinsic evidence independently secured through skillfull investigation." In effect, the Court had three choices: (1) preserve the status quo; (2) reject the status quo by injecting the lawyer at the arrest stage, thereby ensuring the end of confessions; or (3) reach a solution that straddled these two extremes. By choosing the third option, the *Miranda* Court took, in essence, a conservative approach. Although the opinion may have initially been vilified as antithetical to law enforcement, a dispassionate analysis reveals that the *Miranda* majority was a lot more conservative than what knee-jerk reactions indicated.

It is instructive in this regard to examine the historical record as a basis for concluding that *Miranda* was evolutionary. Indeed, the warning to remain silent that has become part of the *Miranda* holding was invoked, unsuccessfully, as early as 1813. The defendant had been indicted for arson and had confessed to the crime after being told by the magistrate that the evidence pointed to his guilt and that "he had better confess." A grand juror objected that the magistrate had not advised the defendant of the right to remain silent in the face of the accusation. Defendant's counsel concurred with the objection, but the trial court rejected the argument, noting that the accused "was presumed to know the law in his favor."[40] Of course, this early invocation of the need to advise the defendant of the right to remain silent is a mere part of the now-familiar *Miranda* warnings; but it also demonstrates that the Warren Court hardly plucked its opinion out of thin air.

Indeed, the *Miranda* warnings had been implemented by the chief of police in the District of Columbia well before the Court issued the opinion. Arguing in the companion case of *Vignera v. New York*, Victor Earle III told Justice Potter Stewart exactly how the warning should be tailored. Paraphrasing the warning given by all police officers in the District, Earle commented that the warnings entailed the right to remain silent, that anything said by the accused could and would be used against him, that he could call "a lawyer, relative, or friend," that he could confer with his lawyer and that if he could not obtain a lawyer, "one will be appointed for you when your case first goes to court." Earle was reticent about the last part of the warning "because it suggests a little bit that you might not be able to get a lawyer now."[41]

It is through this prism that *Miranda* must be viewed. The majority opted for the continued viability of confessions as an instrument of law enforcement. Early in the opinion, Chief Justice Warren acknowledged the obvious: the key to a successful interrogation is privacy.[42] As David Simon points out, a successful interrogator must exert control over the suspect.[43] If the *Miranda* Court wished to correct a perceived imbalance between the interrogator and the suspect, its nod in the direction of maintaining that privacy belied any solicitude for the suspect.

The irony in *Miranda* lies in the majority's recognition that a suspect who does not ask for counsel is the person most in need of a lawyer's assistance.[44] In assessing the lack of need for "station house" lawyers, the majority predicated *Miranda*'s protections on an affirmative request by the suspect for counsel.[45] This anomaly has prompted critics to offer proposals to "Mirandize" *Miranda*; that is, to demand that all suspects in custody have a "nonwaivable" right to "consult" with an attorney before any police interrogation.[46] The problem with this facile solution is that it would deprive the interrogator of a confession. Any lawyer worth his or her fee knows to tell a suspect not to make a statement to the interrogator. Deprived of the three pillars for a successful interrogation—isolation of the suspect (i.e., privacy), control over the process (a derivative of the first corollary), and the opportunity to preclude the suspect from saying anything without an attorney[47]— the police would have to rely solely on extrinsic evidence to make a case.

If *Miranda* struck a blow for interrogation, how is it that it is perceived as enhancing the rights of the criminal suspect? Again, the key lies in the control exerted by police over the interrogation process. In dissent, Justice Harlan aptly remarked that police officers who "use third-degree tactics and deny them in court are equally destined to lie as skillfully about the warnings and waiver."[48] Justice Harlan's observation is corroborated by the facts in *Miranda*. In a footnote, the majority cited the discrepancy in the testimony by two officers who questioned Ernesto Miranda. One officer testified that Miranda was never warned that anything he said would be used against him in court. The other testified that both officers had warned Miranda of this fact.[49] This conflicting testimony highlights the obvious: someone was not quite telling it like it was. Who, after all, would contradict this testimony if it was internally consistent? The suspect would, of course, but he would probably lose the swearing match in court.[50]

The irony of *Miranda*, therefore, is that it did not necessarily dispel the compelling atmosphere of custodial interrogation. Rather, it reinforced the notion that confessions are necessary and proper. Stephen Schulhofer put it best: "far from handcuffing the police, the warnings work to liberate the police. Miranda's much-maligned rules permit the officer to continue questioning his isolated suspect, the very process that the Court . . . found to be in violation of the fifth amendment."[51] Within the sociopolitical context in which it arose, however, *Miranda* was not quite anomalous. As the preceding discussion has demonstrated, the problem of crime was uppermost in the minds of politicians and the public.[52] Within one week of issuing *Miranda*, the Court let it be known that it did not ignore the apparently incongrous aspects of its ruling and that, much like politicians and the American public, it was acutely conscious of the pernicious effect of crime on the social fabric.

Miranda Unravels: Why It Really Wasn't Revolutionary After All

A decision that is often not emphasized when *Miranda*'s relative merits are debated testifies to what the majority thought about its implications. In *Johnson v. New Jersey*,[53] the Court held that *Escobedo* as well as *Miranda* applied only to cases in which the trial postdated these decisions; that is, neither *Miranda* nor *Escobedo* would apply retroactively.[54] In essence, cases that had been adjudicated prior to those decisions would not be affected by the doctrinal emendations wrought by *Escobedo* and *Miranda*. More important, *Johnson*, issued literally as well as figuratively in conjunction with *Miranda*, was authored by Chief Justice Warren and announced by Justice Brennan. None other than the author of *Miranda* and an influential member of the majority intimated that their intent was evolutionary, not revolutionary.

Explaining the reason behind *Miranda*'s nonretroactivity, Chief Justice Warren noted that although *Miranda* and *Escobedo* promoted reliable confessions by applying a conclusive presumption of coercion in every custodial interrogation, the "danger" was "not necessarily as great as when the accused is subjected to overt and obvious coercion."[55] Indeed, the Court went on to remark that the nonretroactivity of *Escobedo* and *Miranda* would not "preclude persons whose trials have already been completed from invoking the same safeguards as part of an involuntariness claim."[56] In unmistakable terms, *Johnson* underscores the conservative bent underlying *Miranda*. Indeed, one could argue that what the Court contemplated in *Miranda* was not a compromise but rather a continuation of the status quo.

The *Johnson* Court touted rather than criticized the voluntariness standard that *Miranda* purportedly improved. Labeling the voluntariness test "substantive," Chief Justice Warren stressed how the standard had been refined to such a degree that it had "become increasingly meticulous through the years."[57] In fact, the voluntariness test had been expanded to account for the failure to warn suspects of their rights and the denial of access to counsel.[58] After reading *Johnson*, one has the impression that what the *Miranda* majority sought to achieve was a lot less than what its critics would have us believe.

From a pragmatic and political standpoint, moreover, the *Johnson* case reminds us that the Warren Court was cognizant of the problem of crime as reflected in political discourse and popular concerns. In a revealing part of the decision, the majority lays bare the practical necessities behind its holding. Reluctant to release numerous prisoners by applying *Miranda* and *Escobedo* retroactively, the majority noted that such a ruling "would require the retrial or release of numerous prisoners found guilty by trustworthy evidence in conformity with previously announced constitutional standards."[59] "Violence in the streets" was not merely the concern reflected in partisan speeches by savy politicians; it was prominent in the mind of the so-called liberal Warren Court. *Johnson* vividly illustrates what *Miranda* obscures: far from engineering a revolutionary reworking of police investigative practices, the Warren Court merely tinkered with the existing structure.

In fact, the *Miranda* majority may have launched a trend it could not have envisioned; that is, by decreeing amuletic warnings designed to dispel the pressure inherent in custodial interrogation, the Court furnished law enforcement with a potent weapon to sanitize otherwise questionable confessions. It is ironic that Justice William Douglas, a member of the majority in *Miranda*, did not perceive the result the opinion eventually wrought. His cautionary and prescient dissent in *Terry v. Ohio*[60] could easily have been applicable to *Miranda*. In that dissent, Douglas presaged the slippery slope that *Terry* initiated toward the decimation of freedom from unreasonable searches and seizures. In a powerful passage, Douglas pointed to the "powerful hydraulic pressures throughout our history that bear heavily on the Court to water down constitutional guarantees and give the police the upper hand."[61] Paradoxically, what *Miranda* accomplished in the guise of seemingly expanding the right against self-incrimination was, in effect, to "give the police the upper hand."

ATTEMPTS TO OVERRULE *MIRANDA*

The notion that *Miranda* was a prolaw enforcement decision may seem counterintuitive at first glance. Certainly, the opinion was not viewed in this fashion by its detractors. Furthermore, politicians saw a golden opportunity to gain political advantage from a concerted attack on *Miranda*'s underlying premises. Two centrifugal forces combined to strip *Miranda* of its symbolic appeal: Congress repealed it within two years, and Richard Nixon, successfully exploiting fear of crime as a campaign tactic,[62] was elected president. When Earl Warren resigned as Chief Justice shortly after Nixon took the oath of office, he provided the means for Nixon to reshape the contours of the Supreme Court. A changed Court, together with a political and social climate conducive to a narrowing of the constitutional rights of criminal defendants, combined to ensure that *Miranda* would become a welcome "piece of station house furniture."[63]

The Omnibus Crime Control and Safe Streets Act of 1968

If the executive branch invoked the theme of "crime in the streets" to win an election, the legislative branch could not be left behind. To the extent that being "tough on crime" had become a zero-sum game, it became politically expedient to deliver on those promises. Because *Miranda* had been transformed into the archetypal symbol of Warren Court excesses in expanding the constitutional rights of criminals, it was the perfect vehicle to show one's true political colors. Placed in proper context, however, the provision of the act repealing *Miranda* was not as bold a departure from legal tradition as one would imagine.

The irony behind the act was that it was signed by President Johnson, known for his liberal domestic policies and programs. Johnson reluctantly went along with the bill, "the last and in many ways the most conservative piece of domestic legislation of his presidency."[64] The clamor for "get tough" legislation on crime was overwhelming. The bill was not only popular with Congress, it also echoed public sentiment. Although President Johnson pondered vetoing the legislation, the "hydraulic pressures" to which Justice Douglas alluded in *Terry* compelled Johnson to enact the measure.[65]

The statute overruled *Miranda*, in effect decreeing the return of the voluntariness standard that *Miranda* had jettisoned. Embodied in the

United States Code,[66] section 3501 states that in any federal jurisdiction or the District of Columbia, a confession "shall be admissible in evidence if it is voluntarily given."[67] It also sets forth a list of factors to be taken into account in assessing the voluntariness of the confession. These factors include any delay between the defendant's arrest and arraignment, whether the defendant was aware of the nature of the charges, whether he knew about the right to remain silent and that anything he said could be used against him, whether he was advised of the right to counsel before being interrogated, and whether the confession was given in the absence of counsel.[68] The presence or absence of any of these factors, moreover, is not dispositive on the issue of the voluntariness of the confession.[69]

Although section 3501 purportedly overruled *Miranda*, one must ask: what did Congress seek to achieve through this legislative sleight of hand? Either it sought to declare the opinion an unconstitutional piece of judicial rule making, as its critics have charged, or it sought to set up a confrontation in which the Court would be faced with the option of exercising the power of judicial review to revoke the portion of 3501 repealing *Miranda*. A third explanation is that Congress merely wanted to get on the bandwagon of popular opinion by reaffirming a "tough on crime" stance. Finally, Congress could have envisioned a changing political climate in which appointments to the Supreme Court by a conservative, Republican president would provide the new Court with the opportunity to ratify 3501 and overrule *Miranda*.

The Countertrend Begins: *Harris, Hass, Cooper,* and *Tucker*

Inevitably, the last alternative materialized: the changing composition of the Supreme Court altered *Miranda*'s latitude, provoking a counterattack that circumscribed the opinion's reach and divested it of its constitutional status. Not endorsing the purportedly radical solution embodied in 3501, the Court nonetheless found a means to short-circuiting the holding without overruling *Miranda*. Although what the Court wrought was not fundamentally different from the essence of 3501, the means by which it accomplished its mission engendered dismal consequences. Indeed, 3501 did not reject *Miranda* outright; it did, after all, recognize that the warnings played a role in determining the voluntariness of a confession. The statute merely refused to accord the warnings the amuletic status conferred by *Miranda*. The Court would have been better off had it discarded *Miranda* and embraced 3501. Instead, it faces an unsolvable conundrum: critics of the opinion believe that the Court has not gone far enough, and supporters contend that it has violated the spirit, if not the letter, of the opinion.

Harris v. New York: The Assault Begins. Within three years of the enactment of 3501, the Supreme Court launched the *Miranda* counterrevolution. Three opinions formed the basis for the attack. Just as *Miranda* was a 5–4 majority opinion, so was *Harris v. New York*.[70] This time, however, Chief Justice Warren Burger and Justice Harry Blackmun, both Nixon appointees, joined three of the *Miranda* dissenters—Justices Harlan, Stewart, and White—to literally and figuratively "impeach" the opinion.[71] Three years after *Harris*, the Court accomplished the same result that Congress had sought when it enacted 3501: it declared the opinion mere judicial dictum without constitutional force.[72]

In a short opinion, Chief Justice Burger held that statements taken in violation of *Miranda* could be used to impeach the defendant's testimony at trial.[73] Although the *Miranda* Court cautioned that statements taken in violation of its holding should not be used to impeach the defendant's testimony,[74] the *Harris* Court dismissed that portion of the decision as uncontrolling dicta.[75] Although it is not my purpose to critique the opinion, a thoughtful commentator has branded it an "exercise in raw judicial power" and lacking in "candor, meticulousness, and reasoned elaboration."[76]

Pragmatically, *Harris* has far-reaching implications. Allowing statements in violation of *Miranda* to impeach the defendant creates an incentive for police to violate *Miranda*. The defendant loses the benefit of *Miranda* if he or she chooses to testify. Furthermore, limiting instructions are likely to be ineffective, because the jury will probably weigh the statement for its substantive impact.[77] Indeed, the limiting instruction could have the unintended effect of reminding the jury of the statement. If, on the other hand, the defendant is dissuaded from taking the stand, the jury is also likely to disregard instructions and perceive the silence "as evidence of guilt."[78]

Oregon v. Hass: Who Cares If You Want an Attorney? Expanding the parameters delineated in *Harris*, the Court dismissed the prospect of police incentive to violate *Miranda* in *Oregon v. Hass*.[79] In *Hass*, the police ignored the suspect's invocation of his right to an attorney after being read the *Miranda* warnings.[80] Nevertheless, the *Hass* majority held that the defendant's statements could be used to impeach his testimony.[81] Although the Court acknowledged that its holding might induce the police to ignore a suspect's rights under *Miranda*, it rejected such a possibility as "speculative."[82] If such abuse was egregious, the defendant could resort to the voluntariness standard and claim the confession was a product of "coercion" or "duress."[83]

As one commentator presciently noted, "*Hass* constituted an open invitation to the police to disregard the suspect's right to the assistance of counsel."[84] In a case in which the stakes are high, law enforcement agents may decide to defy *Miranda*'s prescriptive requirements in the hope of securing a confession. The "speculative possibility" that the Court dismissed in *Hass* has turned into an objective reality. As one would imagine, this occurred in a "high-profile" case in which the stakes were high and in which the police confronted substantial pressure to solve the crime.

The "Speculative Possibility" Materializes: *Cooper v. Dupnik*. Imagine a metropolitan community in utter fear because a serial rapist is suspected in a "chain of rapes, robberies, and kidnappings" that have occurred over a two-year period. This was the scenario facing the Tucson Police Department and the Pima County Sheriff's Department in May 1986.[85] In an effort to ensure a successful conclusion to this ordeal, a joint task force, consisting of members of the police and the sheriff's office, decided that once the "Prime Time Rapist" was apprehended, they would hold him incommunicado, ignore his right to remain silent and any request to speak with an attorney, and "pressure and interrogate him until he confessed."[86] In fact, the "primary interrogator" in the case had imagined a profile according to which the suspect would "immediately ask for an attorney."[87]

In a sworn deposition, the task force members acknowledged that this strategy, though violative of *Miranda*, would be the "first step in creating the illusion of hopelessness" and that it "might ultimately instill fear."[88] More important, the members of the task force knew that such a confession would not be admissible in the prosecution's case-in-chief. However, they were aware of *Harris*'s and *Hass*'s teachings; the confession might be admissible to impeach the defendant and deprive him "of the opportunity of forming an insanity defense."[89]

The strategy pursued by the task force was reflected in the lead detective's assertion that in major cases he is willing to violate *Miranda*; indeed, the detective stated that he had done so in the past, "in all probability will continue to do it," but "will not do it lightly."[90] The first suspect who was apprehended in the case asked for an attorney and was denied his request; the interrogation continued. The decision was easy. In the detective's words: "We decided it was going to be clear-cut,

forget his Miranda Rights, the hell with it."[91] A consequentialist rationale justified the strategy. Again, in the detective's view, he was
"going to violate this American citizen's rights, but look at the totality
of the circumstances, the big picture, is it worth it, yeah."[92]

After this suspect was released, a second suspect emerged: Michael
Cooper. Tragically, Cooper was misidentified as a suspect due to the
incompetence of a state fingerprint expert who had failed the state's
fingerprint examination.[93] When Cooper was apprehended, the plan
went into effect. Cooper repeatedly denied that he was the "Prime
Time Rapist" and made "two unequivocal" requests for an attorney,
both of which were "deliberatively igored," in accordance with the task
force's plan.[94]

What is remarkable about the case is that even though he faced a
grueling interrogation, Cooper was not "worn down" to admit crimes
he did not commit. Even more astounding is that, in the face of a mistaken fingerprint match, the chief of the investigation nevertheless
insisted that Cooper was the "Prime Time Rapist." Cooper maintained
his innocence in light of overwhelming pressure to confess, and the
lead interrogator even believed that they had the "wrong man."[95]

Cooper was eventually released and was not charged; nevertheless
he filed suit for the violation of his civil rights pursuant to 42 U.S.C.,
section 1983.[96] The position espoused in oral argument by the attorneys representing the law enforcement personnel and their municipalities is telling. Not only did appellants contend, quite properly, that
Miranda violations were not actionable under section 1983 because
they did not transgress[97] the Constitution, they also relied on *Hass* and
Harris for the proposition that statements taken in contravention of
Miranda were admissible to impeach the defendant's credibility.[98]

Even when a defendant invokes *Miranda*'s greatest protection, the
right not to be interrogated without counsel, these cries may seem
plaintive in the face of a concerted police effort to override it. More
important, law enforcement's bad faith when it engages in a flagrant
violation of *Miranda*'s dictates will not prevent the confession from
being admitted into evidence. Rather, the defendant must rely on the
voluntariness standard, which is a constitutional remedy, in order to
keep the confession from being used for impeachment.[99]

Miranda's Constitutional Demise: Michigan v. Tucker.   One
term before it decided *Hass*, the Court dealt a severe blow to *Miranda*
in *Michigan v. Tucker*.[100] Justice Rehnquist, writing for the majority,
declared that the "procedural safeguards" erected by *Miranda* were not
constitutionally mandated; rather, they were "measures to insure that

the right against compulsory self-incrimination was protected."[101] The factual context in *Tucker* is also instructive: it involved evidence derived from a *Miranda* violation. Specifically, the police learned the identity of a witness through questioning the defendant, who was not advised of his right to counsel during the custodial interrogation.[102]

Not only did *Tucker* sever *Miranda* from its constitutional moorings, it also paved the way for rendering the "fruit of the poisonous tree"[103] doctrine inapplicable to *Miranda* violations. Indeed, several courts immediately took the cue from *Tucker* by holding the "fruits" doctrine inapplicable to *Miranda*.[104] It is remarkable, therefore, that more courts did not rely on *Tucker* to accomplish the goal set forth in section 3501—that is, to overrule *Miranda*. One court that did perceive the opening provided by *Tucker* made the logical connection between the Court's divesting *Miranda* of its constitutional status and congressional action overruling it.

In *United States v. Crocker*,[105] the Tenth Circuit Court of Appeals upheld the trial court's order, which applied the provisions in section 3501 in determining the issue of the voluntariness of the defendant's confession.[106] Acknowledging that the Court evaded the question of whether it was implicitly ratifying section 3501 in *Tucker*, the *Crocker* court focused on the obvious: if the *Miranda* warnings were constitutionally required under "any and all circumstances," then it was nonsensical to hold that evidence derived from a Miranda violation was nevertheless admissible.[107] It seems as if the three-judge panel in *Crocker* was trying to nudge the Supreme Court to admit what it was reluctant to confess: *Miranda* was a bad opinion that should have been discarded. Perhaps the Court was reticent to overrule a symbol that had become entrenched in both private and public discourse. Rather than risking the controversy that might erupt upon discarding such a symbol, the Court opted for the expedient of confining it out of existence.

Miranda Takes a Dive: *Tucker* Redux in *Quarles* and *Elstad*

Within a decade of issuing *Tucker*, the Supreme Court served notice that it was not retreating from the fundamental premise outlined in that opinion. It did so within the context of carving out the sole exception to *Miranda*: public safety. In *New York v. Quarles*,[108] the majority held that a concern for public safety justifies dispensing with the *Miranda* warnings, thereby making the suspect's statements admissible in the prosecution's case.[109] Citing *Tucker*, Justice Rehnquist labeled the *Miranda* warnings "prophylactic" and "not themselves rights protected by the Constitution but . . . measures [designed] to insure that the right against compulsory self-incrimination [is] protected."[110] Although Justice Rehnquist acknowledged that he was detracting from the "desirable clarity" *Miranda* supposedly affords, a cost-benefit analysis warranted the exception.[111]

What is revealing about *Quarles* is how *Miranda* has displaced the voluntariness standard as the primary means to contest the validity of a confession. In *Quarles*, four officers with their guns drawn handcuffed the suspect and asked him about the location of a gun.[112] These facts prompted Justice Thurgood Marshall to remark in dissent that "it would strain credulity" to maintain that such questioning "was not coercive."[113] The majority replied to this criticism by inviting the defendant on remand to contend that "his statement was coerced under traditional due process standards."[114] In effect, the corrosive impact of *Miranda* is readily apparent in *Quarles:* the opinion lulls counsel into a false sense of security when a *Miranda* violation seems plausible. In a situation in which a due process argument may be viable, the possibility of raising it may be foregone because of *Miranda*'s beguiling attraction.

In conjunction with *Tucker*'s rationale, the Court also endorsed the notion that a voluntary confession in the absence of *Miranda* warnings should not preclude the admission of subsequent statements by the defendant. *Oregon v. Elstad*[115] presents a fascinating glimpse into the Court's ambivalence toward *Miranda*. The *Elstad* majority framed the issue succinctly: "whether the Self-incrimination clause of the Fifth Amendment requires the suppression of a confession, made after proper *Miranda* warnings and a valid waiver of rights, solely because the police had obtained an earlier voluntary but unwarned admission from the defendant."[116] Indeed, the majority opinion, authored by Justice Sandra Day O'Connor, displays in bold relief the manifold inconsistencies that plague the Court's *Miranda* jurisprudence.

While stressing the "prophylactic" nature of the *Miranda* warnings, Justice O'Connor points out that a *Miranda* violation does not necessarily contravene the Fifth Amendment. Rather, it merely triggers a "presumption of coercion."[117] Citing both *Tucker* and *Quarles*, Justice O'Connor employs the sobriquet "preventive medicine" to describe *Miranda*, and she continues by emphasizing that it "provides a remedy even to the defendant who has suffered no constitutional harm."[118] One cannot fail to notice the utter non sequitur underlying this argument.

The Fifth Amendment prohibits coercion in extracting a confession. *Miranda*, in turn, presumes coercion from the failure to warn a suspect or from failure to obtain a proper waiver. Yet it is possible to contravene *Miranda* and not violate the Constitution—that is, coerce the suspect into confessing. If one were to attempt to explain this to a layperson, I would venture to guess that most adults with a modicum of common sense would throw up their hands in exasperation and say, "Nonsense!"

At another point in the opinion, Justice O'Connor tries to praise *Miranda* by remarking that the Court is by no means "retreating" from the "bright-line" rule of *Miranda*.[119] Ironically, on the preceding page Justice O'Connor laments the "murky" and "difficult" questions of when custody begins or when an unwarned statement will be admissible.[120] One the one hand, *Miranda* is commended as furnishing a welcome "bright-line" rule governing custodial interrogation; on the other hand, it is scorned for raising difficult issues relating to custody and admissibility. The Court cannot have it both ways. Either *Miranda* is good precedent or it is bad precedent that the Court reluctantly tolerates. Rather than considering it to be "preventive medicine," it seems the majority classifies *Miranda* as a laxative.

Furthermore, though not reaching the question, the *Elstad* Court gave impetus to lower courts that may have been disinclined to apply the "fruit of the poisonous tree" doctrine to any nontestimonial fruits of *Miranda* violations.[121] This exclusion has far-reaching pragmatic effects. For example, in a murder case in which the defendant gives an unwarned statement disclosing the whereabouts of the murder weapon, the weapon would be admissible that the "fruits" doctrine is not applicable to a *Miranda* violation.[122] Consider the absurdity underlying the Court's rationale: the presumptively "coerced" statement is suppressed, but the fruit of the statement is nonetheless admissible. Why bother excluding the defendant's admission when the fruits are more compelling from an evidentiary perspective? Does *Miranda* really help the defendant while also deterring police misconduct, in this instance? I think not.

Indeed, an example provides ample basis for the conclusion that *Elstad* furnishes an incentive for the police to disregard *Miranda*'s dictates. Consider a defendant who is suspected of murdering his parents.[123] After detectives "interview" the suspect at his home, they transport him to the station and take him to a "small, windowless room," where he is "interviewed continuously for two hours." During that sustained custodial interrogation, the detectives not only fail to administer the *Miranda* warnings, they also deceive the suspect into believing that his father has emerged from a coma and has identified him as a suspect. The detectives ridicule the suspect's exculpatory story as "ridiculous" and "absurd."[124]

Of course, the suspect breaks down, wonders whether he suffered from a blackout when he perpetrated the crime, and states that "it's coming to" him. At this time the police administer the warnings, obtain a waiver from the suspect, and secure a "full confession."[125] Though conceding it is a "close question," the appellate court affirms the admissibility of the confession, citing *Elstad*. The first confession did not involve sufficient coercion to render the subsequent waiver involuntary. Because the first confession was not involuntary—that is, the product of a constrained and unfree will—the second confession was, given the waiver, not suppressible as the fruit of the first "tainted" confession. Although the first confession is not admissible, the carbon copy of it is allowed in.[126]

Notice the successful tactic employed by the detectives in this case. To remove the possibility that the suspect will invoke *Miranda*, they purposely avoid administering the warnings. Within two hours, they soften up the suspect until he relents and gives up. Then they administer the warnings, in the hope of securing a valid waiver and a confession admissible against the defendant in the prosecution's case. They succeed admirably. *Elstad* provided them with the means to circumvent *Miranda* and yet have the benefit of the confession. Notice that, unlike *Harris* and *Hass*, in this case the admission of the inculpatory statements are not predicated upon the defendant taking the stand. Rather, the confession is admissible in the prosecution's case. The police can have their cake and eat it, too. They can willfully violate *Miranda* without suffering any adverse consequences. One wonders, under this state of affairs, just how much of a "prophylactic" *Miranda* truly is!

Edwards v. Arizona

Despite the erosion of the opinion's "prophylactic" effect, one facet of *Miranda* has withstood dilution: the seemingly absolute prohibition of interrogation when a suspect invokes the right not to be questioned without an attorney. In *Edwards v. Arizona*,[127] the Court held that once the accused expresses the desire not to be questioned without the presence of an attorney, he "is not subject to further interrogation by the authorities until counsel has been made available to him, unless the accused himself initiates further communications, exchanges, or conversations with the police."[128] Thus the police cannot further interrogate the suspect, even if they subsequently manage to persuade the accused to change his mind and waive his rights.

Consistently, the Court has refused to recede from this holding. It is curious how attempts to limit *Edwards'* reach have proven unsuccessful. Perhaps the most wide-ranging extension of *Edwards* occurred in *Arizona v. Roberson*,[129] where the majority expanded its scope by refusing to make *Edwards'* protection offense-specific. In that case, *Edwards* was triggered following a suspect's request for counsel even though he was questioned about a different crime.[130] Thus, the protective shield erected in *Edwards* remains effective, regardless of the scope and nature of subsequent police investigations.

Extending *Edwards* to its logical limits, the majority in *Minnick v. Mississippi*[131] heaped effusive praise upon the clarity and certainty of the *Edwards* rule.[132] Consultation with an attorney is not sufficient to protect the suspect once he or she has invoked the right to counsel under *Edwards*. Rather, when the suspects asks for an attorney, "interrogation must cease," and "officials may not reinitiate interrogation without counsel present, whether or not the accused has consulted with his attorney."[133] It is evident, therefore, that a suspect who unequivocally demands an attorney before being questioned receives the full panoply of *Miranda*'s "prophylactic" safeguards.

More intriguing than *Minnick*'s holding is Justice Scalia's acerbic dissent. Decrying the extension of *Edwards*, Justice Scalia derisively refers to *Minnick* as "the latest stage of prophylaxis built upon prophylaxis, producing a fairyland castle of imagined constitutional restriction upon law enforcement."[134] He construes both *Edwards* and *Minnick* as misguided efforts to protect suspects from "their own folly." Justice Scalia also observes that the "sharp-witted" criminal would never confess.[135] He is right about that, but he is wrong about the characteristics of the suspect likely to invoke the right to counsel under *Miranda*. With all due respect to Justice Scalia, he is the one who inhabits the fairyland. In the real world of criminal investigation, *Edwards* and its progeny protect the shrewd criminal, not the dim-witted one. Indeed, the irony behind Miranda is that it has been interpreted in such a fashion as to protect the few, the brave, the tough, and the recidivist; it does not protect the many, the cowed, the intimidated, and the frightened.

Two insightful commentators confirm this rather prosaic yet rational observation. David Simon describes the tale of two professional hit men who "matched" each other "body for body" as Baltimore's "premier contract killers." Every instance in which they were brought into police headquarters for questioning yielded the same result. They were read *Miranda*, invoked the right to an attorney, and the process unceremoniously ended.[136] Indeed, these consummate criminals knew exactly what to do in the stationhouse. *Miranda* was indeed their staunchest ally. The close quarters and police-dominated ambience failed to threaten these men into submission. What is ironic about all of this is that *Miranda* has wound up protecting not the poor, indigent, intimidated suspect the Warrent Court sought so fervently to shield from police domination. Rather, it is the tough, hardened criminal who has the requisite emotional makeup to resist the "inherent" pressures of custodial interrogation.

On the other side of the coin, Janet Ainsworth perceptively notes how women, African Americans, and ethnic minorities suffer from the strictures the Supreme Court has placed on the *Miranda* norms.[137] Stressing the importance of an "unequivocal" assertion of the need for an attorney as a precondition for a suspect to terminate custodial interrogation, the Court in *Davis v. United States*[138] ensured that these groups would be unduly disadvantaged. In mandating that the suspect "must unambiguously request counsel" in order to stop custodial interrogation by the police, the *Davis* majority sided with the hardened, shrewd criminal suspect. By rewarding "direct and assertive" speech patterns, the Court discriminated against the indirect speech patterns characteristic of the powerless: females, African Americans, and ethnic minorities.[139] Given these realities, it is naive to contend that *Miranda* either hampers police from questioning suspects or provides a "veritable fairyland" of constitutional protection for criminals.

Whatever protections *Edwards* seems to offer, therefore, are more than offset by *Davis*'s stringent command: without an unequivocal request for counsel, *Miranda*'s safeguards are evanescent. "Maybe I should talk to a lawyer" simply will not do. In fact, such a statement will not even require the interrogators to stop questioning the suspect in order to clarify what he or she means or desires.[140] The standard, rather, as set forth in *Davis*, puts the burden on the suspect to "articulate his desire to have counsel present sufficiently clearly that a reasonable police officer in the circumstances would understand the statement to be a request for an attorney."[141] The arbiter of whether

the suspect made an unequivocal request is the officer at the station—
that is, the person in control of the inherently compulsive interrogation process.

Even if an *Edwards* violation occurs, the incriminating statement may
nonetheless be admissible under the *Quarles* public safety exception.
The question posed by the conflict between the two cases is simple:
Does the public safety exception trump *Edwards*? At least three courts
have given an affirmative response to this knotty issue. Although
Quarles permits the police to dispense with the *Miranda* warnings when
dealing with a threat to the public safety, it does not resolve the issue
of whether police may ignore an unequivocal request for counsel if they
do decide to administer the warnings. The first court to grapple with
the problem, the Ninth Circuit Court of Appeals, found logic to dictate
that *Quarles* would indeed trump *Edwards*.[142] This conclusion flows
quite naturally from the premises underlying the public safety exception.

To the extent that *Miranda* is a mere "prophylactic safeguard" and
not a constitutional ruling, it makes sense to apply the public safety
exception after a suspect has requested counsel. As the Ninth Circuit
succinctly put it, "Society's need to procure the information about the
location of a dangerous weapon is as great after, as it was before, the
request for counsel."[143] Indeed, the motivation behind the questioning
of the suspect is not to "badger" the suspect into submission; rather,
it is presumably to quell the threat to the public safety. In these circumstances, the remedy the defendant must pursue is to claim that his
statements "were obtained coercively, disregarding *Edwards'* prophylactic rule."[144] Underscoring the obvious, the Ninth Circuit opinion
reveals the degree to which *Miranda* has been rendered irrelevant. The
message conveyed to the defendant is to seek suppression through the
traditional, constitutional means, not through the vicarious, "prophylactic," judicially crafted rule.

Consistent with this rationale, at least two other appellate courts
concur with the assessment offered by the Ninth Circuit in *United
States v. DeSantis*.[145] Although *Quarles* is rooted in the notion that the
Miranda warnings might deter a suspect from answering questions
prompted by a concern with public safety, and such deterrence evapo-
rates once the warnings are read to the suspect, the public safety is
nonetheless applicable. Again, the "danger to the public and police
from hidden traps and discarded weapons is as evident after the
Miranda warnings have been given as before."[146] In short, if custodial

interrogation is objectively prompted by a concern for public safety, the only recourse left open to the defendant is the constitutional one: *Miranda* just will not do.

Withrow v. Williams.   If *Davis* serves to foil the potential advantages offered by *Edwards*, *Withrow v. Williams* stands as the Court's most forceful affirmation of *Miranda*'s fundamental premises. In *Withrow*, Justice David Souter, writing for the majority, refused to preclude a defendant from raising a *Miranda* claim on a federal habeas review of a state conviction.[147] Distinguishing *Miranda* from the Fourth Amendment's exclusionary rule at issue in *Stone v. Powell*,[148] Justice Souter described *Miranda* as protecting a "fundamental trial right" and furthering "the correct ascertainment of guilt."[149] The irony behind the majority opinion lies in the divergence between labeling *Miranda* a mere "prophylactic," on the one hand, and a "fundamental trial right," on the other hand. Attempting to couple two diametrically opposed conceptions of the doctrine yields a quagmire from which the Court cannot escape.

In a perceptive dissenting and concurring opinion, Justice O'Connor exposed the flaws attending *Miranda*'s jurisprudence. In a telling critique of the doctrine's transformation, O' Connor aptly describes *Miranda*'s "presumption of coercion" not as an "impenetrable barrier to the introduction of compelled testimony" but as "leaking like a sieve."[150] Riddled with ambiguities, qualifications, and the "public safety exception," *Miranda* is hardly a formidable obstacle to law enforcement. Rather, the pejorative label it has inherited, a "prophylactic," and a leaking one at that, underscores its utter banality.

Dickerson v. United States.   It seems that the Court's holding in *Dickerson v. United States* has generated a new round of debates among academics, who either expected more from the majority opinion or who determined that the opinion generated more questions than it answered.[151] Paul Cassell hoped that the Supreme Court would uphold the Fourth Circuit opinion, in which the court held that section 3501 overruled *Miranda*. Other scholars have pointed to the incongruity the Court has perpetuated; *Miranda* is a "constitutional" opinion, yet the precedents stripping it of constitutional status and restricting its reach remain valid. Perhaps the Chief Justice, who wrote the majority opinion, has figured out, as I have argued, that in its current diluted form, *Miranda*, is a boon rather than an obstacle to the police. It is worthwhile, therefore, to explore the chief facets of the *Dickerson* holding as a means of assessing its importance or, more accurately, its irrelevance.

As he saw it, Chief Justice Rehnquist, writing for the majority in *Dickerson*, believed that the central issue was "whether the *Miranda* Court announced a constitutional rule or merely exercised its supervisory authority to regulate evidence in the absence of congressional direction."[152] If *Miranda* announced not a constitutional rule, but merely an evidentiary standard, then Congress could have superseded *Miranda* with 3501. The straitjacket from which the Chief Justice had to escape was, as we have seen, the series of opinions referring to the *Miranda* opinion as a mere prophylactic rather than a rule predicated on the Fifth Amendment's privilege against self-incrimination. In essence, the Chief Justice offered three reasons to support the majority's conclusion that, notwithstanding the constitutional erosion of *Miranda* that it had fostered, the opinion stood on constitutional footing.

The fundamental underpinning of the *Dickerson* holding was that *Miranda* extended its reach to state courts. Taking that proposition to its logical conclusion, Chief Justice Rehnquist stated the obvious: the Supreme Court of the United States does not hold supervisory power over state courts. To buttress this rationale, the *Dickerson* majority cited *Withrow*, which allowed habeas corpus proceedings for *Miranda* violations.[153] Because habeas corpus remedies are available only to prisoners being held in violation of the Constitution or law or treaties of the United States, then it follows that *Miranda* must have been anchored by the Constitution. Along the way, however, the *Dickerson* majority was forced to concede that the "language" in some of its opinions, such as *Tucker*, *Quarles*, and *Elstad*, undermined *Miranda*'s constitutional legitimacy.

The second and third bases for the *Dickerson* holding rested on statements in the *Miranda* majority opinion reflecting its belief that it was "constitutional rule"; and the "*Miranda* Court's invitation for legislative action to protect the constitutional right against coerced self-incrimination."[154] Those two justifications for *Miranda*'s constitutional stature belie the extent to which the Court has winnowed its basic safeguards and its fundamental rationale. It is almost as if the *Dickerson* opinion were the Court's attempt at fixing a doctrine that no longer holds any sway over the criminal justice system. Upholding its diluted or nonexistent impact upon police interrogation practices is a futile exercise.

Yale Kamisar, the preeminent scholar on the *Miranda* doctrine, put this banal exercise in proper perspective when he observed that the Chief Justice in *Dickerson* probably opted to "reaffirm" *Miranda*'s constitutional status while also preserving "all the qualifications and exceptions the much-criticized case had acquired over the decades."[155] Indeed, Chief Justice Rehnquist recognized that in its current form *Miranda* poses little, if any, obstacles to law enforcement. He noted that the Court's post-*Miranda* jurisprudence has "reduced the impact of the *Miranda* rule on legitimate law enforcement while reaffirming the decision's core ruling that unwarned statements may not be used as evidence in the prosecution's case in chief."[156] This statement is partially accurate: not only has the Court eviscerated, rather than reduced, the impact of the case on law enforcement, it has also, in the process, decimated rather than reduced the opinion's core holding.

Where does that leave the once-vaunted but much maligned *Miranda* doctrine? Quite simply, it leaves it where most of the Court's criminal justice jurisprudence lies: in an illogical, indefensible, and anomalous intellectual quagmire. Ultimately, *Dickerson* could not undo three decades of case law that stripped *Miranda* of its essential moorings. As one of the participants in a symposium on *Dickerson* aptly noted, the Court "breached its duty to provide a justification for *Miranda* or *Dickerson* and squandered an opportunity to rationalize contradictory case law regarding *Miranda*'s exceptions."[157] It is difficult, if not impossible, to rationalize contradictory case law or a doctrine whose fundamental premise has been obliterated by cynics purporting to ratify it while ensuring its practical demise. There is no other way to describe the Court's meandering path in the *Miranda* field. It is difficult to revive a terminal patient; that is the reason scholars have found *Dickerson* wanting.

THE FUTURE OF *MIRANDA*

Beyond the truism that *Miranda* doesn't have much of an impact on protecting the suspect from the presumed compulsion inherent in custodial interrogation, there lies a more important tenet: *Miranda* has a detrimental effect on the ability of a defendant to suppress a putatively coercive or involuntary confession. Citing *Johnson*, Justice O'Connor in *Withrow* highlights the obvious proposition: "It is entirely possible to extract a compelled statement despite the most precise and accurate of warnings."[158] More to the point, *Miranda* exerts a centrifugal force on defense counsel: it diverts attention from the critical issue of whether the confession was the product of a constitutional violation rather than of the "prophylactic" *Miranda* doctrine. Furthermore, *Miranda* in its current diluted form serves as a useful law enforcement adjunct: a so-called *Miranda* waiver provides the government with a means to argue that an otherwise coerced or involuntary confession was constitutionally secured.

Lulling Counsel into a False Sense of Security: *Miranda*'s Seductive Appeal

Two examples illustrate how *Miranda* obscures the more central question on which the defense counsel should focus: whether the confession was involuntary under the due process clause of the Fourteenth Amendment or was coerced under the self-incrimination clause of the Fifth Amendment. The two cases that amply support this proposition are *Withrow v. Williams* and *New York v. Quarles*. I will discuss how in both cases the defense attorneys lost the war to win the battle.

Robert Williams was a suspect in a double murder which occurred in Romulus, Michigan, in the mid-1980s. Police went to Williams' house, took him to the police station, deliberately avoided giving him the *Miranda* warnings, and ultimately extracted an incriminating statement from him. Though initially denying involvement in the murders, Williams relented when the lead detective gave him an ultimatum: tell the truth or "we'll lock you up" and "you can tell your 'false' story to a defense attorney and she can try to prove the police are wrong."[159] Of course, Williams proceeded to acknowledge that he provided the murder weapon to the trigger man, who told him where he had disposed of the weapon and other incriminating items.[160] It was at this juncture, forty minutes into the interrogation session at the station, that the police advised Williams of his *Miranda* rights. Williams then gave more incriminating statements.

Although the trial court suppressed statements obtained two consecutive days after the initial interrogation because of a delay in arraignment under Michigan law, it nevertheless declined to suppress the statements given after Williams' arrest, ruling that Williams had been given a "timely warning of his *Miranda* rights.[161] After exhausting his state remedies, Williams filed a pro se petition for habeas corpus in federal district court, basing his claim for relief solely on a *Miranda* violation.

Granting relief, the district court found, although neither side had raised the issue, that Williams' statements after he received the *Miranda* warnings were "involuntary under the Due Process Clause of the Fourteenth Amendment."[162] The "totality of the circumstances" revealed that the police inducements of lenient treatment in exchange for the "truth" had overborne Williams' will. Unremarkably, the Sixth Circuit Court of Appeals affirmed the district court's decision, finding that the statements Williams made after being administered *Miranda* were involuntary.

Similarly, defense counsel in *New York v. Quarles*[163] relied exclusively on *Miranda* in an attempt to suppress a confession given without the benefit of the warnings. Although the police questioned the suspect in a supermarket, they did so with guns drawn. One would surmise that questioning by police with guns drawn and pointed at the suspect is a classic example of compulsion. Indeed, Justice Marshall remarked that it "would strain credulity" to think otherwise.[164] Again, *Miranda*'s seductive appeal prompted the defendant to overlook the obvious: the statement could well have been suppressible on "constitutional" rather than on "prophylactic" *Miranda* grounds.

Pragmatically, the centrifugal force that *Miranda* exerts on the more critical issue of whether an incriminating statement is unconstitutionally obtained cannot be understated. If the defendant overlooks the issue, several pernicious effects are discernible. First, if the confession is suppressed on *Miranda* grounds, the prosecution may still, pursuant to *Harris* and *Hass*, introduce the incriminating statements to impeach the defendant's testimony, if he or she elects to take the stand. If the statements are not suppressed because they are deemed to have been given in compliance with *Miranda*, a confession that may have been excluded on constitutional grounds will be admitted at trial. Even if the constitutional issue is raised on appeal, the Court has held that the introduction of a coerced confession at trial is subject to harmless error analysis.[165] Thus a coerced statement that should not have played a role at trial could be erroneously admitted due to misplaced reliance on *Miranda*; nevertheless it may not affect the ultimate outcome because of the harmless error doctrine.

Of course, I have already emphasized that the public safety exception may nullify the protective barrier erected by *Edwards*. Even the magic incantation of the words "I want an attorney" will not preclude the admission of a confession if the public safety exception is deemed applicable. Defense counsel may believe that a foolproof *Miranda* remedy may prevent the prosecution from introducing a confession in its case when, in reality, the public safety exception may furnish a means to admit it. In terms of providing a false sense of security, the potential impact of the public safety exception to override *Edwards* is devastating.

If defense counsel succeeds in overcoming the formidable obstacles erected by the qualifications and exception to *Miranda*, and the incriminating statements are suppressed, the victory may be a hollow one; if the violation does not reach constitutional dimensions, the defendant will not be able to file a civil suit under the civil rights statute. As we have seen,[166] *Miranda* violations are not actionable under 42 U.S.C., Section 1983. To the extent that the defendant may desire to institute actions against the offending municipality and thereby obtain a monetary judgment, *Miranda* will get him zip.

How to Sanitize an Otherwise Coerced Confession: Using a *Miranda* Waiver to Argue That a Confession Was Voluntary

Besides deflecting counsel's attention from the more critical issue of whether a confession was the product of coercion, *Miranda* provides an ancillary benefit to law enforcement: it enables the police to employ a waiver to demonstrate that a confession was the result of the suspect's free will and intellect and not the product of police coercion. I will rely upon an especially poignant case to illustrate the point. It involves the tragic kidnapping and murder in Miami of nine-year-old Samuel James "Jimmy" Ryce in September 1995 and the eventual capture of the suspect, Juan Carlos Chavez. The Ryce case captivated the community because of its chilling details and the sensitivity of the public when a young victim becomes the source of an extensive community, statewide, and national search.[167]

Juan Carlos Chavez became the prime suspect nearly two months after Jimmy Ryce's disappearance, when Chavez's employer discovered Jimmy's backpack inside a trailer in which Chavez resided.[168] Chavez was promptly arrested later that evening by a team of FBI agents and a sergeant from the Metro-Dade Police Department.[169] He was kept in police custody for seventy-five hours.[170]

Police detectives interrogated the suspect for thirty hours before he was allowed to sleep.[171] During that period, the suspect was interrogated by three different teams of detectives, not counting the polygraph examiner, who administered two polygraph examinations.[172] Detectives secured *Miranda* waivers from the suspect a short time after the interrogation began at headquarters and approximately ten and a half hours after the first waiver, after which they confronted Chavez with the negative results of both polygraph examinations.[173] At that time, they let the suspect get some sleep within the cramped confines of the interrogation room. The defendant slept on the "carpeted floor of the interrogation room."[174] Chavez had minimal breaks during this thirty-hour interrogation session; he was questioned by three teams of detectives, excluding the polygraph examiner, and slept for six hours in the imposing, antiseptic edifice of the police "interview room."[175] Because Chavez was placed in police custody at 7:35 P.M. on December 6, 1995,[176] and was first allowed to sleep at 1:30 A.M. on December 8, 1995, the span of time in which he was deprived of sleep exceeded thirty hours (it is safe to assume that he had been awake since the morning of the date he was arrested). Therefore, at a minimum, the suspect did not sleep for forty hours.

The interrogation resumed the next morning, after the suspect had slept for six hours. At the forty-two hour mark of the interrogation, detectives secured a waiver from Chavez of his right to appear before a magistrate twenty-four hours after his arrest.[177] When the interrogation continued, a member of the public defender's office contacted the homicide office and attempted unsuccessfully to gain access to the suspect.[178] At the forty-four-hour mark of the interrogation, Chavez finally broke down and acknowledged participation (though accidental) in the victim's death and acknowledged that he had disposed of the victim's body, but he refused to disclose its location unless the police could promise that he would receive the death penalty for his actions.[179] This statement was given to the fourth shift of detectives who participated in Chavez's interrogation. The remainder of the interrogation involved the detectives's successful attempt to get Chavez to tell the entire story behind his actions and to reveal the whereabouts of the victim's body.[180]

Naturally, the interview concluded with a sworn, transcribed incriminating statement, preceded by the administration of the *Miranda* rights and the purported waiver of those rights.[181] It is revealing that the prosecution stressed the suspect's *Miranda* waivers in its argument that the incriminating statements were "knowingly intelligently and voluntarily made."[182] How much these so-called rights meant to Chavez is problematic, at best. He is a Cuban immigrant who emigrated to America in a raft a mere four years before he was arrested for the Ryce murder.[183] Significantly, he had served in the Cuban military.[184] To what extent would an immigrant with limited knowledge of the English language who had grown up and lived in a totalitarian regime be conversant with the nuances of a radically different criminal justice system? This rhetorical question takes on added meaning because Chavez fled Cuba in order to avoid a prison sentence for theft of military equipment. Again, Janet Ainsworth's observation comes to light: it is unlikely that Chavez would know enough to utter the magic words unequivocally in the Spanish language, "I want an attorney."[185]

Rather than assisting the suspect, what *Miranda* wrought for Chavez was an argument that a seventy-five-hour interrogation that resulted in various incriminating statements was voluntary and thus constitutional. On the third page of the prosecution's response to the defendant's motion to suppress the confession, the state emphasized the suspect's waiver of the *Miranda* rights on three separate occasions.[186] It took the trial court judge less time to underscore the waivers in his order finding that the defendant's statements were voluntarily made.[187] Indeed, the trial court began its legal analysis on the issue by pointing to the suspect's three waivers of *Miranda* during the course of the interrogation.

Imagine for a moment a world without *Miranda*. Without the waivers, would the prosecution and the trial court have found it more difficult to establish that Chavez's incriminating statements were "voluntarily" given? Does not the case seem redolent of *Ashcraft v. Tennessee*,[188] in which the Court held that a thirty-six-hour continuous interrogation of the suspect "was inherently coercive" and not voluntary? This holding is enlightening in view of the fact that the officers in *Ashcraft*, much like in the Chavez case, maintained that they were "kind and considerate" throughout the questioning. Quite simply, what the officers had in the Chavez case that the officers in *Ashcraft* lacked was the great *Miranda* warnings to sanitize a clearly involuntary confession.

Most thoughtful commentators would concur with the judgment that "incessant or protracted interrogation . . . or deprivation of food or sleep for twenty-four hours, while not really damaging to psychological health, have the forbidden tendency to overbear the will and induce nonvoluntary 'cooperation.'"[189] Someone who had experienced police interrogation tactics firsthand commented that a sympathetic judge would have "qualms about calling a confession or statement truly voluntary . . . after a suspect has spent more than twelve hours in an isolated chamber without the benefit of counsel."[190] I would think that however conservative an opinion *Miranda* might be, the majority, including Chief Justice Warren, would recoil at the perverse results generated by its tortured doctrine.

If *Miranda* Is "Bad," Even for the Suspect, with What Should We Replace It?

Miranda's most stern critic, Paul Cassell, proposes taping an interrogation session as the only effective means of eliminating "swearing contests" between police and suspect regarding the voluntariness of a confession.[191] Cassell, together with Richard Uviller,[192] must be hopelessly naive about the psychology attending the police interrogation process. The isolation the suspect feels in the interrogation room, which provides the police with the control necessary to extract an incriminating statement from a suspect, would be foregone if interrogations were taped. Why would the police, especially in a high-profile murder case such as that of Chavez, want to tape a confession and possibly lose their greatest advantages: control and domination as well as the unquestioned ability to win the "swearing match"? It is not surprising, therefore, that the homicide detectives in the Chavez case failed to "preserve" the defendant's statements on audiotape. In contrast to England, which has required recorded interrogations since 1984, only three states have some sort of recording requirement.[193]

In fact, Professor Cassell concedes the obvious when he points out that in many jurisdictions where the police record interrogations, the "videotaping was at the discretion of the interrogating detective."[194] More important, Cassell observes that a "mandatory taping regime" might prompt serious objections from law enforcement entities.[195] It would be counterintuitive, to say the least, for the police to readily cede the natural strategic advantage they possess over the criminal suspect by allowing the intrusive eye or the uninvited ear into the interrogation room.

Other practical considerations militate against recording interrogations. We know that technology is hardly foolproof. How do you account for gaps in the tapes? Would the court treat the gaps as a presumption against the voluntariness of a confession? Would a "good faith" standard suffice to establish the voluntariness of a confession? One extreme could construe such a gap as a violation of the requirement of recording and suppress the incriminating statements.

Cassell suggests an alternative to recording that would replace the current warnings with truncated advisories that apprise the suspect that she will see a lawyer only when the police "bring her before a judge," thus dispensing with the "Miranda offer of counsel."[196] This accomplishes little if anything. Direct observers of the interrogation process note that even the current regime of warnings produces a farce. The theory that warnings dispel the compelling atmosphere of custodial interrogation is an abject failure.[197] Similarly, Uviller concludes, "Most people I have spoken to say the warnings have become largely an empty ritual, embarrassing to cops and superfluous to suspects."[198] A modified version of a failed experiment fulfills an empty promise.

The Only Solution: Do Away with the Warnings Altogether

My solution to this dilemma is quite simple yet radical. I propose that we do away with *Miranda* altogether. In determining whether an incriminating statement or confession is voluntary—that is, the product of a free will and intellect—courts should apply the old voluntariness standard. Further, my proposal goes beyond what section 3501 proposes in overruling *Miranda*. I would not consider the administering of *Miranda* warnings to the suspect to be part of the equation in determining whether a confession comports with the Constitution. Indeed, I would preclude the government from offering a waiver by the suspect as a means of persuading the trial court that a confession was voluntarily given. This position is consistent with my argument that police ought not to hide behind either the warnings or a waiver in order to shield an otherwise involuntary confession from scrutiny. Because *Miranda* serves primarily as a useful adjunct to law enforcement, the police should not be able to hide behind its false beneficence.

CONCLUSION

It is no secret that the police have been transformed into *Miranda*'s most fervent supporters. In *Withrow v. Williams*, for example, the Police Foundation filed an amicus curia brief on behalf of the doctrine.[199] I have provided compelling reasons that more than explain law enforcement's enthusiastic endorsement of a failed doctrine. Those who defend *Miranda* as a symbol and as a "means" to the noble end of not coercing suspects into confessing[200] are, I believe, gravely mistaken. As for its detractors, such as Cassell, they must be warned that they just might get what they ask for in the overruling of the doctrine. Instead of more admissible confessions, a regime entirely without *Miranda* just might result in fewer involuntary confessions being admitted into evidence. In the long run, Cassell ought not to be disturbed or disappointed by the Court's "affirmation" of *Miranda*'s constitutional status in *Dickerson*. In essence, the *Miranda* doctrine in its decimated form presents few if any roadblocks to police interrogation tactics. Rather, the doctrine merely serves as a useful adjunct to law enforcement. In the process of "losing" the *Dickerson* case, Cassell won a victory for law enforcement. Chief Justice Rehnquist implicitly acknowledged this truism in speaking for a majority of the Court in *Dickerson*.

NOTES

1. 120 S. Ct. 2326 (2000).
2. *United States v. Dickerson*, 166 U.S. 667 (1999), rev'd *United States v. Dickerson*, 120 S. Ct. 2326 (2000).
3. *See, e.g.*, Paul G. Cassell and Bret S. Hyman, *Police Interrogation in the 1990s: An Empirical Study of the Effects of* Miranda, 43 U.C.L.A. L. Rev. 839 (1996) (suggesting that *Miranda* has reduced the confession rate); George C. Thomas III, *Is Miranda a Real World Failure? A Plea for More (and Better) Empirical Evidence*, 43 U.C.L.A. L. REV. 821 (suggesting insufficient evidence exists of *Miranda* effect on confessions); Richard A. Leo, *The Impact of Miranda Revisited*, 86 J. CRIM L. & CRIMINOLOGY 621 (1996) (arguing that older, post-*Miranda* empirical studies failed to establish a negative effect on confession rate); Paul G. Cassell, Miranda's *Social Costs: An Empirical Reassessment*, 90 NW. U. L. REV. 387 (1996) (maintaining that *Miranda* "has resulted in a lost confession in one out of every six criminal cases"); Stephen J. Schulhofer, Miranda *and Clearance Rates*, 91 NW. U. L. REV. 278 (1996) (arguing that Cassell's figures and conclusions with respect to confession rates and *Miranda* are based on "selective descriptions of the data," and "partisan characterizations of the underlying material"). What these conflicting and divergent conclusions reflect is the reality that the true effect of Miranda on the confession rate is unknown and unknowable. The renewed debate is just that: a polemic whose conclusion rests in large part on the ideological predilections of the partisans. As Richard Leo aptly concludes, "we must dispense with the polemics that characterize much of the discussion of *Miranda*'s impact in legal scholarship." Leo, supra at 648.
4. *See, e.g.*, *Oregon v. Elstad*, 470 U.S. 298 (1985); *New York v. Quarles*, 467 U.S. 649 (1984); *Harris v. New York*, 401 U.S. 222 (1971).
5. *See* OFFICE OF LEGAL POLICY, U.S. DEP'T OF JUSTICE, REPORT TO THE ATTORNEY GENERAL ON THE LAW OF PRE-TRIAL INTERROGATION 115 (1986).
6. 507 U.S. 680 (1993).
7. Irene Merker Rosenberg, Withrow v. Williams: *Reconstitutionalizing* Miranda, 30 HOUSTON L. REV. 1684, 1692 (1993).

8. *Davis v. United States*, 512 U.S. 452, 458 (1994).

9. 498 U.S. 146 (1990).

10. *See United States v. Mobley*, 49 F. 3d 688 (4th Cir. 1994) (although distinguishable from fact of *Quarles*, public safety exception to *Miranda* applies even if suspect invokes *Miranda* right to an attorney); *United States v. DeSantis*, 870 F.2d 536 (9th Cir. 1989) (same); *Trice v. United States*, 662 A.2d 891 (D.C. App. 1995) (same).

11. *See Oregon v. Hass*, 420 U.S. 714, 722 (1975).

12. President Eisenhower uttered these words in a speech to the Republican National Convention the night before Senator Barry Goldwater's nomination for president of the United States. Republican National Convention, *Official Report* at 186 (1964) as quoted in LIVA BAKER, MIRANDA: CRIME, LAW AND POLITICS 40 (1983).

13. *Id.* at 39, citing Uniform Crime Reports.

14. *Id.* at 40.

15. *See* Robert Weisberg, *Criminal Law, Criminology, and the Small World of Legal Scholars*, 63 U. COLO. L. REV. 521, 524 (1992).

16. In *Johnson v. New Jersey*, 384 U.S. 719 (1966), Chief Justice Warren, in an opinion announced by Justice Brennan, held that *Miranda* was not to be applied retroactively. Rather, it would apply only to "cases in which the trial began after the date of our decision one week ago." *Id.*at 721. The Court justified its decision by noting that the nonretroactivity of both *Miranda* and *Escobedo* would "not preclude persons whose trials have been completed from invoking the same safeguards as part of an involuntariness claim." *Id.* at 730.

17. SAMUEL WALKER, POPULAR JUSTICE: A HISTORY OF AMERICAN CRIMINAL JUSTICE 222 (1980).

18. *Id.* at 223.

19. *Id.* at 222–25.

20. *Id.* at 228.

21. JEROME H. SKOLNICK, JUSTICE WITHOUT TRIAL 245 (2d. ed. 1975).

22. 372 U.S. 335 (1963).

23. *Id.* at 342–44. *See* also ALFREDO GARCIA, THE SIXTH AMENDMENT IN MODERN AMERICAN JURISPRUDENCE: A CRITICAL PERSPECTIVE 9–10 (1992).

24. Yale Kamisar, *The Gideon Case 25 Years Later*, NY TIMES, March 10, 1988, at A27, col. 1., cited in Garcia, *supra* note 23 at 9.

25. These are the terms used to describe Gideon by the noted legal scholar Lawrence M. Friedman. LAWRENCE M. FRIEDMAN, CRIME AND PUNISHMENT IN AMERICAN HISTORY 302 (1993).

26. Baker, *supra* note 3 at 10–11.

27. *Id.* at 15–16.

28. Report, Attorney General's Committee on Poverty, February 25, 1963, at 44–45, quoted in Baker, *supra* note 12 at 16.

29. 377 U.S. 201 (1964).

30. 378 U.S. 478 (1964).

31. *Massiah*, 377 U.S. at 202–3.

32. 360 U.S. 315 (1959).

33. *Id.* at 326–27.

34. *Id.* at 326 (Douglas, J. , concurring).

35. *Massiah*, 377 U.S. at 206.

36. 378 U.S. 478 (1964).

37. James Thompson's argument is quoted in Yale Kamisar, Wayne R. Lafave, & Jerold H. Israel, Modern Criminal Procedure 465 (8th ed. 1994). Thompson relied on *Carnley v. Cochran*, 369 U.S. 506, 513 (1962) for the proposition that if the right to counsel was made available at arrest, it would not depend on a request and that a waiver therefore would have to be knowingly and intelligently made.

38. *Michigan v. Tucker*, 417 U.S. 433, 439 (1974).

39. Quoted in Kamisar, *supra* note 37 at 472.

40. *United States v. Charles*, 25 Fed. Cas. 409, no. 14,786 (C.C.D.C. 1813), reprinted in Philip B. Kurland & Ralph Lerner, eds. The Founders Constitution 275 (1987).

41. Quoted in Kamisar, *supra* note 37 at 473.

42. *Miranda*, 384 U.S. at 448–49.

43. David Simon, Homicide: A Year on the Killing Streets 213 (1991). Indeed, Simon observes that the two principal goals of the successful interrogator are control of the process and to stop the suspect from invoking the right to an attorney under *Miranda*.

44. *Miranda*, 384 U.S. at 471.

45. *Id.* at 474.

46. Charles J. Ogletree, *Are Confessions Really Good for the Soul?* 100 Harv. L. Rev. 1826 (1987).

47. See Simon, *supra* note 43 at 213. I have added privacy as a dimension of control and the opportunity to call on a lawyer since it is a logical corollary of control and is acknowledged by the *Miranda* majority as critical to a successful interrogation.

48. *Miranda*, 384 U.S. at 505 (Harlan, J., dissenting).

49. *Id.* at 491, ft. 66.

50. As Justice Stevens poignantly stressed in dissent, "When an inculpatory statement has been obtained as a result of unrecorded, incommunicado interrogation . . . officers rarely lose 'swearing matches' against criminal defendants at suppression hearings." *Davis v. United States*, 114 S. Ct. 2350, 2363 n. 7 (1994) (Stevens, J., dissenting).

51. Steven J. Schulhofer, *Reconsidering* Miranda, 54 U. CHI. L. REV. 435, 454 (1987).

52. See the section in this chapter entitled "The Historical, Social, and Political Background of *Miranda*."

53. 384 U.S. 719 (1966).
54. *Id.* at 721.
55. *Id.* at 730.
56. *Id.*
57. *Id.*, citing *Reck v. Pate*, 367 U.S. 433 (1961).
58. *Id.* at 731, citing *Haynes v. Washington*, 373 U.S. 503 (1963) and *Spano v. New York*, 360 U.S. 315 (1959).
59. *Id.*
60. 392 U.S. 1 (1968).
61. *Id.* at 39 (Douglas, J., dissenting).
62. *See* Baker, *supra* note 12 at 244–46. In this regard, Nixon had to contend with the vitriolic appeals to law and order by George Wallace. Wallace's visceral reaction to crime related to the ease with which criminals were released and the social explanations proferred for criminal behavior. His speech posited a criminal who "knocks you over the head" and would be released "before you're out of the hospital and the policeman who arrested him will be on trial." The defendant's actions would be in turn justified by "some psychologist [who] says 'well, he's not to blame, society's to blame. His father didn't take him to see the Pittsburgh Pirates when he was a little boy." *Id.* at 243–44.
63. Simon, *supra* note 43 at 211.
64. JAMES T. PATTERSON, GRAND EXPECTATIONS: THE UNITED STATES, 1945–1974 651 (1996).
65. *Id.*
66. 18 U.S.C. Sec. 3501.
67. *Id.* Section 3501 (a).
68. *Id.* at Section 3501 (b) (1–5).
69. *Id.*
70. 401 U.S. 222 (1971).
71. Professor Geoffrey Stone employed this pun in his incisive article surveying the vagaries of *Miranda* in the Burger Court. Geoffrey R. Stone, *The* Miranda *Doctrine in the Burger Court*, 100 SUP. CT. REV. 99 (1977).
72. *Michigan v. Tucker*, 417 U.S. 433, 444 (1974).
73. *Id.* at 224–25.
74. *Miranda*, 384 U.S. at 377. The majority remarked that "statements merely intended to be exculpatory by the defendant are often used to impeach his testimony at trial. . . . These statements are incriminating in any meaningful sense of the word and may not be used without the full warnings and effective waiver required for any other statement." For a critique of the case, *see* Alan Dershowitz and John Hart Ely, Harris v. New York: *Some Anxious Observations on the Candor and Logic of the Emerging Nixon Majority*, 80 YALE L. J. 1198, 1208–10 (1971).
75. Chief Justice Burger stated that the impeachment issue "was not at

all necessary to the Court's holding and cannot be regarded as controlling."
Harris, 401 U.S. at 224.

76. *See* Stone, *supra* note 71 at 114.

77. *Id.* at 112.

78. *Id.* (citations omitted).

79. 420 U.S. 714, 723 (1975).

80. *Id.* at 715. Defendant, after realizing he "was in a lot of trouble," told
the police he wanted to call his attorney. The police officer replied that Hass
would be able to do so "as soon as we [get] to the office." *Id.* at 715–16.

81. *Id.* at 723–24.

82. *Id.* at 723.

83. *Id.*

84. *See* Stone, *supra* note 71 at 129.

85. *Cooper v. Dupnik*, 924 F.2d 1520 (9th Cir. 1991), (hereafter *Cooper I*),
rev'd en banc 963 F.2d 1220 (9th Cir.), cert. denied, 113 S.Ct. 407 (1992)
(hereafter *Cooper II*).

86. *Cooper II*, 963 F.2d at 1224.

87. *Id.*

88. *Id.* at 1225.

89. *Id.*

90. *Id.* at 1226.

91. *Id.* at 1226.

92. *Id.* at 1227.

93. *Id.* at 1228. In fact, the identification technician, who had supposedly
found a match between latent fingerprints taken from the scene and the suspect, had not done any major fingerprint work for at least six, and possibly
nine years, when he linked Cooper to the crime. *Id.*

94. *Id.* at 1229.

95. *Id.* at 1233.

96. 42 U.S.C. Section 1983 provides in pertinent part: "Every person
who, under color of any statute, ordinance, regulation, custom, or usage, of
any State . . . subjects, or causes to be subjected, any citizen of the United
States . . . to the deprivation of any rights, privileges, or immunities secured
by the Constitution and laws, shall be liable to the party injured in an action
at law, suit in equity, or other proper proceeding for redress." Cooper also
alleged nine counts under state tort law. *See Cooper I*, 924 F.2d 1524 n.4. The
state claims were dismissed, and thus were not addressed in the federal
appeal.

97. *See Cooper IIB.3 infra* and accompanying text.

98. *Cooper II*, 963 F.2d at 1235–36.

99. *Mincey v. Arizona*, 437 U.S. 385 (1978).

100. 417 U.S. 433 (1974).

101. *Id.* at 444.

102. *Id.* at 435–37.

103. In *Wong Sun v. United States*, 371 U.S. 471 (1963) applied the exclusionary to evidence derived from a constitutional violation.

104. *See* Stone, *supra* note 71 at 123, n. 132 (citing cases relying on *Tucker* to avoid applying "fruits" doctrine to *Miranda*).

105. 510 F.2d 1129 (10th Cir. 1975).

106. *Id.* at 1138.

107. *Id.*

108. 467 U.S. 649 (1984).

109. *Id.* at 655.

110. *Id.* at 654.

111. Justice Rehnquist observed "that the need for answers to questions in a situation posing a threat to the public safety outweighs the need for the prophylactic rule protecting the Fifth Amendment's privilege against self-incrimination." *Id.* at 657.

112. *Id.* at 655.

113. *Id.* at 684–85 (Marshall, J., dissenting).

114. *Id.* at 655 n.5.

115. 470 U.S. 298 (1986).

116. *Id.* at 303.

117. *Id.* at 306–7.

118. *Id.* at 307.

119. *Id.* at 317.

120. *Id.* at 316.

121. *See* David A. Wollin, *Policing the Police: Should* Miranda *Violations Bear Fruit*, 53 OHIO ST. L.J. 805 (1992) (finding that the "trend has been decidedly in favor of admissibility"). *Id.* at 810.

122. *Id.* at 807.

123. *Tankleff v. Senkowski*, 1998 WL 29961 (2d Cir. N.Y.).

124. *Id.* at 2.

125. *Id.* at 2–3.

126. *Id.* at 8.

127. 451 U.S. 477 (1981).

128. *Id.* at 484–85.

129. 486 U.S. 675 (1988).

130. *Id.* at 677–78.

131. 498 U.S. 146 (1990).

132. *Id.* at 151.

133. *Id.* at 153.

134. *Id.* at 166 (Scalia, J., dissenting).

135. *Id.*

136. Simon, *supra* note 43 at 210.

137. Janet Ainsworth, *In a Different Register: The Pragmatics of Powerlessness in Police Interrogation*, 103 YALE L.J. 259 (1993).

138. 512 U.S. 452, 459 (1994).

139. Ainsworth, *supra* note 137 at 316–19.

140. This is what the suspect had said in *Davis. Davis*, 512 U.S. at 455.

141. *Id.* at 459.

142. *United States v. DeSantis*, 870 F.2d 536, 541 (1989).

143. *Id.*

144. *Id.*

145. *See United States v. Mobley*, 40 F.3d 688 (4th Cir.1994); *Trice v. United States*, 662 A.2d 891 (D.C. App. 1995).

146. *United States v. Mobley*, 40 F.3d at 692.

147. *Withrow v. Williams*, 507 U.S. at 683.

148. 428 U.S. 465 (1976). In that case, the Court held that "when a State has given a full and fair chance to litigate a Fourth Amendment claim, federal habeas review is not available to a state prisoner alleging that his conviction rests on evidence obtained through an unconstitutional search or seizure."

149. *Withrow*, 507 U.S. at 691–92.

150. *Id.* at 712 (O'Connor, J., concurring and dissenting).

151. Indeed, a symposium issue containing eleven articles and entitled, *Miranda* after *Dickerson*: The Future of Confession Law, appeared in the March 2001 issue of the Michigan Law Review. 99 MICHIGAN L. REV. 879–1247 (2001).

152. *Dickerson v. United States*, 120 S.Ct. 2326, 2333 (2000).

153. *Id.*

154. *Id.* at 2334.

155. Yale Kamisar, *Foreword: From* Miranda *to Section 3501 to Dickerson to.*, 99 MICHIGAN L. REV. 879, 889 (2001).

156. *Dickerson v. United States*, 120 S. Ct. at 2336.

157. Susan R. Klein, *Identifying and (Re)formulating Prophylactic Rules, Safe Harbors, and Incidental Rights in Constitutional Criminal Procedure*, 99 MICHIGAN L. REV. 1030, 1071 (2001).

158. *Id.*

159. *Id.* at 683.

160. *Id.* at 684.

161. *Id.*

162. *Id.* at 685.

163. *See* notes 105–6 and accompanying text.

164. *Quarles* at 684–85 (Marshall, J., dissenting).

165. *Arizona v. Fulminante*, 499 U.S. 279, 295 (1991).

166. See *supra* notes 88–90 and accompanying text.

167. *See* Response to Defendant's Amended Motion to Suppress Evidence at 1, *State v. Chavez* (Fla. Cir. Ct. 1995) (No. 95–037867) [hereinafter Response to Motion to Suppress Evidence].

168. *Id.*

169. *Id.* at 3.

170. *Id.* at 21.

171. *Id.* at 5–12.
172. *Id.* at 5–6.
173. *Id.* at 6.
174. *Id.* at 12.
175. *Id.*
176. *Id.* at 3.
177. *Id.* at 13.
178. *Id.* at 13–14.
179. *Id.* at 14–15.
180. *Id.* at 14–19.
181. *Id.* at 19.
182. *Id.* at 23.
183. *Id.* at 3.
184. *Id.*
185. See Ainsworth, *supra* note 137 and accompanying text.
186. *See* Response to Motion to Suppress Evidence at 23.
187. *See* Order Denying Defendant's Amended Motion to Suppress Evidence at 2, *State v. Chavez* (Fla. Cir. Ct. 1995) (filed in 1995 and subject to the *Miranda* mandates).
188. 322 U.S.143 (1944).
189. RICHARD UVILLER, TEMPERED ZEAL 189 (1988).
190. Simon, *supra* note 43 at 219.
191. Paul Cassell, Miranda*'s Social Costs: An Empirical Assessment*, 90 NW. U. L. REV. 387, 488 (1996). Professor Richard A. Leo also has proposed a constitutional rule that requires "as a matter of due process the electronic videotaping of custodial interrogations in all felony cases." Leo, *supra* note 3 at 624.
192. Uviller, *supra* note 189 at 186–87.
193. Gail Johnson, *False Confessions and Fundamental Fairness: The Need for Electronic Recording of Custodial Interrogations*, 6 B.U. PUB. INT. L. J. 719 (1997).
194. Cassell, supra note 191 at 490.
195. *Id.*
196. *Id.* at 496–97.
197. Simon, *supra* note 43 at 211.
198. RICHARD UVILLER, VIRTUAL JUSTICE 124 (1996).
199. Steven Schulhofer, Miranda*'s Practical Effect: Substantial Benefits and Vanishingly Small Social Costs*, 90 N.W. U. L. REV. 500, 559 n. 250 (1996).
200. *Id.* at 562.

CHAPTER 4

THE GRAND JURY: A MODERN-DAY DINOSAUR

INTRODUCTION

In theory, the grand jury is the most egalitarian institution in the modern-day criminal justice system; in practice, it is the most autocratic. How does one explain this glaring paradox? Although there are various explanations for this irony, it is important to emphasize that the contradiction must be placed in its proper historical context. A facile conjecture would attribute the transformation of this democratic institution into an arm of the government to a judiciary bent upon easing the prosecutor's burden of formally charging suspects with serious crimes. Another theory would ascribe the change to the fidelity of the judiciary to the independence of the grand jury from the judicial and executive branches of government. Finally, one could surmise that the metamorphosis occurred due to the inexorable development of a criminal process confronting manifold challenges: the massive historical shifts in the social, economic, and political landscape that transpired after the grand jury was incorporated into the Bill of Rights at the end of the eighteenth century.

Almost three decades ago, the Supreme Court grudgingly conceded that the grand jury no longer served its historic function.[1] As we have seen, however, the historical record does not confirm the "mythology"[2] typically associated with the institution. Grand juries were subject to the abuse of and manipulation by the executive branch of the government since the institution emerged during the reign of Henry II. Nevertheless, in colonial America the grand jury exercised its autonomy not only by the members being elected in town meetings, as was the custom in Massachusetts Bay, but also through its fierce resolve not to indict individuals subject to political persecution, as exemplified by the two New York grand juries that refused to indict John Peter Zenger.[3] This independent tradition continued through the emergence of the new nation, although federal grand juries, in contrast to state grand juries, were more vulnerable to executive influence—especially during the 1790s, at the height of the political struggle between the Federalists and the Republicans.[4] Rather than serving as an instrument of the people's will, the federal grand jury seemed to cater to the whims of a distant, central government. By contrast, local grand juries remained firmly entrenched as "accepted" and "essential" parts of "American democratic government."[5]

It did not take long for this hallowed part of the American democratic culture to come under intense scrutiny and attack. The assault began in England during the early part of the nineteenth century, instigated by none other than the utilitarian Jeremy Bentham, who questioned the efficiency of a group of laymen as opposed to a legally trained prosecutor. Soon, American academics took up the cause, followed by state constitutional conventions and legislative assemblies. From Chief Justice Joseph Story to noted criminal law scholar Francis Wharton, the critics of the grand jury in America focused on its legal naivete, prompting these commentators to recommend that it serve only at the instance of the government. Culminating with the abolition of the grand jury in 1859 by the State of Michigan, the efforts by the opponents of the grand institution began to bear fruit. Once described as the "bulwark of liberty," the not-so grand jury had come to be viewed by some as antithetical to the principles of a democratic polity.[6]

What accounted for such a startling change in the viewpoint of influential members of the American community? After all, only a few decades had passed before the grand jury became the subject of impassioned disapproval. Michigan was not alone; opponents of the institution voiced their discontent in Indiana, Oregon, Wisconsin, Kansas, and Nevada.[7] Succinctly emphasizing the gist of the argument against the grand jury, attorney James Sullivan noted during the Michigan constitutional convention that no prosecutor could be more "arbitrary and/or dangerous" than a secret *ex parte* body whose secret sessions resembled the Star Chamber.[8] Neither in its country of origin nor in its adopted land, therefore, did the grand jury elicit the prestige and adulation that we seem to accord it in our quest to "mythologize" its origins and history. Perhaps its central place in the panoply of constitutional rights, along with the community participation that underlies its nature, makes us loath to jettison our romantic and quaint misconceptions.

Indeed, the misconceptions regarding the grand inquest stem from this fragmented view of its history in America. From the early nineteenth century until modern times, the body has been the subject of controversy. As the United States grew and underwent geographical, political, economic, and social transformations, the grand jury responded to these events. From westward expansion to the Civil War, through industrialization and urbanization and the emergence of corporate America, the grand inquest became intertwined with these historical developments. Westward expansion was favorable to the pristine operation of the grand jury; the Civil War marked a watershed in the use of the grand jury in gauging public opinion and curbing military overreaching; industrialization and urbanization witnessed the emergence of the institution as a weapon to check the excesses associated with the rise of big business and corrupt political machines. Throughout these historical periods, opposition to the grand jury because it was inefficient, overbearing, or a mere tool of the prosecutor infused the polemic about its relative merits. Supporters of the institution always stressed its democratic character.[9]

It is not surprising that the grand institution has alternately provoked praise and opprobrium. On the one hand, the grand jury embodies the ultimate democratic ideal: a body composed of citizens empowered to charge wrongdoers with crime, to defend their brethren from baseless accusations, and to address the community's most pressing social, economic, or political crises. Counterbalancing these advantages are the potential for the grand inquest to wreak considerable harm. In the worst case scenario, both the grand jurors and the prosecutor, acting in secret and without any constraints, may indeed resemble the deliberations of the Star Chamber. Further, to the extent the grand inquest is composed of citizens devoid of legal expertise, it may not be the most efficient mechanism for determining whether probable cause exists to issue an indictment.[10]

The reason for this apparent irony is the structure and purpose of the grand jury. Having both accusatory and investigative functions, the institution simultaneously serves communitarian and antistatist goals. To the extent it performs its "historic" role by protecting the ordinary citizen from the "overzealous" prosecutor, the grand inquest stands against the overwhelming power of the state. By the same token, grand jurors may also seek to eradicate crime in the community by fervently investigating and indicting those suspected of disturbing community tranquility and welfare. In doing so, the grand inquest may place the community's interest ahead of the individual's and abuse its awesome power. In seeking to root out the social, economic, or political ills besetting the community, the grand institution may trample upon individual rights. Exacerbated by the legal naivete of its members, this phenomenon goes against the "American libertarian tradition [that] does not encourage obedience to the state and the law."[11] Therein lies the conundrum that the true historical record seems to reveal: a love-hate relationship with the only institution in the criminal justice system that seemingly advances contradictory aims.

Having placed the grand jury within its proper historical and analytical context, I propose to examine its current shortcomings. I do so from the perspective of how the grand jury is generally functioning in modern-day America. In particular, I will emphasize the U.S. Supreme Court's opinions defining the role of the modern grand inquest. One might question this limited framework. I believe it is justified because the grand jury plays a most prominent role in the federal system, not in the states. No event has underlined this truism more than the impeachment trial of President Bill Clinton. Kenneth Starr relied on the grand jury to uncover potential crimes committed by the president of the United States. The president's testimony evoked the power of the grand jury to snare a suspect within its far-reaching web. Although the president's testimony was atypical, principally because it was prompted more by political considerations than by personal or prudential motives, it underscored for the public the supposed right of the jury to "every man's evidence." The grand jury's role in the Clinton-Lewinsky imbroglio also reflected the domination of the federal grand jury by a federal prosecutor, who controls its deliberations unburdened by any significant restraints.

Reflecting the thesis of this work, I will further emphasize the links between the grand jury and the self-incrimination clause of the Fifth Amendment. Indeed, the Clinton impeachment saga teaches a formidable lesson in underscoring the tie between these two clauses of the Fifth Amendment. Represented by some of the best legal talent in the country, the president could not, because of political considerations, afford to invoke the privilege against self-incrimination and refuse to testify before Starr's grand jury. A similarly well-placed and wealthy target would have the benefit of counsel, who would advise him to invoke the Fifth unless the prosecutor offered immunity from prosecution in exchange for the testimony. Notice my caveat: not all targets will necessarily enjoy the benefits afforded by the president's extensive legal team; nor would they be able to consult with their lawyers during the grand jury session. They would have to ask to be excused from the grand jury's secretive room in order to obtain counsel's advice.

Beyond the relationship between the grand jury and the privilege against self-incrimination, I will delve into the cases that have undermined the fundamental tenets of the institution. Specifically, it is important to underscore the manner in which the Supreme Court has allowed the institution to become, in effect, the federal prosecutor's unfettered domain. This development, along with the lack of protection afforded witnesses who confront the imposing environment of the grand jury room, have disentangled the institution from its foundational moorings. Finally, this chapter will assess the nexus between the new role played by the grand jury and the safeguard against double jeopardy embodied in the Fifth Amendment.

THE CONTRADICTORY AIMS
OF THE GRAND JURY

The function of the grand jury has been described as twofold: to determine whether probable cause exists to charge an individual with a crime, and to protect citizens against unfounded criminal accusations.[12] A corollary of this function is to interpose a body of citizens, independent of either the prosecutor or the judge, between the citizen and a formal criminal accusation.[13] Expressing a fundamental dichotomy, these aims reveal the singular place the guarantee of a grand jury indictment occupies in the cluster of protections afforded criminal suspects and defendants in the Bill of Rights. The guarantees embodied in the Fourth, Fifth, Sixth, and Eighth Amendments to the Constitution provide safeguards to both the public at large and to criminal suspects and defendants in the form of constraints against the overwhelming power of the government. Yet, as Justice Douglas aptly observed, the grand jury "is the only accusatorial body of the Federal Government recognized by the Constitution."[14] Herein lies the duality underlying the grand jury; it is simultaneously vested with the responsibilities of protecting the community from the scourge of crime and safeguarding citizens from accusations that lack a reasonable foundation.

This dichotomy is accentuated by the untrammeled investigative power the institution enjoys. As the Supreme Court has emphasized, grand jurors are free to act on "tips, rumors, evidence offered by the prosecutor, or their own personal knowledge."[15] Similarly, the Court's interpretive gloss has lifted evidentiary burdens, typically associated with trials, from the grand jury: the institution need not rely on trustworthy evidence or ensure that evidence it examines is free from constitutional taint as a precondition for issuing an indictment.[16] Many safeguards accorded criminal suspects and defendants in the Bill of Rights complement each other. For example, the confrontation and compulsory process clauses of the Sixth Amendment are sides of the same coin; they permit the defendant to cross-examine his accusers while also allowing him to summon witnesses on his behalf to present a defense.[17] By contrast, the grand jury clause of the Fifth Amendment, as it has developed both historically and through legal interpretation, is a contradiction in terms.

To discern how this inconsistency emerged requires a careful look at how the Supreme Court has attempted to reconcile the grand jury's accusatory and libertarian roles. The Court has not done this successfully. Perhaps it would have been unrealistic to expect the Court to simultaneously permit the grand inquest to perform its accusatory role while holding potential excesses stemming from this vast power in check. This task was rendered more difficult by the stark reality that the prosecutor had come to assume a prominent role in directing and supervising the accusatory body. Like the conductor of an orchestra, the prosecutor pulls the strings of the players: the citizens who compose a body that in theory is independent of the prosecutor and the courts. As we shall see later in this chapter, the Court has conferred on the prosecutor the same procedural advantages traditionally accorded to the grand jury: freedom from any constraints, even to the point of condoning the prosecutorial violations of federal rules designed to govern the conduct of grand jury proceedings.

Detailing this interpretive journey is necessarily a selective enterprise. Several opinions, however, are representative of an unmistakable trend in which the Court displayed its bent against placing any roadblocks in the path of the grand jury's accusatory function. Beginning in the 1950s and culminating in the 1970s, the Court established an irreversible trend in which it refused to recognize limits upon the institution's investigative and accusatory prerogatives. Presaging the death knell of the federal grand jury's role as a "bulwark" between the citizen and the government, the opinions provide a revealing glimpse into the Court's failure to reconcile the two competing visions inherent in the body's institutional functions. In essence, the sole "accusatory body" enshrined in the Bill of Rights assumed its anomalous role in full force, unfettered by the conflicting purpose of safeguarding the citizen from unfounded or impulsive indictments.

THE RIGHT TO UNDISCRIMINATING EVIDENCE

When the U.S. Supreme Court held in 1884[18] that the right to an indictment by a grand jury for a felony or other serious crime was not applicable to the states through the operation of the Fourteenth Amendment's due process clause, it pronounced that the institution was not fundamental to fairness in the criminal process. As we have seen, given the historical controversy in which the structure and function of the grand inquest is shrouded, one can understand the Court's reluctance to extend the guarantee to a grand jury indictment or presentment to the states. Rejecting the notion that the ancient grand jury offered protection from unwarranted accusations, Justice Matthews, speaking for the Court, reminded us that the "primitive" grand jury was not as grand as the "mythology" enshrouding it. He emphasized that the grand body "heard no witnesses in support of the truth of the charges to be preferred, but presented upon their own knowledge, or indicted upon common fame or suspicion."[19] Those who would invoke its ancient lineage as a bulwark of liberty, therefore, ought to acknowledge, he observed, "that it is better not to go too far back into antiquity for the best securities for our 'ancient liberties.'"[20]

While Justice Matthews' apothegm serves us well, regardless of the liberty we happen to be extolling, he also had to concede that the strength of our common law heritage lies in its adaptability to changing circumstances. The question confronting the Supreme Court was whether it should place any limits on the grand jury's investigatory and accusatory functions. Presented with this challenge, the Court could choose from extreme ends of the spectrum: erecting no limits on what evidence the grand jury could consider in deciding whether probable cause exists to issue an indictment; or crafting palpable barriers to the kind of evidence grand jurors could consider in fulfilling their duties. In between these absolutes lay a nebulous center that would have to be adjusted according to the facts, peculiarities, and necessities of each particular case. Would the Court scrupulously adhere to the "primitive" version of the grand jury, or would it create a new model designed to cope with social, political, and economic growth and the concomitant vagaries of a sprawling criminal justice process? It is difficult to envy the Court's formidable task, especially since it was far removed by its composition from the everyday world of criminal justice.

Until the middle of the twentieth century, the Court provided few hints of how it would resolve this knotty quandary. In the early part of the century, however, Justice Brown furnished an abbreviated glimpse of the matter. Grappling with the emerging corporate structure and the role of the grand jury in investigating and prosecuting corporate violations, Justice Brown noted in passing that "while the grand jury may not indict upon current rumors or unverified reports, they may act upon knowledge acquired either from their own observations or upon the evidence of witnesses given before them."[21] Although this brief passage, not part of the holding or dicta in the case, appears as almost an afterthought, it reflects Justice Brown's acute awareness of the impending storm. How would the Court resolve the delicate balance between providing the grand jury with sufficient flexibility to uncover increasingly complex crimes while simultaneously curbing the abuse of power that could arise from unlimited investigative forays?

The answer to this question came in a case that foreshadowed the Court's reluctance to tread upon the historical accusatory role performed by the grand inquest. In *Costello v. United States*,[22] Justice Hugo Black, writing for the Court, held that a grand jury indictment was not subject to challenge because it was based solely upon hearsay evidence. The facts of the case were emblematic of a crime that required extraordinary measures of investigation: a complex tax evasion scheme that the government established at the defendant's trial through the testimony of one hundred and forty-four witnesses and the presentation of three hundred and sixty-eight exhibits.[23] Rather than presenting such a daunting array of evidence to the grand jury, the government instead relied on the hearsay testimony of the three investigating officers in the case.

Justice Black's rationale rested on two pillars: grand jurors should not be burdened by "rigid," "technical," or "evidentiary" rules, as shown by the grand jury's traditional role; and to require that only competent evidence underlie a grand jury indictment would convert the proceeding into a preliminary hearing or mini-trial on the merits, a result at odds with the history and functions of the grand jury.[24] Resting on solid precedent, the *Costello* holding relied upon the Court's prior ruling in *Holt v. United States*,[25] in which the majority rejected the challenge to an indictment because it was based partly on incompetent evidence. The opinion, however, contains an important caveat. Concurring in the *Costello* opinion, Justice Harold Burton voiced reservations about permitting the grand jury to issue an indictment without having heard or seen "substantial" or "rationally persuasive" evidence.[26] Although that situation was not applicable to the facts in *Costello* because the officers summarized the substantial evidence against the defendant to the grand jurors, Justice Burton was apprehensive lest the holding be extended to immunize any indictment, regardless of how flimsy or inadequate the evidence upon which it rested. Indeed, Justice Burton was echoing the Court's concern in *Hale v. Henkel* that an indictment not rest merely on "rumors" or "unverified" reports.

The tenor of the *Costello* opinion did not appear to assuage Justice Burton's apprehension. Indeed, Justice Black seemed to reject the notion that an indictment by a legally constituted grand jury was unassailable in the face of an evidentiary challenge. Grand jurors should be free from technical evidentiary constraints, and neither history nor "justice or the concept of a fair trial" demanded such restrictions.[27] In effect, Justice Black intimated that such deficiencies would be rendered moot at trial, because only competent evidence is admissible at trial; thus, although the grand jurors would be free to indict upon rumors, innuendo, and hearsay evidence, the government would have to convict upon trustworthy evidence, thereby correcting any seeming injustice attached to such a flimsy indictment.

Confronting the delicate task of balancing the institution's contradictory purposes, Justice Black opted not to counteract the potential abuse of the grand jury's awesome power with any evidentiary obstacles. His remedy seemed eminently sensible: the proof required at trial would nullify either a prosecutor's or a grand jury's attempt to secure an indictment for whatever improper or invidious reasons. The problem with this rationale is that it runs counter to the protective role of the grand institution: to safeguard citizens from unfounded criminal accusations. Implicit in the *Costello* opinion is the conclusion that the grand jury's accusatory function is incompatible with its libertarian purpose to the extent that the protective function hampers grand jurors' ability to consider any evidence in determining whether sufficient probable cause exists to issue an indictment. One can read *Costello* to mean that the two contradictory aims of the grand jury are fundamentally irreconcilable and that the accusatorial role is more important to the smooth operation of the institution than the protective function is.

Leaving no doubt that the untrammeled investigative purpose of the grand jury was essential, the Court held scarcely two years after *Costello* that grand jurors could rely on statements secured in violation of the witness's Fifth Amendment privilege against self-incrimination.[28] In *Lawn v. United States* targets of a grand jury investigation appeared and testified before the jurors, were not advised of their privilege against self-incrimination, and produced incriminating records while criminal charges were pending against them.[29] Quoting at length from *Costello*, the *Lawn* opinion reaffirmed the precept that any evidence could be considered by the grand jury, regardless of its infirmities.

THE PROTECTIVE WALL COLLAPSES: *BRANZBURG, CALANDRA, DIONISIO, MARA*

In the early 1970s, any protective facade the grand inquest may have retained gave way to the law enforcement, investigative imperative. Given the convulsions shaking the foundations of the criminal justice system in the wake of an unprecedented rise in crime in the 1960s, combined with the election of a president who campaigned on restoring law and order, it was inevitable that the jurisprudential trends reflected in *Costello* and *Lawn* would be reinforced.[30] Inevitably, the libertarian side of the grand jury functional equation was bound to vanish. The manner in which this underlying purpose of the grand institution evaporated warrants close review. If the grand jury was to become a mere adjunct to the prosecutor, and if it lacked the competence to perform its accusatory duties, then one must wonder why it has obdurately persisted as a prominent feature of federal prosecutions. Recent proposals to either reform or abolish the grand jury, as we have seen, are not without historical precedent. Why, we must ask, is the grand jury still with us when its country of origin has abolished it? Are we justified in keeping it, or are we undermining whatever symbolic remnant there is, if any, of its supposedly egalitarian and libertarian ethos? Such questions are necessary to analyze the decisions in the 1970s that ratified the predominant motif of the modern institution as an instrument of law enforcement.

Perhaps no other decision signified the complete shift in focus of the grand jury from a "bulwark of liberty" to a law enforcement tool as *Branzburg v. Hayes*.[31] Justice White, writing for the majority, summarized the issue and holding in the case starkly and simply at the outset of the opinion: requiring journalists to appear and testify before state or federal grand juries does not abridge the freedom of speech or press set forth in the First Amendment. From a common-sense perspective, the issue and holding appear unremarkable. When probed more deeply, however, the majority opinion leaves an indelible mark. The majority opinion, as well as the vigorous dissent it elicited, reflected a Court loath to place any restraints in the law enforcement role played by the grand inquest; or, more appropriately, to temper the need to ferret out crime with a modicum of solicitude for the rights of citizens or, for that matter, of other constitutional guarantees in potential conflict with its accusatory role.

Foreshadowing the law enforcement concern with the distribution and use of drugs that would dominate the criminal justice system in the last three decades of the twentieth century, *Branzburg* involved several newspaper reports involving the manufacture, sale, and consumption of drugs in Louisville and Frankfort, Kentucky.[32] When summoned by a grand jury to testify about his observations and knowledge of the drug trade as reflected in his newspaper accounts, Branzburg invoked statutory privileges for reporters as well as the Kentucky Constitution and the First Amendment to the U.S. Constitution. His reason for refusing to testify rested on the belief that his confidential sources would be compromised and, collaterally, so would his effectiveness as a reporter.[33] In conjunction with Branzburg's case, the Court consolidated two other cases that raised the same issue.[34] Branzburg's case is more compelling, however, as a symbol for how the newly constituted Supreme Court, composed of a Chief Justice as well as other justices appointed by President Nixon, would deal with the scourge of crime and, particularly, the grand jury's purpose within the criminal justice system.

The *Branzburg* opinion reflected the fundamental dichotomy of the grand jury as an institution: it posed the conflict between its crime-fighting function and its protective role in stark terms. Though in a different format, as the clash was between the right of the grand inquest to investigate crime versus the privilege of the reporter to shield his sources, the duality underscored the anomalous place the institution occupies in the criminal justice process. More to the point, the *Branzburg* majority opted for a categorical approach to the contradictory purposes of the grand body; it unmistakably refused to place any obstacles in the path of the institution's accusatory role.

What Branzburg proposed was not an ironclad right not to reveal sources when subpoenaed by a grand jury. Rather, he sought several preconditions as requisite to the duty of a journalist to reveal the nature of criminal activity he witnessed or learned about in the course of investigative reporting. Specifically, as Justice Stewart suggested in dissent, the grand jury would have to establish three requirements in order to compel the reporter's testimony: (1) the information sought is relevant to the investigation; (2) it is reasonable to believe that the reporter has the information; and (3) there is no equally effective alternative means of obtaining the evidence that would not impinge on First Amendment liberties.[35]

Rejecting such a compromise, the *Branzburg* majority instead stressed "the longstanding principle that 'the public . . . has a right to every man's evidence,' except those persons protected by a constitutional, common-law, or statutory privilege."[36] As a corollary to this principle, Justice White, speaking for a slender majority, emphasized that other than the Fifth Amendment privilege against self-incrimination, the Court was not disposed to create any new privileges that would restrict the grand jury's investigative and accusatory powers.[37] Indeed, Justice White expressed skepticism toward the prospect of recognizing privileges, even those as hallowed as the right against self-incrimination, that would impede the search for the truth.[38]

Unabashedly proclaiming that "the investigation of crime by a grand jury implements a fundamental governmental role of securing the safety of the person and property of the citizen," Justice White left no doubt that "the role of grand jury as an important instrument of law enforcement" was the institution's paramount, if not sole, purpose.[39] This unilinear view of the grand institution by the *Branzburg* majority prompted Justice Lewis Powell, in his concurring opinion, to rebut Justice Stewart's point in dissent that the opinion presaged the annexation of the media as "an investigative arm of the government."[40] Although that metaphor may have been overblown, it underlined the conflicting aims of an institution historically subject to the social and political forces influencing the criminal justice system. Furthermore, the majority opinion minced no words in delineating a monolithic view of the grand jury: other than the Fifth Amendment privilege against self-incrimination, no obstacle could inhibit the ability of the inquest to probe every nook and cranny of the criminal world, no matter how chimerical or farfetched the investigation might seem to an outside observer.

Within a scant year and a half after setting this monolithic tone in *Branzburg*, the Court reaffirmed the principle that no constitutional roadblocks, other than the privilege against self-incrimination, would hamper the grand jury's discretion in its decision to issue an indictment against a criminal suspect. However, even as *United States v.*

Calandra[41] reveals, when a witness does invoke the privilege against self-incrimination and refuses to answer questions posed by the grand jury, a conferral of immunity from prosecution will compel the witness to answer the grand jury's inquiries.[42] Evincing fidelity to *Branzburg*'s rationale, the *Calandra* Court held that a witness subpoenaed to testify before a grand jury could not refuse to answer questions because they were based on evidence gathered in violation of the Fourth Amendment's proscription of illegal searches and seizures.[43] More important than the holding, however, is the majority's philosophical opposition to any impediments on the grand jury's power to investigate any crime and to accuse any individual formally with a crime regardless of the nature and character of the evidence employed to issue the indictment.

Quoting from *Branzburg*, as well as emphasizing the historic and functional role of the grand inquest, Justice Powell, writing for the majority, noted the "wide latitude" accorded grand jury investigations of criminal violations. He reminded us that the institution "is a grand inquest," not circumscribed in its investigative and accusatory functions by subject matter limitations or "doubts" about whether an individual has committed a crime.[44] Although Justice Powell reiterated the oft-quoted shibboleth that the grand "inquest" has a dual role in both ensuring "effective" law enforcement and safeguarding individuals from unwarranted criminal prosecutions, he unequivocally placed the weight of the Court on the side of law enforcement. In light of the trend launched by *Costello*, the *Calandra* opinion ratified the Court's solicitude for the grand "inquest's" accusatory role. Juxtaposing the contradictory goals of the grand institution, Justice Powell in one breath cites the historic role of the grand jury in protecting citizens from unfounded criminal accusations, and in the next breath he notes that it should not be concerned "by doubts whether any particular individual will be found properly subject to an accusation of crime."[45]

Herein lies the rub of the Court's predicament in attempting to balance the competing aims of the grand "inquest." It is, after all, a wide-ranging inquest, not an institution concerned with whether sufficient evidence exists for a petit jury to find beyond a reasonable doubt that an individual has committed a crime. If probable cause, which is a minimal standard of proof, is all that the grand jury must find to issue a valid indictment, then not much is required for it to do the prosecutor's bidding. Indeed, the modern Court has defined the quantum of proof required to establish probable cause as a mere "fair probability" or "substantial chance" of criminal activity.[46] Surely that

criterion is in tension with the notion that the grand jury is supposed
to protect the innocent from unwarranted accusations. A great potential error rate is built into the concept of probable cause, a rate that is
at odds with the notion of protecting individuals from unfounded
criminal accusations.

Exacerbating this thin reed of proof necessary to the finding of probable cause is the *ex parte* and secret nature of grand jury proceedings.
As one thoughtful commentator has observed, the modern grand jury
does not act as a fact finder; rather, it merely hears the prosecutor's
one-sided version of the facts.[47] Coupled with the difficulty laypersons
may encounter in applying the admittedly mushy, nebulous, and "fluid"
probable cause standard, one must marvel at the persistence of the fiction that the grand inquest is capable of protecting citizens from unwarranted criminal charges. Although one could argue that laypersons
are ill-equipped to apply the probable cause standard because, unlike
police officers and magistrates, they receive no on-the-job training in
the concept,[48] it is counterintuitive to suppose that even if the grand
jurors applied the concept fairly, the innocent would be protected from
unwarranted charges.

Let us return to *Calandra* in order to underline the absurdity of the
Court's putative loyalty to the dual functions of the grand jury. Precisely because the grand inquest is an *ex parte*, secret proceeding, not
bounded by procedural or evidentiary rules governing trials, it would
have been anomalous for the *Calandra* Court to have placed the Fourth
Amendment in the path of the institution's nearly unfettered investigative, accusatory powers. Justice Powell properly harkened to *Costello*
and *Lawn* for the proposition that evidentiary, even constitutional,
imperatives had no role in the grand jury room. The *Calandra*
majority's rationale flowed logically from these tenets; permitting the
witness to invoke the exclusionary rule because of a Fourth Amendment violation would convert the grand jury process into an adversary
proceeding much like a trial, thus seriously impeding its accusatory
function.[49]

Repeating what would become a recurring motif, the *Calandra* Court
stressed that any potential abuse stemming from the grand jury's reliance on evidence obtained as a result of a Fourth Amendment violation would be "substantially negated" by the inadmissibility of the
evidence at the victim's trial.[50] Notice how this justification is incompatible with the liberty-protective role of the grand jury. In effect, the
Court seems to be acknowledging that the grand inquest may indict
an individual on constitutionally infirm evidence, or its derivative fruits,

and the remedy would lie in seeking a dismissal through suppression before trial. Of course, this rationale is consistent with *Costello*'s teaching that the grand jury need not be concerned with procedural or evidentiary niceties in determining whom to indict. Again, the realities of the institution's operation conflict with its civil libertarian purpose. The *Calandra* majority's justification, moreover, is buttressed by the exceptions to the Fourth Amendment's exclusionary rule crafted by the Court.[51] After all, if evidence gathered by a Fourth Amendment violation is admissible at trial through an exception, it hardly seems logical to exclude such evidence from the grand jurors' consideration or to litigate the issue of whether the exception is applicable in the case at hand before presenting the evidence to the grand jury.

Just as *Calandra* continued longstanding precedent stressing the primacy of the grand inquest's accusatory role, the companion cases of *United States v. Dionisio*[52] and *United States v. Mara*[53] acknowledged what had become transparent: the evisceration of the institution's role in protecting citizens from unfounded accusations. Both opinions stand for the unremarkable proposition that compelling witnesses properly subpoenaed before a grand jury to furnish voice and handwriting samples as a basis for comparison to other evidence violates neither the prohibition of unreasonable seizures contained in the Fourth Amendment nor the privilege against self-incrimination enshrined in the Fifth Amendment. More remarkable, as we have seen, is the Court's concession that the grand inquest was just that: an inquest, not a mechanism for safeguarding citizens of unwarranted indictments. Even more telling is the unanimity of the Court's recognition that the protective role of the grand jury was a facade, a shibboleth to be repeated as a way of justifying the continued vitality of the institution in the federal criminal justice process.

Justice Stewart, writing for the majority in *Dionisio*, observed that "the grand jury may not *always* [emphasis added] serve its historic role as a protective bulwark standing solidly between the solid ordinary citizen and the overzealous prosecutor."[54] I suppose Justice Stewart was reluctant to concede the obvious by employing the qualifier *always*, because a more categorical statement would have rendered superfluous the grand jury protection embodied in the Fifth Amendment. By contrast, Justice Douglas's dissent in *Mara* left nothing to the imagination. He put it succinctly: "It is, indeed, common knowledge that the grand jury, having been conceived as a bulwark between the citizen and the Government, is now a tool of the Executive."[55] By the early 1970s, therefore, the proverbial cat was out of the bag; the highest

Court in the land no longer entertained the illusion that the contradictory purposes of the grand jury were reconcilable in the modern federal criminal justice system. The problem for the Court was how to maintain the legal fiction behind the historic and functional purpose of the grand jury in light of this amazing concession. As we shall see, the Court steadfastly clung to this fiction as it sought to prop up an institution whose symbolic historical vestiges endured despite modern practices.

SELF-INCRIMINATION AND THE GRAND JURY: A STRAINED RELATIONSHIP

A peculiar paradox, representing a corollary to the conflicting aims of the grand inquest, has permeated the history of the institution. We have seen how the grand jury was conceived as a body free to gather any information, from diverse sources, in its mission to protect the community from harm inflicted by criminal activity. Of course, the best source of that information is the person or persons suspected of having committed the crimes. Entitled to everyone's evidence, the grand jury should therefore not allow the critical witness to escape from its freewheeling investigative arm, but how does this crucial role square with the witness's privilege against self-incrimination? If she testifies under oath before the grand jury, her testimony could be used against her at trial. Although counsel is available at trial to invoke this critical right on her behalf, a lawyer may not be available to safeguard the witness's privilege at the grand jury stage.[56] More important, should the witness, before she is questioned, be informed of the privilege and warned of the legal consequences of uttering self-incriminating remarks in the secret chambers of the grand inquest? These difficult questions have not generated satisfactory answers from the judiciary, an inherent product of the tension between the contradictory purposes of the grand jury.

It is fitting that a grand juror testified to this tension as early as the nineteenth century. Consider the case of *United States v. Charles*,[57] decided by a federal district court in 1813. The defendant had testified before a grand jury against another suspect. Subsequently, the prosecutor sought to use this testimony at a different proceeding against Charles by calling some of the grand jurors to repeat the substance of his testimony before the grand jury. One of those grand jurors "testified that the prisoner [Charles] was not told that he need not answer any questions tending to criminate himself." The defendant's counsel then argued to the court that the grand jurors' testimony was inadmissible because Charles was not warned of his privilege against self-incrimination. An astute lawyer, therefore, identified the fundamental dichotomy between protecting a citizen's rights and fostering the grand jury's investigative and accusatory role. Before the witness potentially sealed his fate, fair play demanded that he be warned of his privilege against self-incrimination. Otherwise, the grand jury witness's sworn testimony would become the prosecutor's greatest sword.

Implicit in the *Charles* opinion is the precept that the privilege against self-incrimination applies to a grand jury proceeding. The Supreme Court ratified this principle in *Counselman v. Hitchcock*.[58] Acknowledging that the Sixth Amendment applies to formal criminal accusations, the Court distinguished the privilege against self-incrimination as broader than the Sixth Amendment, because the Fifth Amendment applied to "criminal cases."[59] What the Supreme Court did in *Counselman* was to recognize the obvious. Even though the grand jury merely represents the first stage of the criminal process, it would be incongruous not to afford a witness the benefit of the privilege against self-incrimination when he can be legally compelled to appear and testify before the grand jury.

In a remarkable flight through time, the issue posed by *Charles* in 1813 came alive more than a century and a half later when the Supreme Court had to decide whether a witness who was subpoenaed to testify before a grand jury should be given the *Miranda*[60] warnings. Although *Miranda* casts a broader net than merely warning the target of a grand jury investigation that he need not answer incriminating questions, the question joined in 1976 by the Supreme Court in *United States v. Mandujano*[61] revived the prescient inquiry raised by the defendant's counsel in *Charles*. Within the criminal context, *Mandujano* graphically illustrates the irreconcilable conflict in the modern grand jury's competing functions; it also manifests the Court's ultimate and irrevocable drift toward a doctrine in which the inquisitorial aspect of the grand jury reigns supreme. *Mandujano*'s factual predicate, moreover, dovetails with the theme emblematic of the modern criticism leveled at the grand inquest: an institution serving as the prosecutor's "agent."[62]

Mandujano was a low-level drug operative in San Antonio, Texas, during the early 1970s. He was a bartender who was suspected of dealing heroin. Mandujano agreed to secure heroin for an undercover agent; however, the deal was not consummated. He was subpoenaed to testify before a grand jury investigating local drug trafficking.[63] When he appeared, the prosecutor informed him of his obligation to answer the prosecutor's questions, except for the ones that might elicit incriminating responses. Mandujano's reply was deceptively simple: "Do I answer all the questions you ask?" The prosecutor reiterated his previous peroration: he was required to answer all questions except those that might tend to incriminate him. Then the prosecutor asked Mandujano whether he had legal representation; the witness replied that he did not have the resources to hire a lawyer. The colloquy resumed when the prosecutor informed Mandujano that even if he had retained counsel he could not be present at the secret grand jury proceeding, but he could wait outside the grand jury room in the event that he needed legal advice.[64]

The predicament confronting a grand jury witness who is a target of the inquest's investigation is daunting. This quandary is compounded if the witness lacks the money to retain an attorney, as Mandujano's case illustrates. Alone in a room controlled by a prosecutor steeped in the nuances of the criminal law, while facing fellow citizens expecting answers to the prosecutor's questions, must be an intimidating experience for most people. It surely must have provoked Mandujano's candid response to the prosecutor's litany: "Do I answer all the questions you ask?" What other options did he have? He could have invoked his Fifth Amendment privilege against self-incrimination with respect to each and every question posed by the prosecutor and thereby avoided any legal jeopardy stemming from his responses. Of course, he did not have an opportunity to discuss the scope of the privilege or its proper invocation with counsel, because he lacked the funds to retain an attorney. Why would Mandujano respond to the prosecutor's questions, commit perjury concerning the abortive heroin transaction with the undercover agent, and risk criminal prosecution when the prosecutor warned him of his privilege against self-incrimination and of the risk of a perjury charge if he lied under oath? Surely such an outcome seems to defy common sense and the instinct for self-protection.

Perhaps we ought not be so harsh in passing judgment upon Mandujano's dilemma. It is easy to dispassionately analyze Mandujano's situation with the benefit of hindsight. We can empathize with his plight, however, if we put ourselves in his shoes. Here is a man suspected of drug dealing who has been summoned before a grand jury. His first encounter is with the prosecutor, who proceeds to give him a speech about his obligation to testify truthfully. He adds the caveat that he need not furnish incriminating information. Yet what is the purpose of the grand jury proceeding: to gather incriminating information about the drug trade to which Mandujano is suspected of being linked. Mandujano's options were to deny involvement and risk being indicted for perjury; answer truthfully and face a certain indictment for his involvement in the heroin transaction; or invoke the privilege against self-incrimination and the prospect that the grand jury would infer guilt from his silence.

Mandujano's predicament reflects the "cruel trilemma" that the Supreme Court identified in *Murphy v. Waterfront Commission*[65] and that the self-incrimination clause is supposed to prevent. What about the warnings the prosecutor gave Mandujano, which he acknowledged and supposedly understood? Did he have time, as the Court pointed out but dismissed as speculative in another case,[66] "to assimilate their significance," especially in the presence of the grand jurors? Isn't it counterintuitive to argue that a target of a grand jury investigation who invokes the privilege against self-incrimination after being placed under oath will not be vulnerable to the grand jurors' inference of guilty from his silence? The Supreme Court's facile response to this quandary is that the grand jury's historic role is investigative rather than adjudicative; it does not determine guilt or innocence, which is the petit jury's function.[67]

From a legal perspective, the Court's response to Mandujano's plight is sound; from a common-sense vantage point, it is preposterous. The putative target of a grand jury inquest realizes that invoking the "Fifth" whets neither the prosecutor's nor the grand jurors' appetite for the facts from "the mouths of those having knowledge of the unlawful conduct."[68] When coupled with the positive "warning" that he is legally obligated to testify before a grand jury, what message does the witness elicit? The answer, rather simply, is Mandujano's not-so-implicit response to the prosecutor's peroration: I had better answer all of your questions. Indeed, Mandujano represents the quintessentially vulnerable target of a grand jury investigation: an indigent suspect who does not have the benefit of the advice of counsel either preceding or during his grand jury appearance. He is left to fend for himself in a "secret" room occupied by a prosecutor and a host of grand jurors, both of whom are eager for answers from the persons with the most pertinent information: the suspects.

That brings us to the issue in *Mandujano*: whether putative grand jury targets should be given the *Miranda* warnings before testifying. After reaffirming the tenet that a witness who has been properly summoned must testify before a grand jury unless he or she invokes the privilege against self-incrimination, Chief Justice Burger, speaking for a plurality, answers the question in the negative. Before he does so, however, the Chief Justice takes pains to emphasize the familiar shibboleths: the grand inquest is an essential adjunct to the criminal justice system; it simultaneously guards against arbitrary and unfounded accusations. More important, Chief Justice Burger observes that the witness has the burden not only of invoking the privilege but also of convincing the court, if the question is raised by the prosecutor, that the invocation of the privilege is not a "subterfuge."[69] In rather stark terms, the witness bears the onus of invoking the privilege and of justifying it if the invocation is called into question. These are rather formidable requirements, especially for an unrepresented target like Mandujano. Again, however, the accusatory and investigative aims of the grand jury take precedence, despite the Court's reaffirmation of its protective role.

Why shouldn't such a vulnerable witness, a target of a grand jury investigation, be entitled to the *Miranda* warnings as a precondition to testifying? Chief Justice Burger notes that a fundamental difference marks a grand jury inquiry apart from the custodial interrogation by the police; he quotes *Miranda* for the proposition that in the grand jury room, "there are often impartial observers to guard against intimidation or trickery."[70] In sum, the coercive pressures inherent in custodial interrogation are absent in a grand jury room, thereby reducing if not eliminating the prospect that the suspect will be cowed into confessing. Reflecting an implicit disapproval of the *Miranda* holding, Chief Justice Burger remarks that expansion of the *Miranda* doctrine is unwarranted.[71] What about the fact that Mandujano faced the prosecutor or the grand jury without advice from an attorney, either before or during his appearance? Chief Justice Burger rejoined that the Sixth Amendment right to counsel had not yet attached, for that right is triggered only upon the initiation of formal charges against the suspect.[72] In essence, only those suspects with sufficient funds to retain an attorney may enjoy the benefit of such advice. There is a difference, in sum, between judicial compulsion exercised in the grand jury context and police compulsion inherent in custodial interrogation. One may require a lawyer to assist a suspect; the other does not.

There is a certain appeal to the plurality's distinction between custodial interrogation and the questioning of a suspect in a grand jury. The chief evil that *Miranda* is supposed to guard against is incommunicado interrogation in the hostile environment of a police station. As we shall see, what gives police the upper hand in custodial interrogation is the isolation of the suspect in a police-dominated environment. Chief Justice Burger was correct in differentiating the grand jury interrogation context by emphasizing the presence of citizens who can testify as to what transpired in the confines of the grand jury room and who can protest if the prosecutor attempts to browbeat the witness into submission. It was a grand juror, you will recall, who in the *Charles* case testified that the witness was not warned about the privilege against self-incrimination before he testified to the grand jury. Bolstering the *Mandujano*'s plurality opinion was language from *Miranda* distinguishing custodial from other types of interrogation.

Let us move from the surface appeal generated by these distinctions into the realm of reality. The *Mandujano* case serves as the perfect vehicle for our critique. Here is an indigent defendant, alone in a room full of citizens expecting answers from the person who is most qualified to provide explanations. The prosecutor, who controls the proceedings and will conduct the interrogation, provides legalistic warnings. The isolation also exists here, except the control is not exerted by a police officer who is trained in how to manipulate the suspect's emotions in order to obtain a confession. Rather, the person in control is a lawyer steeped in the nuances of the privilege against self-incrimination and in the mechanics of grand jury practice. The isolation and secrecy of the grand jury proceeding is ameliorated by the presence of the grand jurors. How much of a palliative the grand jurors provide, however, is questionable, as they are not there to comfort the witness but to get answers from him. It didn't take Mandujano long to figure out who was in control of the grand jury room: the prosecutor, not the grand jurors. How daunting a prospect this must have been for Mandujano is corroborated by his compliant responses to the prosecutor's legally arcane warnings.

The flip side of this situation is the difference in the legal stakes involved in a grand jury proceeding versus a custodial interrogation. A suspect is free to argue at trial that her confession is the product of coercive police tactics and thus unreliable, the law enforcement version to the contrary notwithstanding.[73] Confessions secured at the police station are not, as a rule, given under oath in the presence of laypersons not connected with law enforcement. By contrast, a grand jury proceeding is a solemn legal proceeding, and the first step in the encounter for the witness is the administration of the oath by the prosecutor. The witness then bears the burden of invoking the privilege against self-incrimination in front of the grand jurors. If the witness furnishes incriminating information to the grand jury, this testimony under oath is transcribed by a court reporter. It is difficult to argue that these self-incriminating responses were the product of coercion when the prosecutor has the argument the *Mandujano* Court provided: the answer was given under oath, in the presence of a body of disinterested citizens, not to police officers with a vested interest in obtaining a confession from the suspect. One is not subject, moreover, to criminal prosecution for lying to a police officer; one is liable for perjury, as the *Mandujano* case demonstrates, for lying to a grand jury.

As Justice Marshall pointed out in his *Mara* dissent, moreover, the target of a grand jury subpoena must respond to the subpoena, thereby meaning that he has been "officially restrained for some period of time."[74] As we have seen, the restraint differs from the restraint associated with custodial interrogation, but only in degree, not in kind. In a sense, the compulsion attaching to a grand jury subpoena may exceed the potential coercion associated with custodial interrogation. The only distinguishing factor, the presence of the grand jurors, is counterbalanced by the control exerted by the prosecutor and the legal implications flowing from the formal nature of the grand jury proceeding.

Those legal ramifications are enormous. In a case known for restricting *Miranda*'s scope and for labeling that opinion a mere "prophylactic," the Court observed that "a defendant's right not to be compelled to testify against himself at his own trial might be practically nullified if the prosecution could previously have required him to give evidence against himself before a grand jury."[75] It is axiomatic, given my previous argument, that if the suspect confesses to the grand jury, it becomes nearly impossible for him to counteract the effects of the incrimination at trial. As I have stressed, a qualitative difference exists between an extrajudicial statement given to law enforcement officers on their own turf and a confession under oath furnished to a grand jury.

Beyond this perceptible difference lies a striking paradox: the potential for the grand jury to circumvent a suspect's desire to invoke her privilege against self-incrimination under the *Miranda* doctrine. Imagine the following scenario. The police unsuccessfully attempt to interrogate a suspect. The suspect invokes his right to remain silent, or more effectively, not to speak with the police without the presence of an attorney.[76] A grand jury, through the prosecutor, issues a subpoena for the suspect to testify. Because this summons does not constitute custodial interrogation, which is the chief evil *Miranda* seeks to prevent, the doctrine is not applicable. Furthermore, the suspect is now forced to invoke the Fifth Amendment privilege without the benefit of a full-fledged *Miranda* warning and in the presence of both the prosecutor and the grand jurors. Although the Court has held that silence in response to the *Miranda* warnings cannot be used at trial against a suspect,[77] the grand jurors are now free to construe the target's silence against him, as the grand jury proceeding presumably falls outside *Miranda*'s ambit; it does not constitute custodial interrogation, nor does it present the circumstances in which the target will be coerced into confessing.

Here we have, therefore, the inevitable clash between the privilege against self-incrimination and the grand jury's traditional inquisitorial role. As Justice Brennan acutely observed in his *Mandujano* concurring opinion, "the fundamentals of the Fifth Amendment privilege may be subverted by talismanic invocation of the role of the grand jury in our constitutional system."[78] What Justice Brennan wistfully sought was a reconciliation of these competing principles.[79] Given the fundamentally contradictory functions assigned to the grand jury, however, Justice Brennan's noble ideal is not attainable. If the grand inquest is entitled to everyone's evidence with no constraints other than a privilege that must be invoked by the witness, it is difficult to reconcile the self-incrimination privilege with the investigative goals of the grand jury. Indeed, Justice Brennan ultimately recognizes the irreconcilable conflict by noting that a target under judicial compulsion to testify before the grand jury, the "classic form of compulsion" addressed by the privilege against self-incrimination, "must claim the privilege or else, without any further analysis, he will not be considered to have been 'compelled' within the meaning of the Amendment."[80]

If the Court has presumably attempted to preserve and protect a citizen's Fifth Amendment privilege against self-incrimination, it certainly has not shown solicitude toward that privilege in the grand jury context. Instead, it has pledged fidelity toward the privilege while facilitating its waiver by placing the burden on the witness to invoke it. Only those targets fortunate enough to retain a lawyer upon being summoned to testify are able to counteract the natural advantage the prosecutor enjoys as the sole legal arbiter in the secret confines of the grand jury room. Even those targets with the financial means to hire a lawyer are vulnerable to the extent that they must step outside the grand jury room in order to secure the benefit of legal counsel. The privilege against self-incrimination has given way to the inexorable triumph of the investigative and accusatory role of the federal grand jury.

IMMUNITY, SELF-INCRIMINATION, AND THE GRAND JURY: CURIOUS BEDFELLOWS

Contrasting with the legal restraints upon the police in the rare circumstance in which a suspect invokes his *Miranda* rights is the prosecutor's option to compel a target's testimony before a grand jury through a grant of immunity. In essence, this is the equivalent of coerced testimony, because the witness must speak or risk a finding of contempt; in short, "the witness is told to talk or face the government's coercive sanctions."[81] Ironically, the Fifth Amendment privilege against self-incrimination disappears from the legal landscape in the face of a grant of immunity from the government. How does one explain this striking irony? A cynic would reply that immunity is a legal fiction intended to circumvent the privilege through a clever device that magically removes whatever ethical or philosophical aversion we may harbor toward coerced testimony.

The skeptic's opinion is reinforced by the naked power that a grant of immunity automatically confers. We need not delve into the amorphous voluntariness standard the Supreme Court has crafted to determine whether a confession is voluntary or coerced—that is, whether physical or psychological pressures overpowered the defendant's will not to confess.[82] Rather, the grand jury target is given no choice and is punished if she does not speak. Notice the splendid juxtaposition between the privilege against self-incrimination and immunity. The privilege is meant to protect the witness by not attaching sanctions to his desire not to speak; on the contrary, a suspect who is granted immunity is punished if he *doesn't* speak. Nowhere is the contrast between the competing purposes of the grand jury more compelling than in this circumstance. Immunity represents the entitlement of the grand inquest to "every man's evidence" without any qualifications or conditions. By removing the sole obstacle to the grand jury's quest for every bit of evidence, immunity ironically stands the fundamental principles of the adversarial system of adjudication on their head. It is as if a grant of immunity transmutes the adversarial system into an inquisitorial one with a single stroke. Let us therefore explore this ingenious sleight-of-hand and determine whether it withstands logical and legal scrutiny.

From a historical perspective, the wording of the Fifth Amendment is absolute; it simply and categorically states that no person shall be compelled to be a witness against himself. One scholar remarks that "the framers of the Constitution apparently concluded that no amount of evidence could justify compelling a person to supply testimonial evidence against himself in a criminal case."[83] Immunity was not part of the historical framework underlying the Fifth Amendment's self-incrimination clause, although immunity statutes had been deeply embedded in Anglo-American jurisprudence.[84] Accordingly, a short time after the advent of the Bill of Rights, immunity statutes were drafted that compelled a person to testify in exchange for immunity from prosecution.[85] In a series of opinions dating from the late nineteenth century, the Supreme Court has construed the scope and constitutionality of immunity statutes.[86] Culminating with the *Kastigar v. United States*[87] opinion, the Court has determined that a person may be compelled to be a witness against herself, especially before a grand jury, as long as her testimony and its derivative products are used neither to develop a case against her nor in a prosecution for the acts to which her testimony relates.[88] The obvious corollary to this holding is the concept that the privilege against self-incrimination does not "mean that one who invokes it cannot subsequently be prosecuted."[89]

Kastigar involved the launching of a preemptive strike against the targets of a grand jury subpoena. The government, suspecting that the suspects would invoke the privilege rather than testify, sought and received from the district court an order granting the targets immunity in accordance with the pertinent federal statute.[90] When the targets refused to testify before the grand jury after receiving immunity, they were held in contempt and incarcerated until they either answered the grand jury's questions or the term of the grand jury expired.[91] To underscore my previous argument, the targets were punished, through loss of their liberty, for failing to speak. The right to remain silent was rendered superfluous by the conferral of immunity through the appropriate statute.

At the outset of Justice Powell's opinion for the majority, he is careful to point out the venerable principle at the core of the investigative function of the grand jury: the right of the public to "every man's evidence."[92] Flowing from this precept is the need to achieve a "rational accommodation" between the competing values underlying the privilege against self-incrimination and the need for the grand jury to hear the most useful testimony of the people implicated in the crime being investigated.[93] In effect, Justice Powell justified the immunity statutes and the compulsion they inevitably produce as a necessary compromise: a balance between the need of the grand jury to investigate and accuse those who inflict harm on the community through the commission of crimes, and the privilege against self-incrimination's tenet that evidence of the crime should not be extracted from the suspect but developed through means disassociated from the suspect.

The coerced testimony from the target of a grand jury subpoena, however, should not preclude his subsequent prosecution. This is *Kastigar*'s main teaching. If the suspect is forced to speak or risk a finding of contempt and the concomitant loss of liberty, then he should be immunized from prosecution for the crimes to which his testimony relates. Known as *transactional immunity*, this is the protection the petitioners sought in *Kastigar*. The privilege against self-incrimination required no less. Rejecting *Kastigar*'s contention, Justice Powell upheld the constitutionality of the federal immunity statute, holding that use-derivative use immunity was consistent with the Fifth Amendment privilege.[94] To the extent that such immunity precluded the use of the compelled testimony "in any respect," it complied with the values safeguarded by the privilege against self-incrimination.[95] Furthermore, use-derivative use immunity presumably left both parties (the government and the witness) in "substantially the same" position as if the witness had "claimed the privilege."[96]

Justice Powell's opinion represents a minimalist view of the scope of the Fifth Amendment privilege. It attempts to reconcile the privilege with the immunity statutes and the rationale undergirding such statutes. Drawing upon the historical record, the *Kastigar* majority implies that the framers must not have intended to undermine the effect of immunity statutes when they incorporated the privilege against self-incrimination into the body of the Fifth Amendment. The right to "every man's evidence," especially where the evidence could only be unearthed from the suspect, required a broader construction of the privilege than the mere words in the Constitution dictated.

An absolutist view of the privilege against self-incrimination, by contrast, would reject Justice Powell's logic. One facet of this position would maintain that a statute, however rational it may seem, cannot override a constitutional command.[97] Another component of the argument focuses on the plain language of the Amendment and compares its categorical terms to the relativist language contained in the Fourth Amendment.[98] According to this perspective, the Fourth Amendment furnishes only "partial immunity" from governmental searches or seizures, which are permissible upon a showing of probable cause. By contrast, the "framers . . . apparently concluded that no amount of evidence could justify compelling a person to supply testimonial evidence against himself in a criminal case."[99] In essence, one amendment "invites balancing," the other does not. It is axiomatic, therefore, that the privilege should not be superseded by a statute that confers immunity in exchange for coerced testimony. Perhaps this axiom is not compelling in light of the fact that the privilege, as the framers knew it, did not forbid coerced testimony as long as the subject was not placed under oath.[100]

Does immunity magically dissolve the coercion attaching to a subpoena to testify in front of a grand jury? From a common-sense perspective, the unequivocal answer is no. How much comfort could we expect the witness to derive from the protection afforded by use-derivative use immunity? Not much. The fact remains that she must face the prosecutor and the grand jurors alone in the secrecy of the grand jury room. Indeed, Justice Marshall may be correct in arguing that the witness may decide to take his poison and be jailed for contempt rather than assist in an investigation that might lead to his demise.[101] Even if the witness is granted transactional immunity, the fact remains that she must still face the prosecutor and the grand jurors and confess to the crime regardless of her desire not to do so. Practical necessities do not square well with categorical constitutional safeguards.

The irreconcilable nature of the grand jury's conflicting purposes emerges in bold relief in the dichotomy between the privilege against self-incrimination and the grand inquest's craving for evidence of the crime. Immunity is ill-suited for the task of reconciliation. Ironically, a suspect receives a greater measure of legal protection from custodial interrogation by the police under the *Miranda* doctrine than he does in front of the magnificent accusatory and investigative arm of the government: the grand inquest. It should not shock us, therefore, that the same criticisms historically leveled at the institution have returned to haunt us.

THE GRAND JURY "INDICTED" ONCE MORE

At the beginning of the new millennium, the federal grand jury is the subject of scathing attacks, exemplified by an article published in the *American Bar Association Journal* aptly entitled "Indictment of a System."[102] Detailing a host of abuses by prosecutors who have employed federal grand juries as their personal bailiwicks, the author also emphasized the independence of the grand jury from judicial supervision as well as the attempt of the defense bar to reform the existing regime. Proposing a ten-point federal grand jury "bill of rights," the National Association of Criminal Defense Lawyers seeks to revamp the present system by allowing criminal attorneys access to the grand jury room and by excluding unconstitutionally seized evidence as well as requiring prosecutors to provide exculpatory evidence.[103] Unlike the federal government, most states have avoided this morass by either reforming the grand jury rules or eliminating the need for indictments by grand juries as the primary charging instrument in the criminal justice system. In the overwhelming majority of states, the prosecutor issues the formal charge for felonies through an information, bypassing the need for a grand jury indictment.[104]

The renewed debate about the failings of the federal grand jury underscores my argument that its primary role is inquisitorial. It is plausible to find a nexus, moreover, between the manner in which Ken Starr used the grand jury in his investigation of President Clinton and the vigor of renewed calls for institutional reform. Wielding the ultimate weapon at his command, Starr compelled Monica Lewinsky to speak about her affair with the president through a grant of immunity. Furthermore, Starr, as I have previously stressed, in effect compelled the president's testimony before the grand jury because although the president could have invoked the privilege against self-incrimination to avoid legal jeopardy, it was not politically expedient for him to do so. In order to combat this disadvantage, the president accused the Office of the Independent Counsel (hereafter OIC) of violating grand jury rules by leaking secret information to the press. Finally, the poignant moment at which Lewinsky's mother, Marcia Lewis, lost her emotional composure before the grand jury illuminated the unchecked power of a federal prosecutor determined to get his quarry, regardless of the human cost. The Clinton impeachment saga made it clear that, contrary to what the Supreme Court has mechanically intoned, the federal grand jury does *not* protect citizens from "arbitrary and oppressive governmental action."[105]

THE CLINTON IMPEACHMENT: WHY A GRAND JURY IS THE PROSECUTOR'S PUPPET

As one scholar has observed, the grand jury "became the focal point of the heavily criticized investigation of the President's conduct."[106] Although Starr bore the brunt of the censure, it was misplaced. Rather, the Supreme Court, as we have seen, with its one-sided view of the purposes of the grand jury, ought to shoulder the blame. Going a step beyond the previous analysis, I would like to employ the Clinton impeachment imbroglio as a lens through which we can view the effects of unbridled grand jury discretion, courtesy of the highest Court in the land. The untrammeled discretion and control, without any judicial oversight, afforded to prosecutors by the Supreme Court gave Starr wide latitude to manipulate the grand jury process. As one commentator has remarked, "The grand jury investigation led by the Independent Counsel did not violate the constitutional rights of any witnesses, even if the tactics appeared high-handed and the reason for the inquiry politically motivated."[107]

Why were Starr's tactics within the realm of acceptable prosecutorial behavior? Quite simply because Supreme Court precedent permits prosecutors to violate grand jury rules with impunity[108] and to withhold exculpatory evidence from the grand inquest.[109] The OIC could, therefore, mishandle witnesses before the grand jury, leak information from that secret body, and not be concerned that those actions would otherwise preclude the president's potential impeachment or indictment after he left office. In the war waged by the OIC against the most powerful figure in the United States, the arsenal calculated to neutralize the president's power rested with the grand jury. It was natural for Starr to rely on this strategic advantage; any prosecutor worth his or her salt would have been loath not to do so. The painful, at times grueling, interrogation session the president endured in front of a camera, broadcast throughout the world, symbolized the manner in which the grand jury was the chief weapon in the fight to secure the president's impeachment. A strictly offensive weapon for the prosecutor, the grand inquest failed miserably in its purported task of protecting the innocent, such as Lewis, from unwarranted accusation, embarrassment, or harassment.

Striking an immunity bargain with Lewinsky, the OIC was not content solely with her testimony in front of the grand jury. Rather, Starr subpoenaed Lewis in his expansive grand jury investigation. More than any facet of the investigation, the image of Lewis being reduced to tears inside the grand jury room provoked a public outcry against Starr's investigation. Criticizing the IOC's tactics, one legal commentator decried the "aggressive and disproportionate tactics" that "left the public with the justifiable perception that Mr. Starr is conducting a crusade rather than an investigation."[110]

Starr's "crusade" reached its zenith in the episode that triggered Lewis's breakdown in front of the grand jury. The inanity of the questions that precipitated this pathos reflects the potential for abuse of a

witness by prosecutors controlling the grand "inquest." The line of questioning revolved around the nickname that Lewinsky had given Hillary
Clinton during the course of her conversations with Linda Tripp. An
exchange occurred in which two of Starr's prosecutors quizzed Lewis
on the meaning of the word "Babba," which was the nickname.[111] Of
course, any member of the public would have a difficult time imagin-
ing how this issue was relevant to Starr's investigation.[112] As we have
seen, however, formal evidentiary rules do not apply to grand jury proceedings, so Starr's subordinates were not constrained in their fields of
inquiry. When overzealous prosecutors have the rapt attention of citizens who depend on government agents to present information, the
"grand" jurors must endure trivia with aplomb and patience.

A watershed event in the history of the federal grand jury, the Starr
investigation of President Clinton's alleged crimes revealed in stark
terms the transformation of the federal grand jury into a purely accusatorial body. However, the "grand" institution has not only become
a strictly accusatorial body; it has been converted into a prosecutorial
tool subject to little if any judicial supervision. In effect, federal prosecutors are unfettered in their ability to flout the rules of grand jury
practice. This phenomenon has transpired while the Supreme Court
maintains the legal fiction that the grand jury remains independent
from prosecutorial control. The Clinton-Lewinsky saga epitomizes the
fact that the federal grand jury hardly protects citizens (certainly not
Lewis) from arbitrary or oppressive government action. If the grand
body was supposed to protect the accused, moreover, it has not accomplished the goal. Indeed, as one scholar has observed, "although the
purpose of the grand jury is to protect those accused of crimes, few
defendants take comfort in its presence; indeed, the staunchest defenders of the institution are prosecutors."[113] Why shouldn't the prosecutors defend the institution? We have seen that the strategic advantages
prosecutors derive from use of the grand jury are compelling. Certainly
Starr's underlings would attest to that fact!

A HANDS-OFF APPROACH TO THE GRAND JURY

In order to counter the IOC's decided advantage, the president went
on the offensive by attempting to have it held in contempt for leaking
secret grand jury materials to the *New York Times*.[114] Bolstering the
grand jury's supposed independence is the secrecy in which its deliberations occur. Therefore, the Clinton legal team sought to win a
public relations coup by accusing the OIC of undermining the funda-

mental rules governing the grand inquest. As it would ultimately discover, the Clinton legal team did not have the benefit of Supreme Court precedent on its side. Let us scrutinize that precedent in light of the Clinton impeachment.

Imagine the following scenario: federal prosecutors commit several violations of the Federal Rules of Criminal Procedure governing the presentation of evidence to a grand jury. Specifically, the prosecutors "manipulated the grand jury investigation to gather evidence for use in civil audits; violated the secrecy provisions of [Federal Rule of Criminal Procedure] 6 (e) by publicly identifying the targets of the subject matter of the grand jury investigation; and imposed secrecy obligations in violation of Rule 6 (e) upon grand jury witnesses."[115] In addition, the prosecutors administered "unauthorized" oaths to Internal Revenue agents; deliberately had those agents misrepresent evidence to the grand jury; and "deliberately berated and mistreated an expert for the defense in the presence of grand jurors."[116] Indeed, the government "conceded" that it was abusive to the witness both during a recess as well as in front of the grand jury.[117]

To a detached observer, this behavior by the prosecutors would seem to be unfair and merit sanctions. That is not the position espoused by the Supreme Court. Relying on the notion that the supervisory power of a federal district court is limited, the *Bank of Nova Scotia v. United States* decision established that a district court may dismiss an indictment based on such misconduct only if it had prejudiced the defendants. [118] In essence, a conviction erases any prosecutorial misconduct, however flagrant, rendering such actions "harmless." That leaves the remedy of attempting to hold the prosecutor in contempt for his or her misbehavior.[119] The prospect for such a proceeding is slim, confirming a scholar's assessment that "the Court's approach to the prosecutor's actions in grand jury investigations has effectively made that conduct unreviewable by lower courts."[120]

An even more extreme version of such a hands-off approach to prosecutorial control over the grand jury is evident in *United States v. Williams*.[121] In that case, Justice Scalia, writing for the Court, held that a prosecutor has no "binding obligation" to present substantial exculpatory evidence to a grand jury; and, correspondingly, that the lower federal courts have "no authority to prescribe such a duty" pursuant to their inherent supervisory power.[122] Grounded in a separation of powers rationale, Justice Scalia's opinion for the majority justifies its conclusion on the functional independence of the grand jury from the judicial branch.[123]

The flaw underlying Justice Scalia's rationale is the assumption that "the Fifth Amendment's 'constitutional guarantee *presupposes* an investigative body acting independently of either the prosecuting attorney or *judge*.'"[124] Notice how Justice Scalia emphasizes the word "presupposes." One wonders whether he did this in a sarcastic tone. If he had read any literature on the true workings of the modern grand jury, he could not have been serious. As we have seen, the prosecutor enjoys untrammeled control over the grand jury, free from the scrutiny of defense counsel, the judiciary or, for that matter, the public.[125] It defies logic and reality to maintain that the modern federal grand jury is not subject to prosecutorial manipulation or control.

Given these precedents, it becomes clear why President Clinton's attempt to have the OIC held in contempt for leaks of grand jury material to the press was destined to fail. In the ultimate political duel, the OIC had a trump card in the game of spin control for the minds and hearts of the American public: virtual immunity from judicial oversight of their actions with the grand jury investigating the president's conduct. The appellate opinion rejecting the president's stratagem is both ironic and illuminating. It is ironic because the counselor to Starr, Charles Bakaly III, lied about what he disclosed to the press; it is illuminating because it shows both the power and impunity bestowed upon federal prosecutors through the Court's "Alice-in-Wonderland" perception of how grand juries truly operate. This brings us to the reasons behind the conclusion that the OIC violated neither the rules of criminal procedure in grand jury proceedings nor the rights of any witnesses.

During the course of President Clinton's impeachment trial in the Senate, the *New York Times* published an article stating that OIC prosecutors were considering the possibility of seeking a grand jury indictment against the president upon conclusion of the Senate trial.[126] Among the charges the prosecutors were contemplating, according to the article, were perjury in Clinton's Paula Jones case deposition as well as in his grand jury testimony.[127] Immediately after publication of the article, Clinton and the Office of the President filed a motion to show cause why the OIC should not be held in contempt for violation of Federal Rule of Criminal Procedure 6 (e), which prohibits federal prosecutors from divulging "matters occurring before the grand jury."[128]

Responding to this motion, the OIC submitted a statement by Bakaly that he told the *New York Times* reporter who wrote the article that he refused to confirm what either Starr or the OIC "was thinking or doing."[129] Eventually, the OIC "abandoned the argument" that it was not the source of the information for the *New York Times* article, "took administrative action" against Bakaly, and requested that the Department of Justice conduct a criminal investigation on the issue.[130] Ultimately, the district court concluded that the disclosure of the potential indictment of Clinton upon the conclusion of the impeachment trial "revealed grand jury material and constituted a prima facie violation of Rule 6 (e)."[131]

Reversing the district court's finding, the U.S. Court of Appeals for the District of Columbia Circuit held that the disclosures made by Bakaly to the *New York Times* did not constitute a prima facie violation of Rule 6 (e).[132] The court based its ruling on two fundamental grounds: the revelations by Bakaly did not involve "matters occurring before the grand jury"; and the disclosure that Clinton was a witness before the grand jury technically violated Rule 6 (e) but was harmless because the whole nation knew that President Clinton had testified before the grand jury—he had told the American public about it in a nationally televised address.[133]

The appellate court had solid reasons for its holding. The disclosures by Bakaly were not "matters" that were before the grand jury. Rather, they represented possible future actions the OIC might undertake upon the conclusion of the impeachment trial. Even though the court had recognized in previous holdings that Rule 6 (e) encompassed "matters likely to occur before the grand jury, "where the reported deliberations do not reveal that an indictment *has been sought* or *will be sought*," they do not fall within the strict boundaries of the rule.[134] Naturally, one had to be traveling in space not to know at the time the article was written that "a grand jury was investigating alleged perjury and obstruction of justice by the President."[135] While noting the "troubling" nature of the disclosures, especially as they could potentially damage an innocent person's reputation, the court implicitly acknowledged that it had no effective means to either remedy or deter such disclosures.[136]

Let us change the facts to determine whether the president would have had a remedy under different circumstances. Suppose the revelation of the possible indictment of the president or the disclosure that he was a witness would have constituted a "prima facie" violation of Rule 6 (e). Further assume that Starr's successor, Ralph Ray, had opted to seek an indictment against Clinton after he left the Office of the Presidency for perjury and obstruction of justice. Finally, let us presume that Clinton would have been convicted of either or both of the counts. Would there be any significant legal ramifications to the violations of Rule 6 (e) by OIC ?

As you may discern, my question is a rhetorical one. Both *Nova Scotia* and *United States v. Mechanik* would have rendered the violations "harmless" upon the entry of a conviction. A result-oriented jurisprudence that nullifies the prosecutor's misconduct as long as the result is a conviction fosters an attitude of invincibility. This theme gives a possible reason for Bakaly's arrogance in misleading the court as to what he divulged to the press. Although Bakaly's deception did not occur under oath, it nevertheless besmirched the office he represented by displaying the same behavior it was seeking to condemn and deter by recommending the president's impeachment and possible indictment.

Similarly, the OIC was not acting outside the bounds of the law when it demeaned Lewis in front of the grand jury. The American public could not be faulted for not knowing that the Supreme Court had in effect condoned such conduct in one of its opinions. In the *Bank of Nova Scotia* case, you will recall, the federal prosecutors admitted to "berating" and "mistreating" a witness both in front of the grand jury and during the course of a recess from its deliberations. If such behavior does not "substantially influence" the grand inquest's decision to indict the defendant, it is legally irrelevant. How could such inane and irrelevant questions put to Lewis by Starr's subordinates have "substantially influenced" its decision to indict? Furthermore, how does one establish this nebulous criterion? In the highly charged political arena in which the investigation was being waged, the OIC's mistreatment of Lewis backfired against Starr. In a run-of-the-mill case, the prosecutor's misconduct would have been ignored.

This woeful tale demonstrates the proposition that the Supreme Court has eliminated judicial review of prosecutorial misconduct during grand jury investigations. The chief reason the Court has proffered in defense of this doctrine is "that seeking judicial review of the grand jury investigation can devolve into a tactic to delay the prosecution of valid criminal charges."[137] Of course, this rationale dovetails with my thesis: the Court has refused to interfere with the accusatorial and inquisitorial functions of the grand institution while effectively obliterating its purported role in protecting the citizens from potential governmental oppression or opprobrium. The Court seems blithely ignorant of the reality it has fashioned; it is content with intoning a magic aphorism that is loyal to the historical purposes of the grand jury.

An alternative to judicial review has emerged in two statutes designed to provide aggrieved parties redress and to sanction the prosecution after the fact through the application of ethical rules of an attorney's conduct. These two statutes are the Hyde Amendment[138] and the McDade Act.[139] Both laws emerged from congressional anger over the prosecution of one of their own members, Robert McDade, who was acquitted of federal charges involving campaign contributions.[140] The Hyde Amendment allows a criminal defendant to recover attorney's fees in the event she is acquitted, as long as she establishes that the government's position was "vexatious, frivolous, or in bad faith." Seeking to render federal prosecutors accountable for ethical violations, the McDade Act subjects them "to State laws and rules, and local Federal court rules, governing attorneys in each State where such attorney engages in that attorney's duties, to the same extent and in the same manner as other attorneys in that State."

It is unlikely that these statutes will have much of an impact on curbing prosecutorial misconduct in grand jury proceedings. Rather, the statutes leave the fortunes of those defendants and witnesses who bear the brunt of the prosecutors's misconduct subject to the political whims of the legislative branch. I wonder whether Congress would have even considered the Hyde or McDade proposals if one of its members had not, in their view, been the target of "overzealous and lawbreaking officials in the United States Department of Justice."[141] Further, these laws impose daunting challenges to those defendants who attempt to invoke them. The Hyde Amendment is consistent with the Court's grand jury investigation jurisprudence; it requires the defendant to prevail and to prove that the prosecution was vexatious or frivolous. The McDade Act requires a suspect being investigated by a grand jury to run the risk of a more vengeful prosecutor who will no doubt be angered by having to contend with an ethical complaint.

The upshot of the Clinton impeachment story is a runaway federal grand jury dominated by prosecutors with little or no meaningful checks upon the enormous power they wielded. Reform efforts are unlikely to yield significant reform. After all, why would federal prosecutors be willing to surrender the strategic advantages they currently enjoy? The grand jury is too valuable an instrument in their arsenal; to accede to changes that would diminish their power is not realistic in an adversarial system of adjudication.

CONCLUSION

As the "gateway" to the criminal justice system, the grand jury has occupied a prominent place in the history of the adversarial process of adjudication. Enshrouded in controversy almost since its inception, the institution continues to provoke controversy in the bar and in the legal academy. Reform has occurred at the state level, where the grand inquest has become at worst a relic of the past, or at best a minor part of the criminal process. At the federal level, however, the institution continues to play a major role in the criminal justice apparatus. In this respect, the body no longer performs the function that the Supreme Court ascribes to it: a medium to protect the citizen from unwarranted oppression, harassment, or baseless accusations. Rather, the institution has been transformed into the prosecutor's fiefdom, operating as an "inquest" through investigations and accusations but not to shield citizens from potentially oppressive governmental conduct.

Perhaps it was quixotic to expect the grand jury to perform mutually contradictory functions. It is, after all, the only institution enshrined in the criminal provisions of the Bill of Rights that accuses the defendant rather than providing safeguards intended to offset the government's strategic adversarial benefits. Although it was intended to serve the protective goal of interposing a body of citizens as a check upon governmental power, it was manipulated by the executive since the time of its genesis. The Supreme Court, of course, has been loath to abandon the fiction that the grand "old" body still protects society while simultaneously safeguarding fundamental individual liberties. We may sympathize with the Court's need to maintain this pristine illusion. In practice, however, the federal grand jury in its present form appears to wreak more havoc than its defenders may wish to acknowledge. Present calls for reform recognize the reality the Supreme Court stubbornly refuses to acknowledge: the institution's schizophrenic goals often get bent in favor of the government, not the ordinary citizen. The Clinton impeachment saga testifies to this sad state of affairs.

More important, the Court has failed in its attempt to balance the competing demands of the privilege against self-incrimination and the investigative function of the grand jury. In effect, the Court has decided that only those fortunate enough to secure the services of a lawyer may have the benefits afforded by the privilege against self-incrimination in the grand jury forum. Through limited immunity safeguards, moreover, the Court has allowed the prosecution to compel a witness to speak. At the first formal contact with the criminal justice system, the witness or putative target of a grand jury investigation is in a weak position vis-à-vis the discretion and power vested in the federal prosecutor. The time has arrived for a candid assessment of the federal grand jury's true colors; the Supreme Court ought to take the mask off the venerable institution and expose its inherent weaknesses.

NOTES

1. *United States v. Dionisio*, 410 U.S. 1, 17 (1972). Justice Stewart, writing for the majority, observed, "The grand jury may not always serve its historic role as a protective bulwark standing solidly between the ordinary citizen and the overzealous prosecutor." *Id.*

2. This is the term employed by Helene Schwartz in her excellent article. Helene E. Schwartz, *Demythologizing the Historic Role of the Grand Jury*, 10 AM. CRIM. L. REV. 701 (1972).

3. See Chapter 1.

4. See MARVIN FRANKEL & GARY NAFTALIS, THE GRAND JURY: AN INSTITUTION ON TRIAL 13 (1977). As Richard Younger observes, federal grand juries in the emergent nation "tended to become instruments of the central government, rather than representatives of the people." RICHARD YOUNGER, THE PEOPLE'S PANEL 47 (1963).

5. Younger at 52.

6. *Id.* at 56–71.

7. *Id.* at 67–71.

8. *Id.* at 66.

9. *Id.*, passim.

10. A perceptive scholar has resurrected the historical argument, with a greater degree of sophistication, that grand jurors do not possess the legal expertise to perform their historic role. *See* Andrew D. Leipold, *Why Grand Juries Do Not (and Cannot) Protect the Accused*, 80 CORNELL L. REV. 260 (1995).

11. SEYMOUR MARTIN LIPSET, AMERICAN EXCEPTIONALISM: A DOUBLE-EDGED SWORD 21 (1995).

12. *Branzburg v. Hayes*, 408 U.S. 665, 686–87 (1972).

13. *Stirone v. United States*, 361 U.S. 212, 218 (1960).

14. *United States v. Mara*, 410 U.S. 19, 28 (1973) (Douglas, J., dissenting).

15. *Branzburg v. Hayes*, 408 U.S. at 701.

16. *See, e.g., Costello v. United States*, 350 U.S. 359 (1956) (indictment may be premised exclusively upon hearsay evidence); *United States v. Calandra*, 414 U.S. 338 (1974) (witnesses subpoenaed to appear and testify before a grand jury may not refuse to answer questions derived from evidence gathered in violation of the Fourth Amendment's prohibition of unreasonable searches and seizures).

17. Peter Westen, *Confrontation and Compulsory Process: A Unified Theory of Evidence for Criminal Cases*, 91 HARVARD L. REV. 567 (1978).

18. *Hurtado v. California*, 110 U.S. 516 (1884).

19. *Id.* at 530.

20. *Id.*

21. *Hale v. Henkel*, 201 U.S. 43, 65–66 (1906).

22. 350 U.S. 359 (1956).

23. *Id.* at 360.

24. *Id.* at 362–63.

25. 218 U.S. 245 (1910).

26. *Costello v. United States*, 350 U.S. at 364–65 (Burton, J., concurring).

27. *Id.* at 364.

28. *Lawn v. United States*, 355 U.S. 339 (1958).

29. *Id.* at 345.

30. For an excellent summary and account of these events, *see* JAMES T. PATTERSON, GRAND EXPECTATIONS: THE UNITED STATES, 1945–74 (1996).

31. 408 U.S. 665 (1972).

32. *Id.* at 667–69.

33. *Id.* at 668–70.

34. *Id.* at 672–79.

35. *Id.* at 739–41.

36. *Id.* at 688.

37. *Id.* at 689–90.

38. *Id.* at 690, note 29.

39. *Id.* at 700–701.

40. *Id.* at 709–10 (Powell, J., concurring).

41. *United States v. Calandra*, 414 U.S. 338 (1974).

42. *Id.* at 341.

43. *Id.* at 354–55.

44. *Id.* at 343 (quoting from *Blair v. United States*, 250 U.S. 273, 282 (1919).

45. *Id.*

46. *Illinois* v. *Gates*, 462 U.S. 213 (1983).

47. *See* Leipold *supra* note 10 at 297.

48. *Id.* at 300–304.

49. *United States v. Calandra*, 414 U.S. at 349–50.

50. *Id.* at 351.

51. Some of the prominent exceptions to the Fourth Amendment's exclusionary rule are: the standing limitation, *see Rakas v. Illinois*, 439 U.S. 128 (1979); the independent source exception, *see Murray v. United States*, 487 U.S. 533 (1988); the inevitable discovery exception, *see Nix v. Williams*, 467 U.S. 431 (1984); the attenuation doctrine, *see Wong Sun v. United States*, 371 U.S. 471 (1963); the good-faith exception, *see United States v. Leon*, 468 U.S. 897

(1984); and the impeachment exception, *see United States v. Havens*, 446 U.S. 620 (1980).

52. 410 U.S. 1 (1973).

53. 410 U.S. 19 (1973).

54. *United States v. Dionisio*, 410 U.S. at 17.

55. *United States v. Mara*, 410 U.S. at 23 (Douglas, J., dissenting).

56. The Supreme Court in dictum has stated that a witness does not have a constitutional right to be represented by counsel when testifying before a grand jury. *In re Groban*, 352 U.S. 330, 333 (1957).

57. 25 Fed. Cas. 409, no. 14,786 (C.C.D.C. 1813), reprinted in Philip B. Kurland & Ralph Lerner eds., THE FOUNDERS' CONSTITUTION 275 (1987).

58. 142 U.S. 547 , 563 (1892).

59. *Id.*

60. *Miranda v. Arizona*, 384 U.S. 436 (1966). Of course, the famous *Miranda* opinion required that a suspect who faced custodial interrogation by the police had to be warned of his right to remain silent, that anything he said might be used against him, that he had the right to an attorney during the interrogation, and that if he could not afford one, an attorney would nevertheless be provided. These warnings were to safeguard the Fifth Amendment privilege against self-incrimination within the hostile environment engendered by custodial interrogation.

61. 425 U.S. 564 (1976).

62. This is the term employed by Justice Douglas in his dissenting opinion in *United States v. Mara*, 410 U.S. 19, 29 (1973) (Douglas, J., dissenting).

63. *United States v. Mandujano*, 425 U.S. at 566–67.

64. *Id.* at 567–68.

65. 378 U.S. 52, 55 (1964).

66. *United States v. Washington*, 431 U.S. 181, 191 (1977).

67. *Id.*

68. The *Mandujano* Court quotes from *Brown v. Walker*, 161 U.S. 591, 610 (1896) for this proposition. *United States v. Mandujano*, 425 U.S. at 574.

69. *Id.* at 574–75.

70. *Id.* at 579, quoting from *Miranda v. Arizona*, 384 U.S. at 461.

71. *Id.* at 580.

72. *Id.* at 581, citing *Kirby v. Illinois*, 406 U.S. 682 (1972).

73. In *Crane v. Kentucky*, 476 U.S. 683 (1986), the Supreme Court held that a suspect is free to question a confession's reliability at trial despite the fact that the court has found the confession to be voluntary and thereby admissible.

74. *United States v. Mara*, 410 U.S. at 44 (Marshall, J., dissenting).

75. *Michigan v. Tucker*, 417 U.S. 433, 441 (1974).

76. See *Michigan v. Mosley*, 423 U.S. 96 (1975) (right of a suspect who is subject to custodial interrogation to cut off questioning and remain silent

must be scrupulously honored); and *Edwards v. Arizona*, 451 U.S. 477 (1981) (once a suspect invokes the right not to be questioned without an attorney, the police must not initiate further contact or interrogation unless suspect initiates further communications or exchanges with the police).

77. *Doyle v. Ohio*, 426 U.S. 610 (1976).

78. *United States v. Mandujano*, 425 U.S. at 590 (Brennan, J., concurring).

79. *Id.* at 590–91.

80. *Id.* (quoting from *United States v. Monia*, 317 U.S. 424, 427 (1943).

81. *New Jersey v. Portash* 450 U.S. 450, 459 (1979).

82. *Id.*

83. Albert W. Alschuler, *A Peculiar Privilege in Historical Perspective*, in R. H. HEMHOLZ, et al. THE PRIVILEGE AGAINST SELF-INCRIMINATION: ITS ORIGINS AND DEVELOPMENT, 183 (1997).

84. *Kastigar v. United States*, 406 U.S. 441, 445 (1972).

85. *See* generally, JOHN HENRY WIGMORE, 8 WIGMORE ON EVIDENCE 2250 (1961).

86. *See, e.g., Counselman v. Hitchcock*, 142 U.S. 547 (1892); *Brown v. Walker*, 161 U.S. 591 (1896); *Ullman v. United States*, 350 U.S. 422 (1954).

87. *Kastigar v. United States*, 406 U.S. 441 (1972).

88. *Id.* at 453.

89. *Id.*

90. *Id.* at 442. The statute is codified at 18 U.S.C. Sections 6002–6003.

91. *Id.*

92. *Id.* at 443.

93. *Id.* at 446.

94. *Id.* at 453.

95. *Id.*

96. *Id.* at 458–59 (quoting from *Murphy v. Waterfront Comm'n*, 378 U.S. at 79).

97. As the Court stated in *Counselman v. Hitchcock*, 142 U.S. at 565, "a mere act of Congress cannot amend the constitution, even if it should thereon engraft such a proviso."

98. Alschuler, *supra* note 83 at 183; Alexander J. Menza, *Witness Immunity: Unconstitutional, Unfair, Unconscionable*, 9 SETON HALL CONST. L. J. 505, 516–19 (1999).

99. *Id.*

100. *Id.* at 193.

101. *Kastigar v. United States*, 406 U.S. at 469 (Marshall, J., dissenting).

102. John Gibeaut, *Indictment of a System*, 87 A.B.A. JOURNAL, 35 Jan 2001.

103. *Id.* at 36.

104. *Id.* at 40 (citing Bureau of Justice Statistics, U.S. Justice Department): twelve states and the District of Columbia require indictments for felony prosecutions, four states require indictments only for capital cases or those cases that carry a life sentence.

105. *United States v. Calandra*, 414 U.S. 338, 343 (1974).

106. Peter J. Henning, *Prosecutorial Misconduct in Grand Jury Investigations*, 51 S.C. L. REV., 1, 2 (1999).

107. *Id.*

108. *See, e.g., United States v. Mechanik*, 475 U.S. 66 (1984) (holding that a prosecutor's violations of Federal Rule of Criminal Procedure 6 are moot if a petit jury returns a guilty verdict); *Bank of Nova Scotia v. United States*, 487 U.S. 250 (1988) (holding that violations of the same rule do not warrant dismissal of the indictment unless the defendant can establish prejudice).

109. *United States v. Williams*, 504 U.S. 36 (1992).

110. Richard Ben-Veniste, *Comparisons Can Be Odious, Mr. Starr*, NAT'L L. J., 21 Dec. 1998.

111. JEFFREY TOOBIN, A VAST CONSPIRACY 282–83 (1999).

112. The Federal Rules of Evidence are not applicable to grand jury proceedings. FED. R. EVID, 1101 (d) (2). Consequently, the irrelevance of this line of questioning to the proceeding does not constrain the prosecutor.

113. *See* Leipold, *supra* note 10 at 261.

114. *In re : Sealed Case No. 99-3091*, 192 F. 3d 995 (D.C. Cir. 1999).

115. *Bank of Nova Scotia v. United States*, 487 U.S. 250, 259 (1988).

116. *Id.* at 260–61.

117. *Id.* at 261.

118. *Id.* at 254. The Court relied heavily on *United States v. Hasting*, 461 U.S. 499, 505–6 (holding that supervisory power ought not to be exercised to reverse a conviction if the error is harmless); and *United States v. Mechanik*, 475 U.S. 66 (1986). The *Nova Scotia* Court adopted the standard set forth in Justice O'Connor's concurring opinion in *Mechanik* that dismissal of the indictment is not warranted unless the violation "substantially influenced the decision to indict," or created great doubt that the decision to indict was not tainted by such violations. *Bank of Nova Scotia* 487 U.S. at 256 (citing *United States v. Mechanik*, 475 U.S. at 78 (O'Connor, J., concurring).

119. *Id.* at 263.

120. Henning, *supra* note 106 at 8.

121. 504 U.S. 36 (1992).

122. *Id.* at 53–55.

123. *Id.* at 47–50.

124. *Id.* at 49, citing to *United States v. Dionisio*, 410 U.S. 1, 16 (1973).

125. Justice Stevens makes this point in dissent. *Id.* at 62–63 (Stevens, J., dissenting).

126. *In re: Sealed Case No. 99-3091*, 192 F. 3d 995 (D.C. Cir., 1999).

127. *Id.* at 997 (quoting from relevant parts of the times article).

128. *Id.*

129. *Id.*

130. *Id.*

131. *Id.* at 997–98.

132. *Id.* at 1001.

133. *Id.* at 1001–5.

134. *Id.* at 1003–4.

135. *Id.* at 1005.

136. *Id.* at 1003–4. The OIC also regretted the disclosures, stating that they revealed "sensitive and confidential internal OIC information." *Id.* at 997.

137. Henning, *supra* note 106 at 47, citing *Bank of Nova Scotia v. United States*, 487 U.S. 250, 254–65; *United States v. Washington*, 431 U.S. 181, 185–88 (1976); *United States v. Dionisio*, 410 U.S. 1, 1–18.

138. Pub. L. No. 10-119, Sec. 617, 111 Stat. 2440, 2519 (1997) (to be codified at 18 U.S.C. Sec. 3006 A).

139. Pub. L. No. 105-277, Sec. 801 (a), 112 Stat. 2681 (1998) (to be codified at 28 U.S.C. Sec. 530 B).

140. *See* 143 CONG. REC. H7791 (statement of Rep. Hyde).

141. Bill Moushey, *Murtha Seeking Prosecutor Limits*, PITTS. POST-GAZETTE, Feb. 3, 1999, at A1. This was the statement attributed to Representative Murtha in the wake of Representative McDade's acquittal on bribery and RICO charges.

CHAPTER 5

DOUBLE JEOPARDY: HAVE WE EVER KNOWN WHAT IT MEANS?

INTRODUCTION

Nor shall any person be subject for the same offense to be twice put in jeopardy of life or limb.

The "deceptively" simple language of the double jeopardy clause has generated reams of judicial and academic debate about its meaning and scope. As we have seen, the history of double jeopardy is a tangled one, riddled with ambiguity and uneven application. As courts and scholars have struggled to make sense of it, the ban on double jeopardy has seemed to bedevil them, leading the Supreme Court to describe its case law as "a veritable Sargasso Sea which could not fail to challenge the most intrepid judicial navigator."[1] Attempting to disentangle this doctrinal mess, legal scholars have fashioned a variety of theories designed to render the clause intelligible. Unfortunately, the academics have failed in their mission to make sense of the double jeopardy principle. Many hypotheses have emerged, without a single one providing a more convincing answer than the other. Some scholars find the answer to the double jeopardy riddle by relying on the concept of verdict finality;[2] others have focused on the fundamental right of juries to nullify the law;[3] one has emphasized the plain language and meaning of the double jeopardy clause.[4] None of these approaches are satisfying for a simple reason: one cannot disarm an octopus; it is logically and practically impossible to do so.

In their valiant efforts to achieve the impossible, jurists and scholars cannot be faulted for their quixotic behavior. After all, by its very nature the law performs the functions of categorizing and prescribing social policy. The problem with double jeopardy law is that neither its history nor its development yields much consensus on its central meaning and scope. From its genesis, therefore, the principle behind double jeopardy has been plagued by inconsistency and ambiguity. Expressing the fundamental value that the government ought not to oppress a citizen by exposing him or her to multiple prosecutions for the "same offense," double jeopardy affirms the premium that the American experiment placed on checking governmental overreaching. Conceptually linked to its sister clauses, the double jeopardy clause of the Fifth Amendment states that once a citizen fully confronts the awesome power wielded by the state, he or she ought to enjoy the benefit of repose. It is puzzling, therefore, to discern the reasons that a clear maxim has become such a tangled web. The answer lies in the rich yet perplexing history of double jeopardy as well as in the complex development of criminal law in America. Contrary to the framework one scholar has developed, double jeopardy law has never been "made simple."[5]

Complexity rather than simplicity governs the double jeopardy ban. It is within this framework that this exercise will attempt to navigate the otherwise impenetrable "Sargasso Sea." Marked by abstruseness and doctrinal inconsistency, the case law confounds rather than illuminates. Similarly, as we have seen, the history is largely "unfathomable." Linked by confusion, the old and the new double jeopardy have managed to exasperate not only judiciary but legal scholars. In a procrustean venture to provide order to this chaos, academics have fashioned, "elegant" and "simple" theories of double jeopardy among others. I am not as intrepid as my colleagues in the academy. Perhaps my choice of words at the outset of this paragraph is ironic: one cannot navigate an unnavigable sea. Instead, what I propose to do is touch upon certain areas of double jeopardy that expose its inscrutable nature. That is the best that one can do. Order cannot be imposed upon analytical chaos.

How, then, shall we proceed to tackle the impossible? The discerning reader needs a road map, however stilted or skewed it may be. Returning to my theme, I will begin with the conflict in case law from the beginning of Anglo-American double jeopardy jurisprudence. Then I will compare the past with the present in order to demonstrate just how much one resembles the other. Let me be clear from the beginning: this is not a comprehensive review of double jeopardy jurisprudence. Others have already accomplished that task, with various degrees of success. Rather, I will attempt to chart the areas that underlie the complexity of the double jeopardy precept, with the purpose of emphasizing that courts and scholars do not have a mutually exclusive "correct" version of what double jeopardy law should look like.

From this perspective, I will emphasize the overriding values of the double jeopardy clause: verdict finality and freedom from government oppression. The two concepts are inextricably intertwined. How they are to be implemented is another matter. In the various contexts in which they are applied, there are three specific areas: mistrials, the starting and ending points for jeopardy, and the definition of what constitutes the "same offense." These are not new questions; they have engaged American courts since the nineteenth century. Nevertheless, the issues have been compounded by the development of new criminal codes that include a host of new offenses, designed chiefly to combat newly emerging white-collar crimes. Furthermore, the ability of the government to charge a defendant with multiple crimes stemming from a single criminal transaction is the natural concomitant of these expansive criminal codes.

In keeping with my primary thesis, I will then return to the links between double jeopardy and the other two clauses relating to the criminal process in the Fifth Amendment. Let us begin our audacious journey.

BACK TO THE FUTURE: MISTRIALS, VERDICT FINALITY, AND GOVERNMENTAL NEGLIGENCE

Justice Frankfurter captured the essence of the bar on double jeopardy when he declared, "Since the prohibition in the Constitution against double jeopardy is derived from history, its significance and scope must be determined, 'not simply by taking the words and a dictionary, but by considering [its] . . . origin and the line of [its] growth.'"[6] We have examined the uncertain history and origin of the double jeopardy principle. The interpretation of the concept and the reach of the constitutional amendment deserve further scrutiny. The pleas of *autrefois acquit* and *autrefois convict* express the fundamental premise that once acquitted or convicted, a criminal defendant should not have to confront the government again in a prosecution for the same offense. This seems to be simple common sense. The seminal case in Anglo-American double jeopardy history belies such simplicity.

In *Vaux's Case*,[7] the defendant, Vaux, had been indicted for poisoning Nicholas Ridley and was acquitted through a special verdict because the indictment was fatally defective for failure to state a crime. He was retried, convicted, and executed. Let us take the words of double jeopardy literally: no one should be tried twice for the same offense. Not only was Vaux retried and convicted for the same offense for which he had been acquitted, he was then put to death! Yet the court held that double jeopardy did not apply to Vaux's predicament. The legal sleight of hand employed by the court in reaching this conclusion was that the accused "was never in jeopardy when charged with an act that was not an offense according to the law." In short, because the defective indictment did not allege a crime, the defendant was never in "jeopardy" for a crime.

Should it have mattered that Vaux's counsel took advantage of the deficiency in the indictment in order to upset the result? Let us compare and contrast *Vaux's Case*, decided by the English courts in the late sixteenth century, with *People v. Barrett*,[8] a New York opinion of the early nineteenth century. In *Barrett* the defendants were acquitted in their first trial. They sought to invoke the plea of *autrefois acquit* to bar a second trial for the same offenses. The prosecution alleged that double jeopardy did not preclude a second trial because the first trial was rendered void because the indictment was deficient because it did not establish venue. The New York appellate court split 3–2 in holding that the defendants could be retried. The three judges who formed the majority relied upon *Vaux's Case* to bolster their rationale that a person is not in jeopardy, regardless of having been tried for the same offense, if the indictment was invalid in failing to set forth a material element of the offense—in this situation, the venue in which the crime was committed.

The two judges in the minority distinguished *Vaux* from *Barrett* on both procedural and policy bases. Justice Tompkins emphasized Vaux's counsel taking "advantage of an insufficient finding in the special verdict." By contrast, *Barrett*'s counsel did not object to the sufficiency of the indictment. In addition, Tompkins pointed to the "acquittal by general verdict" in *Barrett* versus the special verdict, which counsel objected to in *Vaux's Case*. This was critical to another dissenter in *Barrett*, Justice Livingston. He distinguished *Vaux*, in which "the jury had *not acquitted*, nor given *any opinion* on his guilt, but had referred the matter to the court," with the general verdict of acquittal entered by the jury in *Barrett*. To the dissenters, these two crucial differences justified a result different from the one issued in *Vaux's Case*. In effect, they contended that double jeopardy prohibited a retrial in *Barrett*.

More important than the procedural ground was the policy rationale underlying the dissenters' quarrel with the majority opinion. Justices Tompkins and Livingston both believed that the double jeopardy safeguard would be nullified if a prosecutor could employ his or her own negligence as a means of retrying the defendant "*ad infinitum.*" Indeed, Livingston surmised that hundreds festering in prison had been convicted upon defective indictments. Conversely, if an acquittal on a defective indictment occurred, and the prosecutor was "dissatisfied" with the outcome, all he had to do was "to tell the court that his own indictment was good for nothing; that it has *no venue*, or is deficient in other particulars."[9] In the hands of an unscrupulous prosecutor, such a doctrine could foster substantial injustice. To put it simply, the defendant would eventually be convicted or at least "cruelly harassed by such a course of proceeding."

The distinction between *Vaux* and *Barrett* that the dissent in *Barrett* relied upon seems logical and loyal to the values furthered by the ban on double jeopardy. One set of defendants (Barrett) had gone to trial, had not objected to the indictment, and had been acquitted by a jury of their peers. The other defendant (Vaux) had stopped the proceedings short of a verdict by his objection to the validity of the indictment. What if, however, the *Barrett* defendants had been convicted? Presumably they would have the benefit of a second trial if they sought to reverse the conviction, because it was based on a defective indictment. In effect, the defendants would be in a win-win situation regardless of the verdict. If the jury acquitted, double jeopardy would bar a retrial. If the jury convicted, they would have a second chance at a different verdict by upsetting the ruling below due to a legal defect. Perhaps that was the implicit policy rationale guiding the majority of justices in *Barrett*.

On the other side of the ledger, should the government be insulated from its negligence in framing the indictment? It is safe to assume that most prosecutors would not intentionally draft a defective indictment as a safety valve in case the jury acquits the defendant. It works the other way also: a prosecutor would not want to toil in vain, securing a conviction only to have the verdict be overturned because of a defective indictment. If the defense knowingly fails to object to an invalid indictment, should the defendant get the benefit of an acquittal by a jury? Presumably, if a jury acquits on the merits, finding reasonable

doubt as to guilt, why shouldn't the defendant win? Double jeopardy
states that once a defendant confronts the awesome power of the government through a formal charge and trial, he or she should not be
prosecuted or punished again. *Not guilty* means what it says and says
what it means, regardless of the procedural edifices constructed by the
law. It is not the province of the defendant to scrutinize the indictment
for errors; it is the solemn responsibility of the prosecutor to perform
that function. In sum, the prosecutor should not profit from personal
negligence and should certainly not be able to "take advantage of his
own wrong" by intentionally drafting a defective indictment.[10]

Now let us "fast forward" from 1806 to 1973. The U.S. Supreme
Court is set to decide *Illinois v. Somerville*,[11] and the issue is whether
the trial court properly granted the prosecution's motion for a mistrial when the prosecutor discovered, after the jury had been empaneled and sworn in, that the indictment was fatally deficient because it
failed to allege a material element of the crime.[12] The issue in the case
differs from the questions presented in both *Vaux's Case* and *Barrett*
in two respects: in *Barrett* the jury rendered a verdict on the merits;
in *Vaux*, although the jury never reached a verdict, the case was truncated upon a defense request because the indictment was defective. In
Somerville, the trial court declared a mistrial upon the state's motion
and over the defendant's objection. This dilemma raises a fundamental question: in what circumstances, if any, is a court entitled to thwart
a criminal defendant's right to determine his fate through a jury verdict
on the merits?

The seminal case of *United States v. Perez*,[13] was decided by Justice
Story in 1824. When the jury was deadlocked and unable to reach a
verdict, the trial court dismissed the jury without either the defendant's
or the government's consent. The defendant, charged with a capital
offense, objected to a second trial on double jeopardy grounds. Justice
Story rejected the argument, stressing the lack of a verdict and society's
need for a determination of the defendant's guilt. Investing trial courts
with broad discretion in these matters, Story stated that a trial court
could declare a mistrial when "there is a manifest necessity for the act,
or the ends of public justice would otherwise be defeated."[14] This quote
would be transformed into a virtual mantra, repeated by courts in
search of a principled justification for application or rejection of double
jeopardy challenges. More important, the case would furnish a balancing vehicle against which the courts could weigh the defendant's interest in finality and society's stake in determining the defendant's guilt.

How should *Somerville* have been decided, when these competing interests are weighed? A trial on the merits would have been fail-safe for the defendant, with the verdict subject to reversal because of a defective indictment. If the defendant had been acquitted, however, the *Barrett* scenario would have been duplicated, leaving the Supreme Court with the last word on the matter. Instead, the trial was dissolved, due to "manifest necessity" by the trial court, upon the government's request. Who should bear the burden of the mistake by the prosecutor? What if the judge had erred and improvidently declared a mistrial? Just what constitutes "manifest necessity," sufficient to end the trial and potentially start the wheels of the justice carriage once more?

Let us begin with the easy case—that is, the situation in *Perez* in which a jury fails to reach a verdict. No one is at fault. The prosecution, defense, and trial court have presumably labored to arrive at the quintessential aim of the criminal process: a verdict, usually by a jury, occasionally by a judge if a defendant charged with a felony has chosen to waive the right to a jury trial. The "ends of public justice" are foiled in this circumstance, because the system has failed to determine whether the defendant is legally blameworthy for the behavior. Indeed, even the defendant has a stake in being either condemned or legally absolved by the community of the opprobrium associated with a criminal accusation. To the extent that a formal pronouncement has not been declared, society's interest in assessing the defendant's societal wrong has been vitiated.

Beyond this circumstance, the balancing act becomes more delicate. In the rare case in which a court discovers, after the trial has begun, that a juror is biased[15] or disqualified,[16] it is also logical that a mistrial is the only means of averting a potential miscarriage of justice. More difficult cases arise in which the judge or prosecutor—negligently, not intentially—thwarts the defendant's and, for that matter, society's, interest in the adjudication of the case. We have seen how the *Barrett* court resolved this issue in the early part of the nineteenth century. Now let us explore the rationale employed by the U.S. Supreme Court in the latter part of the twentieth century.

Speaking for a bare majority of the Court in *Somerville*, Justice Rehnquist rejected the defendant's argument that double jeopardy precluded a retrial of his case. In the last sentence of his opinion, Rehnquist noted that "the defendant's interest in proceeding to verdict is outweighed by the competing and equally legitimate demand for public justice."[17] In arriving at this conclusion, Justice Rehnquist had to explore a series of cases that could have dictated an opposite result. His trek through this veritable legal quicksand is both illuminating and obscure. It is illuminating in its clever use of *Perez*'s broad language to accord the trial judge the benefit of the doubt in his decision to declare a mistrial. It is obscure because it fails to provide convincing reasons for rejecting Somerville's claims and because it does not furnish even an ill-defined road map for trial courts that are confronting the question of whether to declare a mistrial due to "manifest necessity."

Quoting extensively from *Perez*, Justice Rehnquist began the opinion by noting that Justice Story eschewed "mechanical formulas" in determining when manifest necessity justified a mistrial. He stressed the "broad discretion" afforded the trial court by Justice Story's pithy opinion in *Perez*.[18] Perhaps Justice Rehnquist relied upon *Perez*'s unedifying formula because it would assist him in navigating the bumpy legal terrain that confronted him. Specifically, Justice Rehnquist cited three cases that tilted in Somerville's favor. The oldest case, *Ball v. United States*,[19] did not pose a daunting obstacle. The defendant was indicted on a defective indictment, proceeded to trial, and was acquitted. The Court held that when a defendant has been convicted or acquitted by a jury he is placed in jeopardy and may not be retried.[20] It was not difficult for Justice Rehnquist to distinguish *Ball* from *Somerville*: Ball had gone through the trial and submitted his fate to a jury; Somerville, even though he may have desired to proceed to a verdict, was prevented from doing so when the judge aborted the proceedings before the jury heard a shred of evidence.[21] In *Ball*, moreover, the Supreme Court adopted the dissent's position in *Barrett*: once a defendant subjects himself to a trial and fails to object to an otherwise invalid indictment, if he is acquitted the government cannot put him through another trial.

More difficult than *Ball* for Rehnquist were two recent precedents that seemed to place the burden on the government when either the prosecutor or the trial court erred in declaring a mistrial without the defendant's consent. In *United States v. Jorn*,[22] the judge opted to declare a mistrial when a witness, who was not represented by counsel, faced potential incrimination by taking the stand and testifying. The judge also discovered that there were other similarly situated witnesses who were to take the stand. Hastily pronouncing a mistrial so that the witnesses could receive counsel's advice, the trial court prevented the defendant from resolving his fate through a jury verdict.[23] This abrupt behavior frustrated not only society's stake in guilt determination but also the defendant's interest "of being able, once and for all, to conclude his confrontation with society through the verdict of a tribunal he might believe to be favorably disposed to his fate."[24]

In deference to Justice Rehnquist, I should emphasize that Justice Harlan in *Jorn* also foreswore the resort to mistrial rules "based on categories of circumstances" because of the "elusive nature of the problem."[25] Implicitly, however, Justice Harlan appeared to adopt a guideline that favored the defendant's interest in finality when either the prosecution or the trial court negligently triggers a mistrial. Thus, without prosecutorial or judicial "overreaching," but despite judicial or governmental error, the defendant may not raise the double jeopardy ban in moving for a mistrial. Although he quoted from the nebulous language of *Perez*, Justice Harlan implied that the defendant should prevail under most circumstances when a trial is aborted due to judicial and prosecutorial negligence.[26]

Indeed, prosecutorial negligence was the key issue in *Downum v. United States*,[27] a case remarkably similar to *Somerville*. After the jury had been empaneled and sworn in, the prosecutor in *Downum* sought a continuance because a critical witness for two of the six charges against the defendant was missing. Although the prosecution knew that the witness had not been found and had not been served with a subpoena, it allowed the impaneling of the jury. The trial judge declared a mistrial over the defendant's objection, and the Supreme Court held that a retrial violated the ban on double jeopardy because the mistrial declaration was not justified by manifest necessity.[28] How would Justice Rehnquist distinguish *Downum* from *Somerville*? In both cases, the prosecutor's mistakes had forced him into the untenable position of requesting the judge to declare a mistrial. *Downum* presented an even bigger obstacle than *Jorn* because the judge, not the prosecutor, was to blame for aborting the trial.

Applying the fuzzy criterion set forth in *Perez*, Justice Rehnquist concluded that the trial judge had used his discretion providently in declaring a mistrial in *Somerville*.[29] He distinguished *Downum* on two related grounds. First, the flawed indictment would preclude a just resolution of the case, as it would negate either a fair conviction or an acquittal. Second, and unlike *Downum*, a mistrial declaration in these circumstances did not lend itself to prosecutorial "manipulation," thereby affording the prosecution a strategic advantage by giving the state an opportunity to "strengthen" its case.[30] In effect, Justice Rehnquist artfully avoided the obvious: the prosecution had requested a mistrial in both cases owing to either its negligence or, at worst in

Downum, its deliberate deception of the trial court by announcing that it was prepared to proceed with its case.

The paramount consideration in these cases was the accommodation of the two competing bases of the law of double jeopardy: the defendant's stake in resolving "his confrontation with society through a verdict of tribunal" that might be disposed to acquit him,[31] and society's interest in guilt determination, which by necessity does not "assure a defendant a single proceeding free from harmful governmental or judicial error."[32] More than any other facet of double jeopardy law, the mistrial area joins the "underlying idea" of this simple yet puzzling constitutional safeguard. In what is probably the most quoted passage expressing this ideal, Justice Black stated:

The underlying idea, one that is deeply ingrained in at least the Anglo-American system of jurisprudence, is that the State with all of its resources and power should not be allowed to make repeated attempts to convict an individual for an alleged offense, thereby subjecting him to embarrassment, expense and ordeal and compelling him to live in the continuing state of anxiety and insecurity as well as enhancing the possibility that even though innocent he may be found guilty.[33]

It is clear that human nature prevents an error-free trial in which the defendant's right to a fair trial will not be impaired. When an error occurs, the defendant has the option of requesting a mistrial to repair the damage. If a mistrial is not granted, the defendant might seek to upset a guilty verdict by pointing to either the prosecutor's or the judge's errors or misdeeds. Such a device protects the defendant from either an overzealous prosecutor or an incompetent or biased judge. In these circumstances, of course, the defendant is seeking to either abort the trial or reverse the verdict as a means of protecting the right to, if not a perfect trial, at least a fair trial. The notion that brings these concepts together is that the defendant has a right to seek a just resolution of his or her guilt on the merits, free from either prosecutorial or judicial error, both of which impinge on such an outcome.

Distinct from this precept is the situation posed by *Somerville*, *Downum*, or *Jorn*. However different the facts of those cases may be, they have one thing in common: prosecutorial or judicial error in aborting a trial that the defendant did not seek to terminate. Presumably, the defendant in these cases wanted to end his "confrontation with society." In *Jorn*, the defendant wanted to conclude the trial, an interest distinct from the trial court's misplaced oversolicitude for the self-incrimination rights of several witnesses. *Downum* was willing to proceed with the trial on the four counts on which the prosecution was not missing any critical witnesses; the defendant merely sought a dismissal of the two counts in which the prosecutor *was* missing the crucial witness. Finally, *Somerville*, as we have seen, presents a more difficult issue in that the defendant could obtain either an acquittal or an automatic reversal based on the defective indictment. Nevertheless, as the Court has observed, the essential interest of the defendant in having his fate resolved by a verdict is predicated on the belief that the outcome will be in his favor.[34] Furthermore, the defendant in a *Somerville* scenario still potentially risks the "anxiety, expense, and ordeal" of a second prosecution if the jury convicts upon the defective indictment in the first trial.

Why should the defendant bear the burden of egregious legal errors by the prosecutor or the judge when he is ready to end his "ordeal" in the first trial? *Downum* and *Jorn* suggest that he should not; *Somerville* suggest that he must pay the price. Are Justice Rehnquist's distinctions in *Somerville* compelling? I think not. When a defendant decides to face a jury of his peers, it signifies a monumental decision in our criminal justice system. After all, the vast majority of cases in the process are resolved through plea bargaining. It is not a commonplace occurrence, therefore, to confront the jury and the uncertainties and vagaries associated with that process. It is a solemn occasion, one that ought to be treated with respect and dignity by two of the players responsible for upholding the ideal of justice: the prosecutor and the judge. Both the litigants and the judge must be held to "standards of responsible professional conduct in the clash of an adversary criminal process."[35] To place the onus on the defendant "to compensate for prosecutorial [or judicial] mistake"[36] appears unseemly in an adversarial system of adjudication.

Retreating from its own late-nineteenth-century jurisprudence, the Court in *Somerville* placed double jeopardy law regarding mistrials back into a permanent state of confusion. It is ironic that Justice White's dissent reminded the *Somerville* majority of language the Court employed in *United States v. Ball*, decided in 1896.[37] Castigating the negligence of the prosecutor, the *Ball* Court noted, "This case . . . presents the novel and unheard of spectacle of a public officer, whose business it was to frame a correct bill, openly alleging his own inaccuracy or neglect, as a reason for a second trial. . . . If this practice is tolerated, when are trials of the accused to end?"[38] Giving the trial court wide latitude by relying on the ambiguous language of *Perez*, the *Somerville*

Court sowed doubt and fostered ambivalence in an area that needed some clarity.

Is the "balancing test" the Court crafted useful to trial judges who must decide during a heated trial battle whether to declare a mistrial? Justice Marshall answered that question eloquently when he observed that the test is based on elements "stated on such a high level of abstraction as to give judges virtually no guidance at all in deciding subsequent cases."[39] Perhaps we should not place the blame squarely on Justice Rehnquist for failing to provide trial judges with a modicum of guidance in how to navigate the "Sargasso Sea" of double jeopardy law. Like a pendulum without a center of gravity, the Court's schizophrenic nature in its interpretation of the double jeopardy clause of the Fifth Amendment is nonetheless true to its history and development. In fact, the doctrinal inconsistency evident in *Downum*, *Jorn*, and *Somerville* reminds us of the split opinion of the early nineteenth century reflected in the *Barrett* case. Shrouded in ambiguity from its genesis, the double jeopardy clause, as seen through the lens of the mistrial doctrine, seems destined to remain obscure, no matter how hard the Supreme Court labors to elucidate its meaning and scope.

Lest we overstate the ambiguity attending the mistrial segment of double jeopardy law, it is important to remember the clear part. At least we know that deadlocked juries, biased jurors, and other matters triggering a mistrial outside the province of the litigants and the trial court will not bar a second prosecution. If the defendant seeks to upset the verdict, moreover, unless there is deliberate misconduct by the prosecutor designed to induce a mistrial, he implicitly waives his double jeopardy claim.[40] Here we have a doctrine that exposes the inconsistency that plagues double jeopardy law. In an attempt to define the circumstances that justify a double jeopardy ban when the defendant seeks a mistrial, Justice Rehnquist sought a clear standard rather than a flexible one. Why would the Court prefer a loose criterion in the *Somerville-Jorn* context, but not in a situation in which the defendant is compelled to seek a mistrial because the prosecutor substantially reduces, if not eliminates, his chances of securing an acquittal?

Consider the case of *Oregon v. Kennedy*. A man is on trial for the theft of an oriental rug. The defendant's counsel successfully impeaches the credibility of the state's leading expert witness regarding the value of the rug by getting the witness to acknowledge that he had previously filed a criminal complaint against the defendant. Eventually, the prosecutor sought on redirect to rehabilitate the expert witness by attempting to expose why he filed a criminal complaint against the defendant. Frustrated by a series of objections to this line of questioning, the prosecutor committed a classic overkill error: he asked the witness the question whether he had not done business with the defendant "because he is a crook."[41] Of course, the defendant requested a mistrial, which the trial court immediately granted.[42]

Let us pause for a while and ponder those simple facts. In the middle of the prosecution's case, perhaps a young prosecutor lost his nerve and injected a flagrantly prejudicial remark into the proceedings. At best, the prosecutor was grossly negligent by adverting to the defendant's character. Any law student who has suffered through the counterintuitive rules of evidence knows that in a criminal trial, a prosecutor may not bring up the defendant's character unless it is to establish a relevant issue aside from the defendant's propensity to act in accordance with that character trait.[43] Nothing could be more prejudicial to the defendant charged with theft than a reference to his being a "crook." If the prosecutor was not grossly negligent, then he was incompetent: that is, we must assume that he was unaware of a fundamental rule of evidentiary law or that he forgot it in the heat of battle. The critical double jeopardy question, therefore, is whether a defendant who is deprived of the right to have "his guilt or innocence decided in one proceeding"[44] ought to face a second trial because of a prosecutor's gross negligence or incompetence. Framed in this fashion, then, the issue in *Kennedy* is not much different from the question the Court faced in *Somerville* and *Downum*, even though the distinction remains between the cases because the defendant moves for a mistrial in *Kennedy*.

Indeed, the fundamental question posed by *Kennedy* underlines the contrasting objectives of the double jeopardy ban: the defendant's interest in finality and freedom from governmental oppression versus "society's interest in affording the prosecutor one full and fair opportunity to present his evidence to the jury."[45] Should the prosecutor have a second opportunity to present his case to the jury when he could have avoided it by adhering to the fundamental rules of the law? Notice that in *Kennedy* the prosecutor got a chance to start the trial but aborted it through either his gross negligence or incompetence. By contrast, the prosecutors in both *Downum* and *Somerville* had barely gotten the trial started when they realized that their negligence precluded any further progress. The essential issue remains: Who should bear the burden for the prosecutor's mistakes?

Consistently, Justice Rehnquist answers the question in *Kennedy* in the same way he deals with it in *Somerville*: the defendant should suffer the prosecutor's negligence or incompetence unless he can establish that the prosecutor intentionally provoked a mistrial in order to gain a tactical advantage. Rejecting the "fuzzy" criterion employed by the lower court, Justice Rehnquist instead opts for the "clearer" standard. In fact, the standard the lower court employed, that the prosecutor engaged in "overreaching," was derived from the Court's precedent in *Jorn*.[46] Rather than adhering to this nebulous criterion, Justice Rehnquist lauds the advantages of a firmer standard, emphasizing the "desirability of an easily applied principle" when contrasted with the "broader" and "somewhat amorphous" standard applied by the lower court.[47]

The remarkable transformation in the Court's rationale from *Somerville* to *Kennedy* might prompt cynicism from a judicial skeptic. Pronouncing an almost insuperable barrier for the defendant to overcome, Justice Rehnquist requires the defendant to establish that the prosecutor, through his misconduct, "intended to 'goad' the defendant into moving for a mistrial."[48] It is instructive to observe that the prosecutor in *Kennedy* "testified" that he did not intend to cause a mistrial.[49] What sane prosecutor would admit to such intent? How would the defendant establish that a prosecutor intended to provoke a mistrial? Here is where even Justice Rehnquist's standard promises more than it delivers. How would an appellate court gauge whether the trial was not going well for the prosecutor so that he viewed a mistrial as his only hope? Although he acknowledges that his allegedly clearer standard is preferable, Justice Rehnquist concedes that it is "not entirely free from practical difficulties."[50] This justification is a far cry from the doctrine the Court espoused in the "manifest necessity" cases beginning with *United States v. Perez*, in which it "repeatedly . . . shunned inflexible standards."[51]

Is there a common thread tying the Court's shifting and "amorphous" jurisprudence in this area? Perhaps there is, even at the cost of attempting to steer through the unnavigable waters of a turbulent jurisprudential sea. It seems as if the Court is reluctant to penalize the government for egregious prosecutorial errors, even at the cost of burdening the defendant's interest in finality. At one end of the spectrum, we have cases like *Somerville* in which the prosecutor drops the ball when the players are ready to go but before the first pitch is thrown; and at the other end of the spectrum we have *Kennedy*, in which the prosecutor starts the game and in the heat of the competition throws at the hitters because he momentarily forgot about the fundamental ethics of the game. This raises the fundamental question: Should the prosecution "forfeit" the game or should it get another opportunity to clean up its act and perhaps win the game? The obvious answer for the Court is that, without proof of malicious intent, the prosecutor should always receive another chance to play without any penalties for his errors.

Viewing the mistrial doctrine from the standpoint of the defendant's stake in finality and freedom from oppression, the Court's murky double jeopardy waters do not bode well for either of those interests. The government always has the advantage of starting all over again, whereas the defendant must suffer prosecutorial errors; in turn, society's concern for adjudication of guilt or innocence takes precedence over the defendant's interest in "ending his confrontation" with the government. Justice Black's famous *Green* dicta expressing the fundamental safeguards flowing from the double jeopardy clause emerges in bold relief. Does the Court's mistrial jurisprudence "[compel] the defendant to live in a continuing state of anxiety and insecurity, as well as [enhance] the possibility that even though innocent he may be found guilty"?[52]

It is difficult to answer this question definitively, reflecting the unsettled nature of the deceptively simple double jeopardy clause. From the defendant's perspective, he continues to experience "anxiety and insecurity" when a mistrial is declared, whether he seeks the mistrial because he is left with little choice or whether he objects to it because he wants to end his brush with society. The inescapable fact remains: he must confront the prosecutor and the jury once more and ponder whether another prosecutorial mistake will compel yet another trial. At best, the defendant must bear the vagaries of prosecutorial negligence or incompetence; at worst, if he cannot establish government intent, he must bear the cost of prosecutorial oppression. Either way, the defendant does not have many remedies at his disposal to avoid a second trial after a mistrial prompted by the government's mistakes, however egregious such errors may be. The Court's mistrial jurisprudence, in short, resembles the mistrial jurisprudence that prevailed in the nineteenth century. History has been perdurable in the double jeopardy area; the judiciary has acknowledged as much.

THE SCHOLARS WEIGH IN: DO THEY
PROVIDE THE ANSWERS?

Since the judiciary seems to have conceded the muddled state of its double jeopardy doctrine, it is natural that the legal academy has attempted to fill the void. Whether the academy's extraordinary effort to provide a framework where none exists has succeeded is another matter. Let me start by commending an array of scholars who have been "intrepid" enough to set sail in the so-called Sargasso Sea. Indeed, the scholarship in this sphere of constitutional criminal procedure is perhaps the most creative in what has become, to use my own term, an otherwise "sterile" enterprise. My view differs from that of my distinguished colleagues because I believe that neither history nor doctrine yields much coherence in this confusing area. One can scoff at my indeterminacy in this field by accusing me of shirking my academic responsibility to provide order where chaos might seem to dominate. The unique history and development of the double jeopardy clause, however, leads me to conclude that my colleagues have succeeded in their endeavor to create, as Gordon Wood observers, "necessary fiction."[53] Paradoxically, the Court has been more faithful to the historical record than the academy has in its attempts to provide a coherent framework. Even those who purport to adhere to the language of double jeopardy ignore the historical backdrop.

Let us begin by exploring the way in which the academy has sought to impose order in a seemingly chaotic field. The most prominent and prolific scholar in the field of double jeopardy law is George Thomas III. His seminal work attempts to provide an "elegant" theory of the otherwise jumbled double jeopardy law.[54] The elegance stems from Thomas's primary thesis, which posits that "finality is the fundamental value of the double jeopardy clause."[55] It is difficult to quarrel with this conclusion, given that the language embodied in the clause seems to have finality as its ultimate aim. Not to be tried "twice for the same offense" implies that the defendant is entitled to an end point in the criminal justice process. The problem lies in the difficulty of fitting the Court's meandering jurisprudence into this neat model. Although my brief summary and critique may not capture Thomas's richly nuanced argument, I will nevertheless attempt to compare and contrast it with my "nihilistic"[56] thesis.

Thomas distinguishes his hypothesis from two other double jeopardy theories: the "traditional" and "government oppression" theses.[57] Grounding his theory upon the notion of "verdict finality," Thomas argues that in the "paradigm case," the government may not appeal an acquittal or reprosecute the defendant for the same offense after he has been convicted.[58] By contrast, he critiques the traditional approach, which is aptly summed up in *North Carolina v. Pearce.* The Supreme Court repeats the orthodox formulation as it were a ritualistic incantation. The famous phrase goes as follows: double jeopardy "protects against a second reprosecution for the same offense after an acquittal; it protects against a second prosecution for the same offense after conviction. And it protects against multiple punishments for the same offense."[59] For Professor Thomas, the problem with this theory is that it is underinclusive as well as misleading. It is underinclusive because it fails to account for the "most litigated" area of double jeopardy law, mistrials; it is misleading because, for example, it implies that the term "same offense" has a "self-defining quality."[60]

Thomas takes greater issue with the "Rehnquist-O'Connor" government oppression theory. The gist of that thesis is that government oppression rather than verdict finality is the triggering event for double jeopardy protection.[61] One might be tempted to ask at this juncture: Isn't the protection from governmental oppression the chief evil against which the double jeopardy clause guards? Thomas acknowledges that "at a high level of abstraction" the government oppression theory is correct in identifying that wrong, reflected in persecuting individuals through "multiple use" of the criminal process, as the fundamental goal of the double jeopardy clause.[62] How does this theory differ from Thomas's "elegant" verdict finality thesis? Quite simply, Thomas maintains that the government oppression theory confuses "cause" with "effect." For Thomas, government oppression is not relevant to double jeopardy analysis in the sense that the "effect of the double jeopardy clause is to forbid an entire category of oppressive government conduct (relitigating settled verdicts)."[63] In short, it is the "effect" that matters, not the cause of the effect.

This is, I must admit, a wonderful rhetorical flourish. Thomas differentiates his theory from the government oppression thesis based on what amounts to a semantic distinction. Lest the reader derive a skewed conclusion from my critique, I do not cast doubt upon Thomas's "elegant" theory because it might rest on a rhetorical foundation. Indeed, as L. H. La Rue has demonstrated, constitutional law is meant to persuade, and, as such, it is primarily fiction—not in a pejorative sense, but rather in a positive vein.[64] I believe, however, that it is impossible to disentangle the two concepts; both verdict finality and government oppression are inextricably connected. From an explanatory perspective, Thomas's thesis may be "elegant" and persuasive; from a teleological viewpoint, however, it fails to convince. Indeed, Thomas concedes that the government oppression does explain the "preverdict" cases but does not account for the "verdict finality core" of double jeopardy, which exists regardless of government oppression.[65] In the final analysis, however, isn't verdict finality meant to prevent government overreaching? Of course it is! This is my point: you cannot segregate two concepts that lie at the heart of double jeopardy protection.

At a more germane level, Thomas's theory attempts to provide an "elegant" framework for an otherwise jumbled and incoherent jurisprudence. Acknowledging that double jeopardy is not a "monolithic entity" and that it must accommodate conflicting applications,[66] he also recognizes that "no adequate statement of double jeopardy theory exists today."[67] Although this statement was written in 1989, it is still valid a little more than a decade after its origin. Herein lies the key to the double jeopardy academic exercise. Scholars have attempted to furnish order where chaos reigns supreme. As early as 1983, an astute commentator pointed to the futility of providing compelling double jeopardy analysis predicated on the Court's confusing case law.[68] Although Thomas makes a valiant effort to navigate the "Sargasso Sea," he also does so within the framework of the Court's chaotic jurisprudence. It is counterintuitive to attempt to navigate unnavigable waters.

Another significant scholar who sought to provide a coherent theory of the double jeopardy case law is Peter Westen.[69] He adds a significant dimension to the scholarly debate. Ultimately, however, his theory is as unsatisfying as that of other scholars. This is a function, again, of the materials available to the scholar: an incoherent jurisprudence and an ambivalent and nebulous historical record. Westen focuses on the one area where the double jeopardy law is settled: an unshakable faith in the "absolute finality to a jury's verdict of acquittal."[70] So far has the Court carried this principle that it has left acquittals undisturbed even when "based on an egregiously erroneous foundation."[71] What accounts for this inexplicable consistency in an otherwise unsettled area? This is the inquiry Westen explores, with a view to finding the definitive answer to the double jeopardy riddle.

Westen contrasts the absolute nature of acquittals with the pliant character of convictions. Although the defendant does not implicitly waive his right to finality by appealing his conviction, Westen argues, he is precluded from doing so to safeguard society's interest in punishing the guilty.[72] After refuting a host of reasons for distinguishing convictions from acquittals,[73] Westen arrives at his ultimate conclusion: the primary rationale for the absolute nature of acquittals as a bar to double jeopardy is to ensure the viability of jury nullification.[74] Nullification is, according to Westen, "the only thing that explains why, though a defendant can be retried following an erroneous conviction, he cannot be retried following an erroneous acquittal."[75] Consistent with this premise, Westen maintains that the same principle applies to bench trials, because the trial judge should be afforded the same power to acquit against the evidence as the jury is implicitly granted.[76]

Ultimately, Westen's thesis is flawed in several respects. Do we really know why a jury chooses to acquit a defendant? Let us offer a recent prominent example to test his theory. In the O. J. Simpson case, did the jury acquit the defendant because it believed the prosecution did not establish guilt beyond a reasonable doubt or because it sought to nullify the law? Assume that none of the jurors chose to offer their versions about what transpired during the deliberations. Invariably, people who were disposed to believe that Simpson was guilty would surmise that the jury acquitted against the evidence. People who believed that the prosecution and the Los Angeles Police Department presented such a flawed case that they could not establish guilt beyond a reasonable doubt would surmise that the jury performed admirably in carrying out its legal duty. Who is right in this debate is irrelevant for our purposes. The debate does reveal a glaring deficiency in Westen's thesis: presumably many defendants who were not acquitted despite the evidence fall outside Westen's narrow parameter. How many cases, moreover, fall within the indisputable range of jury nullification? I would guess that an infinitesimal number do. Yet Westen would have us believe that this is the overarching principle guiding the only settled part of double jeopardy jurisprudence.

Not only does Westen's narrow focus seem misplaced, but it also misses what he recognizes is the most prominent facet of double jeopardy law: the problem of whether a defendant may be reprosecuted after a mistrial.[77] To the extent that jury nullification fails as an explanatory principle in this important sphere, then it misses the mark as a compass to the "Sargasso Sea." Once more, we see that scholars are attempting to impose a procrustean solution to an intractable problem: how to reconcile and explain a confusing and sometimes contradictory jurisprudence. It is as if scholars seek to erect the perfect template for an insoluble dilemma.

The most clever advocate for a solution to the double jeopardy puzzle is Professor Akhil Reed Amar. He claims to have found the answer to the riddle in a piece that is aptly entitled *Double Jeopardy Law Made Simple*.[78] Amar contends that the plain language of the double jeopardy clause ought to be interpreted literally and that the clause contains "simple" and "clean" rules.[79] Then he backtracks by maintaining that these "simple" rules must be supplemented with other "commonsense" precepts embodied in the due process clause and the jury clause of the Sixth Amendment.[80] Professor Amar's argument is profoundly anachronistic. Indeed, Amar purports to find a definitive and "simple" answer to what historically and developmentally has been a jumbled and incoherent area. Indeed, he resorts to creating "four boxes" in order to dissect the "Blockburger" (*Blockburger v. United States*)[81] test, which is the threshold test the Supreme Court has crafted to determine whether an offense is the "same" for double jeopardy purposes. As with the other two prominent double jeopardy scholars, Amar tries to "make simple" something that is not amenable to simplification: the Court's "Sargasso Sea" double jeopardy jurisprudence.

Paradoxically, Amar calls into question the only indisputable issue in double jeopardy law: the irrevocable nature of jury acquittals. Although he does not deny the jury's power to nullify the law, he believes that when the trial judge commits legal errors prompting the jury to acquit, the defendant should not receive the benefit of the doubt: a retrial should ensue. He rejects the supposed asymmetry between reversals of convictions based on legal errors sought by the defendant and acquittals grounded on similar legal errors.[82] If the acquittal is based on the jury's exercise of its power to nullify the law, and not on legal errors, then the defendant's right to finality rests on the Sixth Amendment's jury trial clause.[83] Amar categorically assumes that "a defendant has no vested right to a legal error in his favor."[84]

Amar's deft thesis is riddled with irony. He tells us that double jeopardy law may be rendered "simple," yet he complicates the only area of it that is settled. Before he reaches this conclusion, however, Amar quotes language from the Court that the Constitution "surely protects a man who has been acquitted from having to 'run the gauntlet' a second time."[85] If, moreover, double jeopardy is "so simple," why does Amar, who professes to adhere to the text of the Constitution in interpreting the double jeopardy clause, resort to due process as well as the Sixth Amendment's jury clause in order to make sense of such a simple clause? If the clause contains "simple" and "clean" rules, why do you need other rules to make sense of it? In order to fit the Court's jurisprudence and other scholarship into his framework, Amar adeptly borrows from other constitutional rights to make his case. Amar overlooks history and purports to find order in a constitutional clause born out of confusion and ambivalence.

I should not conclude my analysis without acknowledging the contribution these scholars have made to perhaps the most conceptually vexing area of constitutional criminal procedure. They are not to blame for the chaotic genesis and development of a constitutional provision that defies facile description or categorization. Whether finality, jury nullification, or textual exegesis are valid explanatory vehicles misses the point: it is a herculean, indeed futile, task to pluck order from disarray. The academic enterprise, however, inherently seeks rational answers to implacable problems. To the extent that scholars have employed hortatory contrivances as defining principles, they have made the Court's "Sargasso Sea" seem navigable. We are indebted to them because it would be disheartening to introduce an area of law embedded in our constitutional landscape by conceding that nothing explains it. Even my nihilistic approach contains a cohesive element; in effect, my organizing contrivance relies on the historical, political, and jurisprudential ambivalence in which the double jeopardy clause is clothed.

Furthermore, I believe that these scholars have illuminated tenets underlying the double jeopardy clause. As I have argued, both finality and protection from governmental oppression are safeguards that are inherent in the double jeopardy clause. To a much lesser degree, jury nullification and textual interpretation are, at the very least, starting points in the discursive endeavor to make sense of the "deceptively" simple double jeopardy language. Because no one concept neatly fits into the double jeopardy mix, it is natural for scholars to embrace one or the other in an effort to distill its essence. I have veered from this path because, even more so than the Fourth Amendment's ban on unreasonable searches and seizures, the Fifth Amendment's double jeopardy clause has been shrouded in a historical, jurisprudential, and conceptual abyss. Unlike my colleagues in the academy, and against my attempt to steer criminal procedure scholarship away from a fragmented nihilism, I must conclude that the double jeopardy area by itself is not amenable to such a gestalt.

WHEN DOES JEOPARDY BEGIN AND END?

That double jeopardy has traveled a meandering road is evident in the most fundamental question posed by this putatively simple constitutional protection: When does jeopardy begin and end, thereby precluding the government from trying the defendant for a second time? Writing the opinion for the Court on this issue, Justice Stewart succinctly stated the obvious after quoting the language of the double jeopardy clause: "But this deceptively plain language has given rise to problems both subtle and complex, problems illustrated by no less than eight cases argued here this very Term."[86] Promptly, however, Justice Stewart fell into the familiar trap we have seen scholars stumble on: the reductionist tendency to label a difficult question a "straightforward" issue. He framed that issue as "the point during a jury trial when a defendant is deemed to have been put in jeopardy, for only if that point has once been reached does any subsequent prosecution of the defendant bring the guarantee against double jeopardy into play."[87] One is tempted to agree with Justice Stewart's characterization of the issue as straightforward until one reads Justice Powell's thoughtful dissent.[88]

The majority and the dissent in *Crist v. Betz* agree on one thing: historically, a defendant was considered to have been placed in "jeopardy" only upon either a conviction or an acquittal.[89] This English common law rule, however, evolved in America after the ratification of the Bill of Rights and, specifically, the Fifth Amendment's double jeopardy clause. Justice Stewart argued that the precept that jeopardy attached when the jury was sworn came to be constitutionally noticed, though only implicitly, when the Court decided the famous "manifest necessity" case of *Perez* in 1824,[90] eventually becoming "firmly established by the end of the 19th century."[91] The next step for Justice Stewart was to furnish a convincing justification for this apparent transformation.

Finding the rationale in the "interest of an accused in retaining a chosen jury,"[92] Justice Stewart attempts to ground the justification not in history but in the language of the double jeopardy clause. After all, if the point at which jeopardy attaches is merely a product of historical accident or practice, then the *Crist* majority is carving out a constitutional interpretation based on mere historical happenstance. Therefore, Justice Stewart relies on several twentieth-century Supreme Court opinions reiterating the "retention of a chosen jury" rationale to support the majority's holding.[93] As you may discern from this account, Justice Stewart's seemingly "straightforward" issue belies the complexity that characterizes double jeopardy law, which he recognized at the outset of his majority opinion.

Justice Powell, by contrast, found the rule that jeopardy attaches when a jury is sworn to be "the product of historical accident."[94] Making a powerful case for this proposition, Justice Powell's historical account concludes that a rule designed to prevent the "needless discharges of juries" was transformed by state courts into a constitutional double jeopardy right.[95] In a more compelling argument, he pointed to the lack of a rational distinction between the rule that jeopardy attaches when a jury is sworn in and the settled rule that in a bench trial it attaches when "the court begins to hear evidence."[96] As we have seen, the *Crist* majority's rationale rested on the defendant's interest in resolving his dilemma before the same jury. Yet, Justice Powell observes, a defendant who waives his right to a jury trial in the hope of securing a particular judge is not necessarily guaranteed that the same judge will adjudicate his case.[97] If this was the defining reason for determining when jeopardy attaches, then the Court created inconsistent precedents. The majority's justification begins to resemble "an arbitrary exercise of linedrawing."[98]

The *Crist* opinion, in the final analysis, begs the important issue: jeopardy really begins when a person is formally charged with a crime through either an indictment or an information.[99] A formal charge merely begins the process, however; the end may come in a variety of ways, most tellingly when a jury reaches a verdict. Herein lies the critical double jeopardy question: when should a defendant be relieved of having to "run the gauntlet" a second time? If we are balancing the right of the defendant to be free from double jeopardy with society's interest in guilt determination, where do we draw the line? Ultimately, the exercise requires some "arbitrary" delineation. No matter how "straightforward" the issue may seem to Justice Stewart, it defies a simple solution.

From the defendant's perspective, it makes sense to draw the line when the jury is sworn in. The selection and impaneling of a jury represents a solemn decision on the defendant's part that he will not participate in a bargain with the prosecution. The stakes increase markedly when the defendant opts to put his fate in the hands of a group of laypeople without any quid pro quo to counteract the potential risks of a conviction. It is not so much his stake in having a specific jury decide his fate that creates anxiety and oppression, but rather the burden of having to reject once more a bargain with the government and entrusting his fate to a group of strangers from the community. Juxtaposing these risks with society's goal in adjudicating the defendant's guilt or innocence yields a radically different conclusion. When a jury is sworn in and no testimony has emerged, society is stripped of its essential goal in the criminal process: the factual and legal determination that the defendant has either breached a community's most fundamental mores or that society lacks the proof, beyond a reasonable doubt, that justifies stripping the offender from his most precious commodity: freedom. This dichotomy explains the English common law's reluctance to trigger double jeopardy protections without a finding on the merits. It also explains the origins of the manifest necessity doctrine; a deadlocked jury fails to resolve the fundamental question with which the jury is entrusted.

To a large extent, moreover, the dilemma is manifested in the confusing state of the mistrial sphere of double jeopardy law. At the beginning of this chapter, we witnessed the sharp divide separating the majority and the dissenting judges regarding the application of double jeopardy to mistrial contexts. The deep split remains today: the Supreme Court is no closer to providing an overarching or compelling rationale for discerning the appropriate contexts in which double jeopardy should apply when the trial judge declares a mistrial. Although the double jeopardy clause protects the defendant from government oppression and furthers his interest in finality, it says nothing about how to reconcile these safeguards with society's concern with the adjudication of guilt. However "simple" the double jeopardy clause may seem, it is not susceptible to easy answers, especially in the area of mistrials, fraught as it is with ambiguity and conflicting results.

WHAT IS AN OFFENSE?

Ambiguity, confusion, and inconsistency mark the Court's attempts to determine what constitutes an offense for double jeopardy purposes. Again, the deceptively simple language of the clause, that no offender be "put in jeopardy" twice for the "same offense," has generated jurisprudential disarray. How can such a seemingly plain term create such a doctrinal "mess"?[100] Professor Amar argues that this "mess" stems from the Court's reluctance to construe the term *same offense* literally: that is, "same offense" means "same offense."[101] A literal interpretation is a fail-safe manner in which to tackle a difficult issue. It works beautifully, provided one is dealing with a finite and restricted number of offenses whose elements are clearly defined. Once we depart from this plain model, however, complications arise. With the emergence of increasingly detailed and complex criminal codes, the literal interpretation of *same offense* quickly loses its allure and effectiveness.

As the Court has acknowledged, "at common law, and under early federal criminal statutes, offense categories were relatively few and distinct."[102] By contrast, modern times have witnessed an "extraordinary proliferation of overlapping and related statutory offenses," thereby making it "possible for prosecutors to spin out a startlingly numerous series of offenses from a single alleged criminal transaction."[103] It is not surprising, therefore, that the test the Court fashioned in 1932 to determine if two offenses are the same has become a "mess." Apparently straightforward, that formulation provides that "where the same act or transaction constitutes a violation of two distinct statutory provisions, the test to be applied to determine whether there are two offenses or only one is whether each provision requires proof of a fact which the other does not."[104] A standard so simple has been transformed into a complex web by the stunning array of criminal offenses that legislatures have spun in order to stem the flood of crime in modern America.

Rather than delving into this doctrinal and academic imbroglio, it is more fruitful to elucidate a category of cases that does not neatly fit into the same offense mold. Beginning with the seminal case *Ashe v. Swenson*,[105] we will see how the language of the double jeopardy clause, judicial interpretation, and academic analysis all fall short of providing a compelling rationale for a viscerally just result.

In *Ashe*, the defendant was charged with the armed robbery of six poker players and the theft of a car belonging to one of the players. This incident stemmed from a single criminal "transaction": the robbery of the six victims occurred simultaneously during a poker game being played in the basement of a private residence. The prosecution did not consolidate the six robberies in order to establish the defendant's guilt. Rather, it proceeded to try him for the robbery of one of the six victims. At trial, the proof was "unassailable" that a robbery had occurred and that there were six victims. The issue was one of identification of the defendant as one of the robbers; it was unclear whether three or four men perpetrated the robbery. Witnesses failed either to identify the defendant as one of the robbers or their identification was tenuous; the defendant's lawyer, moreover, did not contest the robbery but focused upon undermining the witnesses' identification testimony. The jury acquitted the defendant, justifying its verdict by referring to a lack of sufficient evidence for conviction.[106]

Learning from its mistakes, the prosecution then proceeded to try the defendant for the robbery of a different victim in the poker game. This time they secured a conviction by shoring up the witnesses' identification testimony and by failing to put on the stand a victim whose identification testimony at the first trial was "conspicuously negative."[107] It is clear that the defendant, although he objected to being tried a second time, was not placed in jeopardy for the "same offense." If he did commit the robberies, the defendant committed six distinct "offenses" against six different victims. Yet the conundrum for the Court was to determine whether it was consistent with either the double jeopardy clause or notions of fundamental fairness (due process) to have the defendant "run the gauntlet" twice for the same criminal episode.

Because the Court had held in *Benton v. Maryland*[108] that the due process clause of the Fourteenth Amendment "incorporated" the Fifth Amendment's double jeopardy clause, thereby making the clause applicable to the states, the *Ashe* Court did not have to rely necessarily on due process concepts for its holding. Because the same offense analysis was irrelevant, however, the Court had to find another discursive avenue if it was inclined to apply the double jeopardy clause to the peculiar *Ashe* scenario. Borrowing from the civil area, the *Ashe* majority imported the concept of "collateral estoppel," or issue preclusion, to the criminal process.

Under that approach, once "an issue of ultimate" fact has been adjudicated "by a valid and final judgment," that issue may not be "again litigated between the same parties in any future lawsuit."[109] This framework is not susceptible to facile determination in the criminal arena because jury verdicts are general in nature—that is, the jury does not explain in its verdict its reasons for acquittal. The only contested issue in the case was whether he had been one of the perpetrators to the robbery. As the Court concluded, the jury verdict thereby established that there was a reasonable doubt that "he was one of the robbers."[110] Resting its justification on the hallowed principle that a defendant should not be made to "run the gauntlet" twice after being acquitted, the *Ashe* Court held that collateral estoppel, implicitly embodied in the double jeopardy clause, precluded the second prosecution.[111]

Having resorted to a clever artifice to apply double jeopardy outside the same offense context, the *Ashe* Court had to furnish a rationale for its holding. That justification rested on the notion that the prosecution could not consider the first trial a mere "dry run for the second prosecution."[112] Why did the Court venture from the strict language of the clause, to the point of employing a precept from the civil arena, in order to fit its holding into the double jeopardy peg? Quite simply, it feared that, in view of the proliferation of criminal offenses, the potential for government abuse through successive prosecutions was "more pronounced" than it had been in the past.[113]

More than any other opinion, *Ashe* reflects the inextricable nexus between the finality and government oppression motifs underlying the double jeopardy clause. For the *Ashe* holding recognizes that even though the defendant may not be reprosecuted for the "same offense," he may nevertheless be subjected to government oppression through a seriatim process based on the same criminal transaction.[114] Ultimately, this conjunction raised the fundamental question of whether the double jeopardy clause requires the prosecution to "join" in its charging document related offenses growing out of the same criminal episode.[115] It was an issue that would bedevil the Court in the future,[116] yielding a flip-flop in Court doctrine within three years.[117]

Is the Court's importation of the collateral estoppel principle to the facts in *Ashe* defensible? Not really, according to Professor Amar's "double jeopardy made simple" analysis. Amar does not repudiate the *Ashe* result; he rejects the basis for the holding. Because the defendant was not reprosecuted for the same offense, Professor Amar supports the *Ashe* result on due process rather than double jeopardy grounds.[118] Here is where Amar's theory runs into trouble. If double jeopardy is "so simple," why do we need an amorphous constitutional clause to cover a situation that seems to belong viscerally in the double jeopardy arena? If we need a due process principle to deter the prosecutor from "manipulative bifurcation," either to gain a "strategic advantage" or "to vex defendants," aren't we really talking about double jeopardy in the guise of due process?[119] As the *Ashe* majority aptly noted, isn't this superfluous since the double jeopardy principle was made applicable to the states through the due process clause in *Benton*?[120] Professor Amar cannot have it both ways: either the double jeopardy clause conveniently fits into a series of "boxes," or it defies such categorization and therefore is more complex than Amar concedes.

To buttress my argument, I offer the following case to discern whether the collateral estoppel branch of double jeopardy applies to the facts. The defendant, Canon, is prosecuted for driving while intoxicated. His defense at trial is that his companion was driving the vehicle. The jury acquits the defendant. Subsequently, a witness comes forward and relates to the prosecution that the defendant has bragged that he in essence beat the rap by perjuring himself at trial; in effect, the defendant has supposedly admitted to the witness that he was the driver, not his companion. Truth is stranger than fiction; these are the abbreviated facts of *State v. Canon*.[121] The issue was whether the collateral estoppel principle barred the defendant's subsequent prosecution for perjury. Do these facts fall within the collateral estoppel box of double jeopardy or, for that matter, Professor Amar's due process branch of double jeopardy?

On one level, it seems that *Canon* falls squarely within the four corners of the *Ashe* holding. Although perjury is not the same offense as driving while intoxicated, isn't the prosecution relitigating the same issue as the jury resolved in the first trial, that a reasonable doubt existed whether the defendant was the driver?[122] You may object that Canon is being prosecuted from a different criminal transaction in the perjury case; that is, for lying to the jury in the trial rather than for driving while intoxicated at an earlier point in time.[123] Isn't this a "technical" distinction that does not withstand scrutiny when placed under the *Ashe* umbrella? After all, the only issue the jury resolved favorably for the defendant in the first trial, whether Canon was the driver, will be "necessarily determined" at his second trial.[124]

At a different level, you may instinctively ask: Would not such a holding give a defendant who chooses to testify at his trial a license to commit perjury? Balancing the "competing policies" behind the double jeopardy clause with the "integrity of the truth-finding" process, the *Canon* court opted for a compromise of these interests. Relying on other precedents, the Wisconsin court held that the defendant could be tried for the perjury offense only if the state established four conditions by clear and convincing evidence: that the evidence was newly discovered; that the state was not negligent in failing to discover the evidence; that the evidence was material to the issue; and that the new evidence was not cumulative to evidence already available at the first trial.[125] In effect, this compromise reflected "a narrowly tailored exception" to *Ashe*, designed to punish perjury while protecting the defendant's double jeopardy rights.[126]

Raising more questions than it answers,[127] such a test is emblematic of the complexity pervading double jeopardy law. However the courts may wish to finesse the issue, the collateral estoppel doctrine complicates an area that is already beset with ambiguity and complexity. The perjury wrinkle to collateral estoppel, moreover, conflicts with the finality the Supreme Court has conferred on acquittals despite the legal errors that may have tainted them. Would the Court, for example, reverse an acquittal for the same offense after the defendant boasted that he got away with murder because the judge was either incompetent, corrupt, or inattentive? Not according to the Court's unswerving allegiance to the principle that acquittals are irrevocable. To the extent, moreover, that the collateral estoppel doctrine provides an exception to the "same offense" requirement of double jeopardy, then the perjury "collateral estoppel" exception becomes, in essence, an exception to an exception! Navigating the "Sargasso Sea" in these turbulent waters is a treacherous endeavor.

How treacherous that enterprise has become is evident in a case in which the Court has crafted another exception to the collateral estoppel branch of double jeopardy. This variation involves a rather unusual circumstance, yet one that holds tremendous potential for prosecutors while being fraught with danger for criminal defendants. Imagine the dilemma Reuben Dowling confronted. Charged with federal armed robbery of a bank and other crimes, Dowling fared well in his attempts to deflect the charges. His first trial ended in a hung jury; he was convicted in the second trial, but the conviction was reversed on appeal. The third trial was the charm for the prosecution: the jury convicted Dowling on most counts, and the trial judge sentenced him to seventy years' imprisonment.[128]

When a defendant proves to be so slippery, prosecutors sometimes must resort to whatever weapons are available in their arsenal to prevent, literally and figuratively, an escape. Honing its case for the third time, the federal prosecutor relied upon an evidentiary rule to foil Dowling's potential slippage. Federal Rule of Evidence 404 (b) provides that evidence of other crimes, wrongs, or acts is admissible against a defendant at trial as long as such evidence is not used to prove the defendant's character but rather another relevant point—for example, motive, intent, preparation, or knowledge.[129] Employing this evidentiary rule, the prosecution introduced at Dowling's armed robbery trial, over his objection, testimony by a witness to the effect that Dowling had burglarized her apartment two weeks after the armed robbery and that she had identified him.[130] The only problem was that Dowling had been acquitted of that burglary, along with other crimes stemming from the same incident, before his third armed robbery trial had begun. In short, the government relied on an evidentiary rule to introduce evidence about crimes for which the defendant had been acquitted.

Strictly speaking, these facts do not fall within *Ashe*'s ambit. The acquittal on the burglary and related charges did not determine "an ultimate issue" in the federal bank robbery case.[131] The question,

rather, was whether the spirit behind the collateral estoppel component of double jeopardy barred the government from relying on an
acquittal in order to bolster its evidentiary proof in a different case.
The *Dowling* majority concluded that such a reading was not consonant with collateral estoppel because a jury might have concluded that
Dowling was the man who burglarized the apartment, "even if it did
not believe beyond a reasonable doubt that Dowling committed the
crimes charged" in the burglary case.[132] In effect, the higher burden
of proof in a criminal trial did not automatically translate into a finding of innocence, given the lower burden (the preponderance of the
evidence) required under Federal Rule of Evidence 404 (b). Citing precedents in which the Court has held that the double jeopardy clause
does not preclude civil forfeiture proceedings after an acquittal on the
underlying offense because of the different burdens of proof, the
Dowling majority saw no distinction between *Dowling* and the forfeiture
cases.[133]

Isn't the defendant, however, being made "to run the gauntlet" for
the second time when he has to explain away, in a second criminal case,
the facts for which he has been acquitted? Isn't this at odds with the
Court's treatment of acquittals as sacrosanct, even if they are based on
erroneous foundations?[134] As for the majority's reliance on the civil
forfeiture cases, moreover, aren't those precedents distinguishable
because the acquittals were used in subsequent civil, not criminal,
proceedings?[135] These were the arguments proffered by the *Dowling*
dissent.

Regardless of which side one finds more appealing or persuasive,
Dowling reveals in bold relief the vagaries and nuances attending the
interpretation of the double jeopardy clause. From a broad policy perspective, one can agree with the dissent's argument that the criminal
collateral estoppel doctrine ought to forbid the government from
making a defendant attempt to explain away an acquittal, especially
since that explanation is critical to his chances of acquittal in a subsequent prosecution. Technically, the majority is correct when it maintains that collateral estoppel, as defined in *Ashe*, is not applicable to
the facts in *Dowling*. In essence, the majority is attempting to shorten
Ashe's reach, whereas the dissent vainly sought to broaden it so as to
be faithful to its spirit. To put it bluntly, balancing in the double jeopardy sphere yields unsatisfactory results.

Can we explain either *Ashe* or *Dowling* by reference to the same offense language in the double jeopardy clause or through some other
external source? George Thomas contends that he has an answer to

this quandary. In his erudite volume on the history and law of double jeopardy,[136] Thomas argues that double jeopardy is defined by focusing on the criminal actor's "blameworthy act," and that "same offense" can be discerned only through the legislative definition of what constitutes an offense. To put it in his own words, "to arrive at a definition [of double jeopardy], we need the legislature. But if we need the legislature to flesh out our understanding of double jeopardy, we cannot avoid deferring entirely to the legislature when it speaks clearly to double jeopardy issues."[137] We shall return to this proposition shortly; for now, it is imperative to see how Thomas's thesis fits into the *Ashe-Dowling* conundrum.

The first question we must ponder is why the legislature would preclude a second trial in *Ashe* when it has obviously authorized separate punishments for the robberies perpetrated against six distinct victims? Thomas explains this paradox by referring to his blameworthiness approach to double jeopardy issues. He maintains that if the jury finds that the defendant was not the robber, then this bars subsequent prosecutions for the other robberies, "whether or not the offenses share a definitional identity."[138] Since the actor did not create the "blameworthy state of affairs," he should not suffer any other civil or criminal penalties.[139] Thomas further qualifies his thesis by noting that a second prosecution would not be prohibited if the defense in *Ashe* had been that the money the defendant took from the victims belonged to him.[140]

Does Thomas's thesis provide a coherent rationale for either the *Dowling* or *Canon* holdings? Let us apply his reasoning to both cases, with the caveat that I am extrapolating a result from his thesis that Thomas may not necessarily believe is consonant with its fundamental tenets. How does "blameworthiness," for example, resolve the issue presented in *Dowling*—whether evidence of crimes for which Dowling was acquitted could be used to establish his identity as the culprit in a different robbery? Initially, one would instinctively posit that because Dowling was deemed not "blameworthy" in the first case, if we assume that the jury reached its verdict based on the belief that he was not the culprit, then he should not suffer further civil or criminal penalties stemming from that act.

You may object, however, that Dowling is not being prosecuted for the same "blameworthy" act, but for different and discrete offenses that are divorced from the original criminal acts for which he was deemed not "blameworthy." Instead, Dowling is the unwelcome recipient of an evidentiary rule that permits the admission of other offenses for which the actor has not been adjudicated "blameworthy" in order to bolster the prosecution's case on a relevant issue regarding a different "offense." In short, the actor is not suffering another criminal penalty for the same act; rather, he is suffering a collateral effect from that act in the guise of an evidentiary rule designed to assist the fact finder in determining whether the actor has created a different "blameworthy state of affairs."

Nonsense, the untrained nonlegal observer may object in utter exasperation: Dowling is being punished again; the evidence of a crime for which he has been acquitted is being used to prop up the government's shaky case! However the jury may be instructed to use this evidence, the possibility or probability exists that the evidence of the allegedly "not blameworthy" act may tip the scales in favor of guilt in the case for which the defendant now stands in jeopardy. Does this circumstance fall within the parameters of Thomas's blameworthiness thesis? I do not believe that it does. It is difficult to place *Dowling* in Thomas's definition of collateral estoppel "as a case-sensitive, same-offense claim."[141] Yet, my intuition tells me that there is no valid reason for excluding *Dowling* from Thomas's "blameworthiness" postulate.

If *Dowling* does not quite fit into the Thomas thesis, may we nevertheless confine it within the *Canon* variation on *Ashe*? Again, we run into conceptual difficulties in attempting this delicate task. Canon, after all, was found not guilty by the jury of the offense of driving while intoxicated. Once he is deemed not blameworthy, according to Thomas, he should not suffer any further criminal or civil penalties for that act. Being prosecuted for the act of perjury, one may plausibly maintain, is not the same as being prosecuted for driving while intoxicated. We run, however, into the same conceptual difficulty in *Canon* that we encountered in *Dowling*. Didn't the jury find Canon not guilty for the state of affairs relating to the driving of the automobile? Isn't Canon's testimony inextricably linked to the offense for which he was absolved by the jury?

Thomas might counter that the legislature, in its attempt to preserve the integrity of the adversary process, saw fit to punish perjury separately from any other offense, such as, for example, driving while intoxicated. Therefore, according to his thesis that "legislature defines the scope of double jeopardy," there is nothing amiss in prosecuting Canon for the distinct blameworthy act of lying to the jury about whether he was driving. Why, then, do courts have such a difficult time excluding this scenario from the collateral estoppel branch of double jeopardy? The reason, as we saw, is that it is exceedingly difficult not to apply the issue preclusion rule to the *Canon* case. However the law may wish to categorize it, the second jury would be deciding the same issue the first jury resolved: whether Canon was at least "minimally" credible when he testified that he was not the driver of the car. Furthermore, that was the only contested issue in the case. Without the subtleties and fine legal distinctions, *Canon* at its core is not different from *Ashe*.

Where does Thomas's sophisticated theory leave us? I contend that it does not leave us in any more of a comfortable position than any other viable double jeopardy thesis does. No matter how scholars may wish to reduce an intractable problem into a readily solvable one, the fact remains that double jeopardy is not amenable to conceptual reduction. Indeed, it is ironic that Thomas tells us that double jeopardy is different from other constitutional criminal safeguards, such as the Fourth Amendment protection against unreasonable searches and seizures and the Fifth Amendment privilege against self-incrimination, because we have no "cultural benchmarks" for defining "twice in jeopardy" or "same offense."[142] That leaves matters to the legislature, which cannot anticipate every nuance emanating from criminal statutes. I doubt that the legislatures or even the courts pondered the ambiguities, complexities, or nuances that cases such as *Canon* and *Dowling* have wrought. A simple boat will not navigate the toughest waters of the "Sargasso Sea."

LEAVE IT TO THE LEGISLATURE: IT WILL DETERMINE THE DOUBLE JEOPARDY BOUNDARIES

Because the Court has acknowledged failure in its attempt to provide a coherent double jeopardy theory, and scholars have also failed to accomplish this goal, it follows that another government branch might fill the void. Modern-day legislatures at the state and federal level have supplanted the role of the common law in defining crimes and determining the appropriate punishment for criminal offenses. As we have seen, Thomas argues that the double jeopardy clause is defined by legislative fiat, especially when that command is clear. As such, double jeopardy operates merely as a "procedural" limitation on prosecutors or judges. The logical corollary to this precept is that the double jeopardy constitutional prohibition does not contain "substantive" limitations upon the legislature prerogative to define crimes and regulate punishments.[143]

Doesn't this theory abdicate responsibility for constitutional interpretation to the legislature and thereby run counter to the fundamental principle that the Constitution, and especially the Bill of Rights,
was meant to curb potential majoritarian excesses by the legislative
branch? Isn't this abdication the worst nightmare James Madison envisioned? In the criminal justice context, does this "legislative prerogative" theory in effect "pander to the crime fear in the populace?"[144] As
we have examined, Thomas answers this powerful criticism by relying on "blameworthiness" analysis and by limiting the judiciary's interpretive functions to situations where the legislature has not spoken
clearly to "assigning criminal blameworthiness."[145] The inherent definitional gaps in criminal statutes, I have argued, especially in the double
jeopardy area, leave the courts with interpretational puzzles of the type
exemplified by *Ashe* and its progeny and by *Dowling*'s paradoxes.

What about the clear examples, you may object, in which the legislature unequivocally conveys an intention to punish someone twice for
what amounts to the same offense, although the legislature has clev-
erly drafted two statutes to cover the same criminal act? Would the
successive prosecution of these offenses violate the double jeopardy
bar? *Missouri v. Hunter*[146] raised these questions; unfortunately, the
majority answered only the multiple punishment issue, leaving the successive prosecution question for another day. The ramifications of
Hunter are compelling, for they demonstrate the proliferation of criminal statutes as one of the prominent motifs of modern double jeopardy law. It is ironic that both the Court and scholars have looked upon
legislative intent as the saving grace for the otherwise impenetrable
double jeopardy law. They have searched for the solution to the double
jeopardy conundrum in one of the primary sources of the puzzle. With
that caveat, let us delve into what the legislature supposedly made so
clear in *Hunter*.

Hunter was charged and convicted of first degree robbery, armed
criminal action, and assault with malice.[147] His criminal actions con-
sisted of the armed robbery of a grocery store as well as shooting at
an off-duty police officer who unsuccessfully attempted to foil the robbery. Hunter was sentenced to concurrent terms of ten years for the
robbery, fifteen years for the armed criminal action, and five years for
the assault. He maintained that his fifteen-year sentence for armed
criminal action violated the double jeopardy clause because it
amounted to double punishment for the same offense.[148] In effect,
Hunter argued that the robbery and armed criminal action were the

same crime, thereby subjecting him to multiple punishment for the same offense.

Missouri's legislature defined *armed criminal action* as a felony committed "by, with, or through the use, assistance, or aid of a dangerous or deadly weapon."[149] More important, the legislature made it clear that the punishment for this offense was superimposed upon the substantive crime committed with the weapon.[150] In short, "the net effect of such [a] statute is to enhance (in the pure sense of enlarging) the penalty assessed for the underlying felony."[151] Two questions emerge from this legislative sleight of hand: are the two offenses (the underlying offense and armed criminal action) the same offense and, if so, does the double jeopardy clause prohibit multiple punishments for the same offense? Of course, the Court has acknowledged that the double jeopardy clause "protects against multiple punishments for the same offense."[152] May the legislature override that prohibition, however, by an explicit fiat evincing its intent to enhance the penalty for the predicate offense? That was the issue the majority resolved in *Hunter*.

Deferring to the Missouri Supreme Court's interpretation of the two statutes, the *Hunter* majority conceded that both first-degree robbery and armed criminal action defined the "same crime."[153] The straitjacket the majority had to escape from seemed formidable: the imposition of multiple punishments for the same offense went against precedent and the purpose undergirding the double jeopardy clause. In essence, the *Hunter* majority engineered its escape by finding that the *North Carolina v. Pearce* ban on multiple punishments for the same offense was inapplicable when the legislature explicitly avowed a "contrary intent."[154] The legislature, therefore, is authorized to supersede the Court's constitutional interpretation as long as it explicitly declares its intention to impose multiple punishments for the same offense.

Taken to its logical conclusion, this theory permits the legislatures to spin a multitude of crimes "on the basis of the same act, state of mind, or result,"[155] thereby geometrically expanding the range of punishments for the same transaction. Beyond this conclusion, could the legislature avow that the prosecution could prosecute the predicate felony and the armed criminal action successively without violating the double jeopardy clause? Justice Marshall, in dissent, believed that if Hunter had "been tried for these two crimes in separate trials, he would plainly have been subjected to multiple prosecutions for 'the same offense' in violation of the Double Jeopardy Clause."[156] If this is the core principle supporting the double jeopardy clause, one would not question Justice Marshall's conclusion. Given the superiority accorded legislatures in defining and setting the terms of punishments for criminal offenses, and the logic underlying the *Hunter* opinion, one could cast doubt upon Justice Marshall's analysis.

If multiple punishment for the same offense is part of the Court's tripartite safeguards embedded in the double jeopardy clause, why should it be different from its counterparts? A criminal defendant should neither be tried twice for the "same offense" nor be convicted or punished twice for the same crime. To the extent that the Court is saying that the defendant may be punished twice for the same crime as long as the legislature confirms its intention to inflict multiple punishment, then why shouldn't the legislature override the other two safeguards? Is there a qualitative or normative difference among multiple punishment, successive prosecutions, or multiple convictions for the "same offense"? Such an argument would be critical to the validity of the *Hunter* premise. If the legislature were to pass a law permitting successive prosecutions for first-degree robbery and armed criminal action, would the statute run afoul of the double jeopardy clause? Let us ponder this query, with a peculiar wrinkle added for special effect.

Assume that the prosecution first tried Hunter for the crime of armed robbery. The jury acquitted Hunter, based upon poor eyewitness identification testimony linking Hunter to the crime. Hunter does not contest the commission of the robbery in the first trial; rather, the only issue he raises is whether he is one of the culprits. The state then shores up this weak testimony, tries Hunter for armed criminal action, and secures a conviction. Not only is the prosecution permitted to try Hunter for the same offense, it is allowed to strengthen its case, making the first trial a mere "dry run" for the second prosecution. How can we square this with the successive prosecution ban and also with the *Ashe* collateral estoppel branch of double jeopardy? Notice that in this instance, the prosecution is not trying Hunter for a different offense, as the state vainly attempted in *Ashe*; rather, the prosecution is trying Hunter for the same crime. Therefore, the government would be violating not only the successive prosecution ban but also the issue preclusion tenet embodied in *Ashe*.

The preceding scenario is a crude example of government conduct the Court has implicitly sanctioned in deferring to the will of the legislature. *Garrett v. United States*[157] represents the culmination of judicial abdication to majoritarian attempts to skirt the double jeopardy ban in order to address what is perceived to be a pressing national problem: the pernicious influence of illegal drugs in American culture.

Responding to this threat, Congress in 1970 enacted the Comprehensive Drug Abuse Prevention and Control Act of 1970,[158] which penalized high-level drug operatives for engaging in a "continuing criminal enterprise" (CCE). To put it in Justice Rehnquist's apt phrase, the language in the CCE statute "is designed to reach the 'top brass' in the drug rings, not the lieutenants and foot soldiers."[159] It does so by punishing a defendant who commits at least three "continuing predicate" felony drug offenses with at least five or more persons, occupies a managerial position in the organization, and obtains substantial income or resources from the violations. The CCE statute carries substantial penalties: a minimum ten-year term of imprisonment and a maximum of life imprisonment; and forfeiture of any profits, property, or contractual rights deriving from the continuing criminal enterprise.

Garrett was initially charged in March 1981 with three counts relating to the importation of approximately six tons of marijuana into Washington state.[160] Aware of pending CCE charges in Florida at the time he was negotiating with the government, Garrett attempted to deflect the inevitable by requesting that all impending charges be merged with the Washington proceedings. The motion was opposed by the government and denied by the trial court because no other charges had been filed against Garrett at that time.[161] He ultimately pled guilty to one count of importation of marijuana, with the remaining counts being dismissed "without prejudice to the government's right to prosecute him on any other offenses he may have committed."[162] He was sentenced to five years' imprisonment and a $15,000 fine.[163]

Garrett's fears quickly materialized, for he was indicted for CCE in Florida within two months after his bargain with the federal government in Washington state.[164] The Washington importation was one of the predicate offenses for the Florida CCE indictment, with the prosecution introducing evidence regarding the Washington scheme at trial.[165] Garrett was convicted and sentenced for the three predicate offenses as well at the CCE count; he was sentenced to forty years' imprisonment and a $100,000 fine for the CCE count, consecutive to the five-year term and the fine he received when he pled guilty to the Washington importation offense.

In effect, Garrett maintained that he was prosecuted and punished twice for the Washington importation conviction.[166] Briefly, Justice Rehnquist, speaking for a plurality of the Court,[167] rejected Garrett's contentions, delving into congressional history in concluding that the CCE statute was distinct from the predicate offenses, in both the sense of being a separate offense and in the sense of carrying a penalty in addition to that contained in the predicate offenses.[168] Although Justice Rehnquist acknowledged that both the Washington importation and the CCE violation were the same offense under the *Blockburger* test, he concluded that the *Hunter* legislative intent principle superseded the same offense hortatory formula set forth in *Blockburger*.[169] The logical corollary to this reasoning followed: if Congress meant to define CCE as distinct from the predicate offenses, then it intended to impose separate punishments as well.[170]

The cultural and societal paradigm underlying *Garrett* emerges boldly in Justice Rehnquist's opinion. Pay close attention to the aphorism he invokes to justify successive prosecutions and punishments under the CCE statute: "it would be illogical for Congress to intend that a choice be made between predicate offenses and the CCE offense in pursuing major drug dealers."[171] In sum, whatever offense or category of offenses the legislative branch deems dangerous enough will not fall under the double jeopardy umbrella by definitional fiat. The majority may have disdain for drug dealers and their pernicious influence on American society. Does this deference to the majority have any discernible limits? The unmistakable import of *Hunter* and *Garrett* is that such limits are nonexistent, even when legislative intent must be culled from congressional history and the "structure" of a specific statute.

Let us venture beyond *Garrett* and imagine that the government sought to prosecute a defendant without having obtained a conviction for the predicate offenses. As Thomas sees it, "While these felonies do not have to be manifested in prior convictions, they usually are." This is a natural function of both prosecutorial convenience and the fact that the prior charges and convictions "tip off the authorities to the existence of the criminal enterprise."[172] However, let us return to the *Dowling* opinion, with its perverse twist on collateral estoppel and double jeopardy. Because Congress has not clearly required a conviction as a precondition for CCE prosecution, will an acquittal preclude it? Justice O'Connor surmises that the *Ashe* collateral estoppel bar would furnish protection under that circumstance.[173] Taking the legislative supremacy doctrine to its conclusion, however, would mean that if Congress sought to explicitly override the *Ashe* principle, then its intention would be paramount. The Sargasso Sea of double jeopardy interpretation seems more unnavigable than ever.

Nowhere have the interpretational vagaries besetting the double jeopardy clause seemed more perplexing than in the Court's creation of the dual sovereignty doctrine. The doctrine came under intense scrutiny when the Los Angeles police officers who were acquitted in the beating of Rodney King in state court were subsequently prosecuted in federal court for criminal violation of King's constitutional rights.[174] How could the bedrock principle of double jeopardy law be so blatantly violated? In effect, those officers were acquitted in state courts and were promptly reprosecuted in federal court for the same acts, if not for the same offenses. Enter the dual sovereignty exception to the double jeopardy clause, crated by the Supreme Court, and the protection embedded in the double jeopardy clause mysteriously vanishes.

Rooted in our federal system, the dual sovereignty doctrine was fashioned by the Supreme Court in the mid-nineteenth century.[175] In two cases, the Court noted in dicta that the double jeopardy bar against either successive prosecution or punishment was not applicable when separate sovereigns—that is, state and federal governments—prosecuted or punished a defendant for the same criminal offense. The justification for this odd precept was twofold: the Fifth Amendment only constrained the federal government, and an offender who committed an act that simultaneously violated both a federal and a state statute was neither prosecuted nor punished for the same offense. Dissenting in both cases, Justice McLean aptly labeled the doctrine a legal fiction that ran "contrary to the nature and genius of our government [by punishing] an individual twice for the same offence."[176]

Reaffirming the dual sovereignty principle in the twentieth century, the Supreme Court has slavishly adhered to its counterintuitive premises. From the *United States v. Lanza* opinion in the early part of the twentieth century to the *Heath v. Alabama* opinion in the latter part of the century, the Court has applied this legal fiction to an array of cases in which the defendant has been prosecuted or punished twice for the same offense.[177] In *Bartkus v. Illinois*,[178] the Court held that a defendant could be prosecuted by the state after he was acquitted in federal court for robbing the same federally insured bank. Similarly, the Court held in *Abbate v. United States*,[179] that the federal government could prosecute the defendant for conspiracy to destroy federal communications after he had pled guilty to conspiracy to destroy the same property in state court. To put it simply, as one scholar has ably done, "it seems anomalous that the federal and state governments, acting in tandem, can generally do what neither government can do alone—prosecute an ordinary citizen twice for the same offense."[180]

Perhaps the most egregious application of the dual sovereignty principle occurred in the *Heath* case.[181] Heath arranged with two accomplices to have his wife abducted from her home and murdered. The two accomplices kidnapped the victim from her home in Alabama and transported her across the state line to Georgia, where they committed the murder. The victim's body was discovered in Georgia, and the Georgia authorities arrested and subsequently indicted Heath for the murder. Facing the death penalty, Heath opted to plead guilty to the murder in exchange for a life sentence. Not satisfied with this outcome, the State of Alabama indicted Heath for the murder seeking to obtain the death penalty that Heath had avoided by pleading guilty in Georgia.[182] Heath sought to enjoin the Alabama proceedings by invoking the double jeopardy clause and by claiming that the Alabama court lacked jurisdiction because the crime occurred in Georgia.[183]

When the trial court rejected his double jeopardy claims, Heath opted for a jury trial because he had nothing to lose. Imagine the absurdity of the trial: the potential jurors knew that Heath had pleaded guilty and had been sentenced for the murder in Georgia; yet, the trial court was able to find venire persons who avowed that this knowledge would not prejudice their ability to weigh his guilt based on the evidence presented at the trial.[184] Given this stacked deck against the defendant, the "outcome of the trial was a foregone conclusion."[185] Alabama accomplished its goal: the defendant received the death penalty.

Invoking the dual sovereignty doctrine, the Court held that double jeopardy did not preclude Alabama from prosecuting the defendant after he had pleaded guilty to the same homicide in Georgia. Quoting from *Lanza*, Justice O'Connor, speaking for the majority, observed, "When a defendant in a single act violates the 'peace and dignity' of two sovereigns by breaking the laws of each, he has committed two distinct offences."[186] Prosecution by two sovereign states is not normatively different from prosecution by a state and the federal government. To the extent that the dual sovereignty doctrine rests upon the common law tenet that conceives crime as an offense against the sovereignty of the government, then the only question becomes whether the two entities seeking to prosecute the defendant can be considered separate sovereigns.[187] Unlike municipalities, which derive their power from the state, states are distinct sovereigns who are entitled to exercise their authority to prosecute those who violate their fundamental social norms.[188]

The *Heath* opinion is riddled with ironies. Had Heath's accomplices not transported the victim across state lines, Alabama would have had only one bite of the capital punishment apple. Indeed, Justice O'Connor acknowledges this obvious fact in her opinion; "had these offenses arisen under the laws of one State and had petitioner been separately prosecuted for both offenses in that State, the second conviction would have been barred by the Double Jeopardy Clause."[189] Justice O'Connor, a proponent of the theory that the double jeopardy clause's overriding purpose is to prevent government oppression, sanctions the ultimate in oppression by permitting a sovereign to have the defendant "run the gauntlet" a second time and lose his life in the process. Facilitating "collusion" between two states to secure the defendant's execution[190] seems an affront to the values fostered by the Bill of Rights and our republican form of government.

Another perverse consequence of the state's "sovereign" power is at work in the application of the dual sovereignty doctrine. Heath struck a legal bargain with the state of Georgia when he pleaded guilty in exchange for avoiding the death penalty for his wife's murder. Yet, a different sovereign, Alabama, violated the benefit of this legal bargain with impunity when it successfully prosecuted him and secured the death penalty. If the Georgia authorities struck the bargain in bad faith, confident in the knowledge that Alabama would exact the ultimate penalty because the dual sovereignty doctrine would not present an obstacle to successive prosecution and punishment, government oppression rises to unimaginable levels. This "collusion" theory is not farfetched in view of the fact that Georgia and Alabama authorities pursued dual investigations of the murder "in which they cooperated to some extent."[191] If the evidence against Heath had not been compelling, moreover, Georgia could have initiated prosecution, proceeded to trial, and if it failed to obtain a conviction, then it could have advised Alabama of ways to strengthen its case to ensure a conviction. In essence, the first trial would be merely, as the Court put it in *Ashe*, a "dry run" for the second prosecution.

A more apt metaphor for the Court's double jeopardy jurisprudence than Justice Rehnquist's "Sargasso Sea" might be "the meandering empty and sinking vessel." Not only is double jeopardy doctrine mired in hopeless confusion, it is subject to manipulation by the government. The exceptions to the double jeopardy bar fashioned by the Court to a large extent belie its majestic safeguards. More important, the doctrinal morass leaves the defendant in an awkward position, evident in the *Heath* case: may the defendant invoke the double jeopardy clause to prevent the government from initiating a formal prosecution against him?

DOUBLE JEOPARDY, THE GRAND JURY, AND INCRIMINATION

Given the confused state of double jeopardy jurisprudence, it is difficult for the defendant to predict, with some semblance of accuracy, when the government is precluded from initiating a second prosecution after he has been placed in jeopardy for an offense. The mistrial facet of double jeopardy law leaves a certain amount of doubt regarding the ability of the government to launch a second prosecution. Similarly, the exceptions to the double jeopardy bar place the defendant in the awkward position of guessing at the intentions of a different sovereign with respect to an offense that violates the criminal statutes of dual sovereigns. Although the federal government has, through self-imposed guidelines,[192] restricted its ability to reprosecute a defendant who has run the gauntlet in the state system, this policy may be superseded upon the attorney general's discretion. As we have seen, moreover, the collateral estoppel branch of double jeopardy is also ambiguous and difficult to apply other than in unusual circumstances.

It should not be surprising, however, that the links between the double jeopardy clause, the privilege against self-incrimination, and the grand jury are subject to the vagaries of the "Sargasso Sea" of judicial interpretation: the double jeopardy clause. The extent to which a defendant may be indicted by a grand jury when he has already been subjected to prosecution for the "same offense" is uncertain depending upon the nuances and exceptions to the double jeopardy prohibition. Indeed, the defendant may run the risk of double incrimination, not just self-incrimination, depending on such a fortuitous circumstance as the locus of his offense. Similarly, the defendant may be punished twice for the same offense depending on the legislature's intent to delineate explicitly its intention to double punish for the same act. A stormy sea is by definition unpredictable; however we may wish to tame the "Sargasso Sea," it is not amenable to navigation.

In an intriguing new book on the legal enterprise, Anthony Amsterdam and Jerome Bruner[193] posit that law is shaped by narration, categorization, and persuasion. The problem with Anglo-American double jeopardy law is that it has been lacking in all three areas from its genesis. No coherent narrative exists to support its underlying bases. Attempts to categorize its various facets have been an abject failure; indeed, by its own admission, the Supreme Court has acknowledged its bankruptcy in this sphere. The lack of a coherent narrative and plausible categories, moreover, have contributed to an unconvincing rhetoric, a void that academicians have vainly attempted to fill. Perhaps deconstruction is the first step toward a thorough reconstruction.

NOTES

1. This is the language employed by Justice Rehnquist in *Albernaz v. United States*, 450 U.S. 333 (1981). The concession is remarkable because the Court seldom acknowledges that its jurisprudence on a given area is, at best, muddled.

2. George C. Thomas III, *An Elegant Theory of Double Jeopardy* 1988 U. ILL. L. REV. 827 (1988). Thomas is the leading scholar in the field, producing a vast body of work, which itself attests to the tangled web the Supreme Court has created.

3. Peter Westen & Richard Drubel, *Toward a General Theory of Double Jeopardy*, 1978 SUP. CT. REV. 81.

4. Akhil Reed Amar, *Double Jeopardy Law Made Simple*, 106 YALE L. J. 1807 (1997).

5. *Id.*

6. *Green v. United States*, 355 U.S. 184, 199 (1957) (Frankfurter, J., dissenting, quoting from *Gompers v. United States*, 233 U.S. 504, 610.

7. 76 Eng. Rep. 992 (K.B. 1591).

8. 1 Johns R. 66 (N.Y. 1806), reprinted in Phillip B. Kurland & Ralph Lerner, eds., 5 THE FOUNDERS CONSTITUTION 267.

9. *Id.* at 269.

10. Justice Tompkins employed this oft-stated "salutary maxim" of the common law in *Barrett. Id.* at 267.

11. 410 U.S. 458 (1973).

12. *Id.* at 459–60.

13. 9 Wheat. 579 (1824).

14. *Id.*

15. *Simmons v. United States*, 142 U.S. 148 (1891).

16. *Thompson v. United States*, 155 U.S. 271 (1894). In that case, the juror was disqualified because he was a member of the grand jury that indicted the defendant.

17. *Illinois v. Somerville*, 410 U.S. at 471.

18. *Id.* at 461–62.

19. 163 U.S. 662 (1891).

20. *Id.* at 669.

21. *Illinois v. Somerville*, 410 U.S. at 467.

22. 400 U.S. 470 (1971).

23. *Id.* at 472–73.

24. *Id.* at 486.

25. *Id.* at 485, citing *Wade v. Hunter*, 336 U.S. 684, 691 (1949).

26. *Id.* (citations omitted).

27. 372 U.S. 734 (1963).

28. *Id.* at 737.

29. *Illinois v. Somerville*, 410 U.S. at 468–69.

30. *Id.*

31. *United States v. Jorn*, 400 U.S. at 486.

32. *Id.* at 484.

33. *Green v. United States*, 355 U.S. 184, 187–88 (1957).

34. *United States v. Jorn*, 400 U.S. at 486. "[T]he judge must always temper the decision whether or not to abort the trial by considering the importance to the defendant of being able, once and for all, to conclude his confrontation with society through the verdict of a tribunal he might believe to be favorably disposed to his fate." Justice White noted in his *Somerville* dissent, "Such analysis, however, completely ignores the possibility that the defendant might be acquitted by the initial jury." *Illinois v. Somerville*, 410 U.S. at 474–75 (White, J., dissenting).

35. *United States v. Jorn*, 400 U.S. at 486.

36. *Illinois v. Somerville*, 410 U.S. at 476 (White, J., dissenting).

37. *Id.*

38. *United States v. Ball*, 163 U.S. at 667–68.

39. *Illinois v. Somerville*, 410 U.S. at 483 (Marshall, J., dissenting).

40. *Oregon v. Kennedy*, 456 U.S. 667 (1982).

41. *Id.* at 669.

42. *Id.*

43. Fed. Rule of Evidence 404 A, B.

44. *Oregon v. Kennedy*, 456 U.S. at 682 (Stevens, J., concurring, citing *Arizona v. Washington*, 434 U.S. 497, 503 (1978).

45. *Id.*

46. *Id.* at 670 (citations omitted).

47. *Id.* at 674–77.

48. *Id.* at 676.

49. *Id.* at 669. Justice Powell emphasized this point in his concurring opinion. *Id.* at 680 (Powell, J., concurring).

50. *Id.* at 675.

51. *Id.* at 690–91 (Stevens, J. concurring).

52. *United States v. Green*, 355 U.S. at 187–88. Professor Westen suggests that only two of Justice Black's protections are applicable to the mistrial cases. *See* Westen, *supra* note 3 at 86–87.

53. Gordon S. Wood, *Ideology and the Origins of Liberal America* 44 WILLIAM & MARY QUART. 632–33 (1987).
54. *See* Thomas *supra* note 2.
55. *Id.* at 829.
56. *See* Alfredo Garcia, *Toward an Integrated Vision of Criminal Procedural Rights: A Counter to Judicial and Academic Nihilism*, 77 MARQ. L. REV. 1 (1993).
57. Thomas, *supra* note 2 at 829–34.
58. *Id.* at 828–29.
59. *North Carolina v. Pearce*, 395 U.S. 711, 717 (1969).
60. Thomas, *supra* note 2 at 830–31.
61. *Id.* at 832–33.
62. *Id.* at 837.
63. *Id.* at 834, 871.
64. LEWIS H. LA RUE, CONSTITUTIONAL LAW AS FICTION: NARRATIVE IN THE RHETORIC OF AUTHORITY (1995).
65. Thomas, *supra* note 2 at 871.
66. *Id.* at 831–32.
67. *Id.* at 836.
68. Monroe G. McKay, *Double Jeopardy: Are the Pieces the Puzzle?*, 23 WASHBURN L.J. 1, 8 (1983). Judge McKay called Professor Weston's theory into question because it was based "on the case law generated by [the Court's] confusion to support his thesis."
69. *See* Westen, *supra* note 3.
70. *Burks v. United States*, 437 U.S. 1 (1978).
71. *Fong Foo v. United States*, 369 U.S. 141, 143 (1962).
72. Westen, *supra* note 3 at 124–27, citing *Tateo v. United States*, 377 U.S. 463 (1964).
73. *Id.* at 126–30.
74. *Id.* at 130–32.
75. *Id.* at 132.
76. *Id.* at 132–37.
77. *Id.* at 85.
78. Amar, *supra* note 4.
79. *Id.* at 1809–10.
80. *Id.* at 1809.
81. *Blockburger v. United States*, 284 U.S. 299 (1932).
82. Amar, *supra* note 4 at 1841–47.
83. *Id.* at 1846 (citing Westen, *supra* note 3).
84. *Id.* at 1844.
85. *Id.* at 1827, quoting from *Ashe v. Swenson*, 397 U.S. 436, 446 (1970) (citations omitted).
86. *Crist v. Bretz*, 437 U.S. 28, 32 (1978).
87. *Id.* at 32–33.
88. *Id.* at 40 (Powell, J., dissenting).

89. *Id.* at 33, 40–41.

90. *Id.* at 34, n. 10 (citations omitted).

91. *Id.* at 34.

92. *Id.* at 35.

93. *Id.* at 36 (citations omitted).

94. *Id.* at 40 (Powell, J., dissenting).

95. *Id.* at 45–47.

96. *Serfass v. United States*, 420 U.S. 377, 388 (1975).

97. *Crist v. Bretz*, 437 U.S. at 51 (Powell, J., dissenting).

98. *Id.* at 37. This is the charge Justice Stewart attempts to deflect in the majority opinion.

99. Amar, *supra* note 4 at 1840.

100. *Id.* at 1814. Professor Amar uses this term to describe the Court's seminal case on the issue, *Blockburger v. United States*, 284 U.S. 299 (1932).

101. *Id.* at 1815.

102. *Ashe v. Swenson*, 397 U.S. 436, 445 n. 10 (1970).

103. *Id.*

104. *Blockburger v. United States*, 284 U.S. at 304.

105. 397 U.S. 436 (1970).

106. *Id.* at 438–39.

107. *Id.* at 439–440.

108. 395 U.S. 784 (1969).

109. *Id.* at 443.

110. *Id.* at 444–45.

111. *Id.* at 445–46.

112. *Id.* at 447.

113. *Id.* at 445, n.10.

114. From a much broader viewpoint, this was the point of Justice Brennan's concurring opinion in *Ashe*. *Id.* at 448–60 (Brennan, J., concurring).

115. *Id.* at 459–60.

116. *See, e.g., Illinois v. Vitale*, 447 U.S. 410 (1980); *Grady v. Corbin*, 495 U.S. 508 (1990); *United States v. Dixon*, 509 U.S. 688 (1993).

117. Compare *Grady, supra* (holding that same offense should be synonymous with same conduct for double jeopardy purposes) with *Dixon* (overruling *Grady* because it lacked a "constitutional basis").

118. Amar, *supra* note 4 at 1828–29.

119. *Id.* at 1828.

120. *Ashe v. Swenson*, 397 U.S. at 441–43.

121. 622 N.W. 2d 270 (2001).

122. *Id* at 272. This is the holding of the lower appellate court, which the Supreme Court of Wisconsin reversed and remanded (citations omitted).

123. *Id.* at 274–75.

124. *Id.* at 275.

125. *Id.* at 277–78.

126. *Id.* at 278.

127. *See, e.g.,* Justice Abramson's dissent. *Id.* at 279 (Abramson, J., dissenting).

128. *Dowling v. United States*, 493 U.S. 342, 344 (1990).

129. Federal Rule of Evidence 404 (b). The rule reads as follows: Evidence of other crimes, wrongs, or acts is not admissible to prove the character of a person or to action in conformity therewith. It may, however, be admissible for other purposes, such as proof of motive, opportunity, intent, preparation, plan, knowledge, identity, or absence of mistake or accident, provided that upon request by the accused, the prosecution in a criminal case shall provide reasonable notice in advance of trial, or during trial if the court excuses pretrial notice on good cause shown, of the general nature of such evidence it intends to introduce at trial.

130. *Dowling v. United States*, 493 U.S. at 344–45.

131. *Id.* at 348.

132. *Id.* at 348–49.

133. *Id.* at 349–50 (citations omitted).

134. *Id.* at 355 (Brennan, J., dissenting, citing *Fong Foo v. United States*, 369 U.S. at 143; and *Sanabria v. United States*, 437 U.S. 54, 68–69 (1978).

135. *Id.* at 359–60.

136. GEORGE THOMAS III, DOUBLE JEOPARDY: THE HISTORY, THE LAW (1998).

137. *Id.* at 14.

138. *Id.* at 202.

139. *Id.*

140. *Id.*

141. *Id.*

142. *Id.* at 14.

143. *Id.* at 14–15. Professor Thomas quotes from *Brown v. Ohio*, 432 U.S. 161, 165 (1977) to support his thesis. "The legislature remains free under the Double Jeopardy Clause to define crimes and fix punishments."

144. *Id.* at 17.

145. *Id.* at 17–21.

146. 459 U.S. 359 (1983).

147. *Id.* at 361–62.

148. *Id.* at 362.

149. *Id.*

150. *Id.*

151. *Id.* at 364, n.2, quoting from *State v. Kane*, 629 S.W. 2d 372, 377 (1982).

152. *North Carolina v. Pearce*, 395 U.S. 711, 717 (1969).

153. *Id.* at 368.

154. *Id.* at 367–68. The majority quoted approvingly from *Albernaz v. United States*, 450 U.S. at 340 for this proposition. In *Albernaz*, the Court labeled the *Blockburger* same offense test as a "rule of statutory construction," reversible upon proof of "contrary legislative intent."

155. *Id.* at 371 (Marshall, J., dissenting).

156. *Id.* at 369 (citations omitted).

157. 471 U.S. 773 (1985).

158. 21 U.S.C. § 848.

159. *Garrett v. United States*, 471 U.S. at 781.

160. *Id.* at 775.

161. *Id.*

162. *Id.* at 775–76.

163. *Id.* at 775.

164. *Id.* at 776.

165. *Id.*

166. *Id.* at 777.

167. Justice O'Connor provided the fifth vote with her concurring opinion. *Id.* at 795–98.

168. *Id.* at 777–95.

169. *Id.* at 778–79.

170. *Id.* at 793–95.

171. *Id.* at 785.

172. Thomas, *supra* note 136 at 25.

173. *Garrett v. United States*, 471 U.S. at 798–99 (O'Connor, J., concurring). Justice O'Connor states in pertinent part: "Any acquittal on a predicate offense would of course bar the Government from later attempting to relitigate issues in a prosecution under § 848." (Citations omitted.)

174. A summary of the facts of the case may be found in *Koon v. United States*, 116 S.Ct. 2035 (1996). *See* also, Akhil Reed Amar & Jonathan Marcus, *Double Jeopardy Law after Rodney King*, 95 COLUM. L. REV. 1 (1995).

175. *Fox v. Ohio*, 46 U.S. (5 How.) 410 (1847); *Moore v. Illinois*, 55 U.S. (14 How.) 13 (1852).

176. *Moore v. Illinois*, 55 U.S. (14 How.) at 21 (McLean, J., dissenting). Justice McLean also dissented in *Fox*.

177. *See, e.g., United States v. Lanza*, 260 U.S. 377 (1922); *Bartkus v. Illinois*, 359 U.S. 121 (1959); *Abbate v. United States*, 359 U.S. 187 (1959).

178. 359 U.S. 121 (1959).

179. 359 U.S. 187 (1959).

180. Amar, *supra* note 174 at 2.

181. 474 U.S. 82 (1985).

182. *Id.* at 83–85.

183. *Id.* at 85.

184. *Id.* at 96–97 (Brennan, J., dissenting).

185. *Id.* at 97.

186. *Id.* at 88 (citations omitted).

187. *Id.* at 88–89.

188. *Id.* at 90 (citations omitted).

189. *Id.* at 87–88.

190. *Id.* at 95 (Brennan, J., dissenting).

191. *Id.* at 84.

192. In *Petite v. United States*, 361 U.S. 529 (1960), the Supreme Court recognized the internal policy in which the federal government limits its authority to prosecute an individual who has been subjected to state prosecution for "substantially the same act or acts," unless an assistant attorney general decides otherwise.

193. ANTHONY G. AMSTERDAM & JEROME BRUNER, MINDING THE LAW (2000).

EPILOGUE

At the beginning of this endeavor, I sought to provide a more comprehensive approach to the three clauses of the Fifth Amendment dealing with the criminal process. My goal was twofold: to educate by pointing to the existence of the provisions in the amendment other than the privilege against self-incrimination; and to point out common threads among the discrete clauses. I hope I have furnished a perspective, both historical and legal, that differs from the dominant academic analysis underlying the Fifth Amendment.

To a large extent, the Supreme Court, as the final interpretive arbiter of the Fifth Amendment, has written the post-ratification "story" of these clauses. Although my "story" has taken issue with the way in which the Court has construed and interpreted these clauses, one can certainly take issue with my interpretation, just as I have with the Court's analysis. I make this startling concession in the epilogue because my thesis is intertwined with the historical perspective that constitutional interpretation is largely a work of "necessary fiction." My fiction, therefore, may differ from the Supreme Court's or other legal academician's narrative.

What has informed my narrative is a pragmatic, real-world, view of the criminal justice system. I do not believe that we can examine the world of criminal justice in an ethereal, strictly theoretical, vacuum. Perhaps more than any other part of the legal system, the criminal process reflects the "rough and tumble" of the streets. Examining such a process from the halls of our "ivory tower" skews and distorts the lens through which the system must be viewed.

My critique of the Court's story stems largely from this viewpoint. For example, my critique of both the law of confessions and the role of the grand jury derive from the cognitive dissonance between the Court's opinions and reality. Similarly, the double jeopardy story has had a checkered, confused, and illogical genesis. Its application to the modern criminal process was bound to result in the morass the Supreme Court has labeled a "Sargasso Sea." Perhaps my expectations are grandiose, given the background of most Supreme Court justices. Few Justices have had meaningful experience or contact with the criminal justice system. Alternatively, few Justices, though lacking in such experience, penetrate beyond the abstruse legal arguments and examine the real-world implications of their lofty rulings.

We have reached a stage, however, exemplified by the Court's interpretation of the *Miranda* doctrine, in which the Court seemingly adheres to precedent while simultaneously decimating it. It would be more intellectually honest if the Justices discarded "old" Warren Court doctrine in favor of the prior regime. We may conclude that the Court's jurisprudence lacks coherence and, to a certain degree, legitimacy, because of this doctrinal abyss.

Finally, both the Court and, by and large, academics have failed to acknowledge the link among the criminal provisions of the Bill of Rights, or the relationship among the clauses of specific amendments. At the risk of sounding procustean, I think it would be a salutary experiment to view the criminal justice system from a holistic rather than an insular perspective. It might broaden our horizons and compel us to look at the criminal process through a different prism.

BIBLIOGRAPHY

Ainsworth, Janet, *In a Different Register: The Pragmatics of Powerlessness in Police Interrogation*, 103 YALE L.J. 259 (1993).

Amar, Akhil Reed. THE BILL OF RIGHTS: CREATION AND RECONSTRUCTION (1998).

Amar, Akhil Reed & Lettow, Renee B., *Fifth Amendment First Principles: The Self-Incrimination Clause*, 93 MICH. L. REV. 857 (1995).

Amar, Akhil Reed & Marcus, Jonathan, *Double Jeopardy Law after Rodney King*, 95 COLUM. L. REV. 1 (1995).

Amar, Akhil Reed, *Double Jeopardy Law Made Simple*, 106 YALE L. J. 1807 (1997).

Amsterdam, Anthony G. & Bruner, Jerome. MINDING THE LAW (2000).

Appleby, Joyce. LIBERALISM AND REPUBLICANISM IN THE HISTORICAL IMAGINATION (1992).

Baker, Liva. MIRANDA: CRIME, LAW AND POLITICS (1983).

Banning, Lance. THE SACRED FIRE OF LIBERTY: JAMES MADISON AND THE FOUNDING OF THE FEDERAL REPUBLIC (1995).

Bailyn, Bernard. THE IDEOLOGICAL ORIGINS OF THE AMERICAN REVOLUTION (1967).

Bailyn, Bernard. THE ORIGINS OF AMERICAN POLITICS (1967).

Ben-Veniste, Richard, *Comparisons Can Be Odious, Mr. Starr*, NAT'L L. J. 21 (Dec. 21, 1998).

Bodenhamer, David J. FAIR TRIAL: RIGHTS OF THE ACCUSED IN AMERICAN HISTORY (1992).

Brooks, Peter. TROUBLING CONFESSIONS: SPEAKING GUILT IN LAW AND LITERATURE (2000).

Cassell, Paul G. & Hyman, Bret S., *Police Interrogation in the 1990s: An Empirical Study of the Effects of* Miranda, 43 U.C.L.A. L. Rev.839 (1996).

Cassell, Paul, *Miranda's Social Costs: An Empirical Assessment*, 99 N.W. U. L. Rev. 387 (1996).

Clark, Leroy D. The Grand Jury (1975).

Collingwood, R. G. The Idea of History (1946).

Dershowitz, Alan & Ely, John Hart, Harris v. New York: *Some Anxious Observations on the Candor and Logic of the Emerging Nixon Majority*, 80 Yale L.J. 1198 (1971).

Dumbauld, Edward. The Bill Of Rights and What It Means Today (1957).

Fogelson, Robert M. Big City Police (1977).

Frankel, Marvin & Naftalis, Gary. The Grand Jury: An Institution on Trial (1977).

Friedland, Martin. Double Jeopardy (1969).

Friedman, Lawrence. Crime and Punishment in American History (1993).

Garcia, Alfredo, *Mental Sanity and Confessions: The Supreme Court's New Version of the Old "Voluntariness" Standard*, 21 Akron L. Rev. 275 (1988).

Garcia, Alfredo. The Sixth Amendment in Modern American Jurisprudence: A Critical Perspective (1992).

Garcia, Alfredo, *Toward an Integrated Vision of Criminal Procedural Rights: A Counter to Judicial and Academic Nihilism*, 77 Marq. L. Rev. 1 (1993).

Gibeaut, John, *Indictment of a System*, 87 A.B.A. Journal 35 (Jan. 2001).

Grano, Joseph D. Confessions, Truth, and the Law (1993).

Grano, Joseph, *Voluntariness, Free Will, and the Law of Confessions*, 65 U.VA. L. Rev. 859 (1979).

Hamilton, Alexander, Madison, James & Jay, John. The Federalist Papers (Clinton Rossiter ed., 1961).

Hancock, Catherine, *Due Process before* Miranda, 70 Tul. L. Rev. 2195 (1996).

Handlin, Oscar. Truth in History (1979).

Handlin, Oscar & Lillian. Liberty and Power, 1600–1760 (1986).

Hemholz, R.H., *Origins of the Privilege against Self-Incrimination: The Role of the European ius Commune*. 65 N.Y.U. L. Rev. 962 (1990).

Hemholz, R.H. et.al. The Privilege against Self-incrimination: Its Origins and Development (1997).

Henning, Peter J., *Prosecutorial Misconduct in Grand Jury Investigations*, 51 S.C. L. Rev. 1 (1999).

Hickok, Eugene W., Jr. (ed.). The Bill of Rights: Original Meaning and Current Understanding (1991).

Jefferson, Thomas. Notes on the State of Virginia (1787) in Jefferson Writings (Merril Peterson ed., 1984).

Johnson, Gail, *False Confessions and Fundamental Fairness: The Need for Electronic Recording of Custodial Interrogations*, 6 B.U. Pub. Int. L.J. 719 (1997).

Kamisar, Yale, *Foreword: From* Miranda *to Section 3501 to Dickerson to . . .* , 99 MICH. L. REV. 879 (2001).

Kamisar, Yale, *What Is an Involuntary Confession: Some Comments on Inbau and Reid's Criminal Interrogation and Confessions*, 17 RUTGERS L. REV. 728 (1963).

Kamisar, Yale, LaFave, Wayne R. & Israel, Jerold H. MODERN CRIMINAL PROCEDURE (8th ed. 1994).

Klein, Susan R. *Identifying and (Re)formulating Prophylactic Rules, Safe Harbors, and Incidental Rights in Constitutional Criminal Procedure*, 99 MICH. L. REV. 1030 (2001).

Kurland, Phillip & Lerner, Ralph (eds). THE FOUNDERS' CONSTITUTION (5 vols. 1987).

LaFave, Wayne R., Israel, Jerold H. & King, Nancy J. CRIMINAL PROCEDURE (3rd. ed. 2000).

Langbein, John H., *The Criminal Trial before the Lawyers*, 45 U.CHI. L. REV. 263 (1978).

Langbein, John H., *The Historical Origins of the Privilege against Self-Incrimination at Common Law*, 92 MICH. L. REV. 1047 (1994).

LaRue, Lewis H. CONSTITUTIONAL LAW AS FICTION: NARRATIVE IN THE RHETORIC OF AUTHORITY (1995).

Leipold, Andrew D., *Why Grand Juries Do Not (and Cannot) Protect the Accused*, 80 CORNELL L. REV. 260 (1995).

Leo, Richard A. *The Impact of* Miranda *Revisited*, 86 J. CRIM. L. & CRIMINOLOGY 621 (1996).

Leo, Richard A. & Ofshe, Richard J., *The Consequences of False Confessions: Deprivations of Liberty and Miscarriages of Justice in the Age of Psychological Interrogation*, 88 J. CRIM. L. & CRIMINOLOGY 429 (1998).

Lessig, Lawrence, *Understanding Changed Readings: Fidelity and Theory*, 47 STAN. L. REV. 395 (1995).

Levy, Leonard, *The Right against Self-Incrimination*, In ENCYLCOPEDIA OF THE AMERICAN CONSTITUTION 1570 (L. Levy, K. Karst, & D. Mahoney, eds., 1986).

Levy, Leonard W. ORIGINS OF THE FIFTH AMENDMENT: THE RIGHT AGAINST SELF-INCRIMINATION (2d ed. 1986).

Lipset, Seymour Martin. AMERICAN EXCEPTIONALISM: A DOUBLE-EDGED SWORD (1996).

Madison, James. NOTES OF DEBATES IN THE FEDERAL CONVENTION OF 1787 (A. Koch ed., 1966).

McKay, Monroe G. *Double Jeopardy: Are the Pieces the Puzzle?* 23 WASHBURN L.J. 1 (1983).

McNair, Michael R.T., *The Early Development of the Privilege against Self-Incrimination*, 10 OXFORD J. LEGAL STUD. 66 (1990).

McNaughton, J. *The Privilege against Self-Incrimination: Its Constitutional*

Affectation, Raison d' Etre and Miscellaneous Implications, 51 J. CRIM. L. CRIMINOLOGY & POLICE SCI. 138 (1960).

Menza, Alexander J., *Witness Immunity: Unconstitutional, Unfair, Unconscionable*, 9 SETON HALL CONST. L. J. 505 (1999).

Moglan, Eben, *Considering Zenger: Partisan Politics and the Legal Profession in Provincial New York*, 94 COLUM. L. REV. 1495 (1994).

Moglan, Eben, *Taking the Fifth: Reconsidering the Origins of the Constitutional Privilege against Self-Incrimination*, 93 MICH L. REV. 1086 (1994).

Moore, Ben Perley (ed.). THE FEDERAL AND STATE CONSTITUTIONS, COLONIAL CHARTERS AND OTHER ORGANIC LAWS OF THE UNITED STATES (1877).

Morgan, Edmund S. AMERICAN SLAVERY, AMERICAN FREEDOM: THE ORDEAL OF COLONIAL VIRGINIA (1975).

Nelson, William E., *History and Neutrality in Constitutional Adjudication*, 72 U. VA. L. REV. 1237 (1986).

Office of Legal Policy, U.S. Dep't of Justice. REPORT TO THE ATTORNEY GENERAL ON THE LAW OF PRE-TRIAL INTERROGATION (1986).

Ofshe, Richard J. & Leo, Richard A., *The Social Psychology of Police Interrogation: The Theory and Classification of True and False Confessions*, 16 STUDIES IN LAW, POLITICS AND SOCIETY (1997).

Ogletree, Charles J., *Are Confessions Really Good for the Soul?* 100 HARV. L. REV. 1826 (1987).

Patterson, James T. GRAND EXPECTATIONS: THE UNITED STATES, 1945–1974 (1996).

Penney, Steven, *Theories of Confession Admissibility: A Historical View*, 25 AM. J. CRIM. L. 309 (1998).

Perry, Michael J. THE CONSTITUTION IN THE COURTS: LAW OR POLITICS? (1994).

Pollock, R. & Maitland, F. THE HISTORY OF THE ENGLISH LAW (2nd ed., (1898).

Rakove, Jack N. (ed.). INTERPRETING THE CONSTITUTION: THE DEBATE OVER ORIGINAL INTENT (1990).

Rakove, Jack N. ORIGINAL MEANINGS: POLITICS AND IDEAS IN THE MAKING OF THE CONSTITUTION (1996).

Reid, John Phillip. THE CONCEPT OF LIBERTY IN THE AGE OF THE AMERICAN REVOLUTION (1988).

Rosenberg, Irene Merker, Withrow v. Williams: *Reconstitutionalizing* Miranda, 30 HOUSTON L. REV. 1684 (1993).

Rossum, Ralph, *Self-Incrimination: The Original Intent*, in THE BILL OF RIGHTS: ORIGINAL MEANING AND CURRENT UNDERSTANDING (Eugene Hickock, Jr., ed., 1991).

Rothman, David J., *Perfecting the Prison*, in THE OXFORD HISTORY OF THE PRISON (Norval Morris & David J. Rothman, eds. 1995).

Russell, William Oldham. RUSSELL ON CRIMES (Reprint ed. 1986).

Schulhofer, Stephen J., Miranda *and Clearance Rates*, 91 N.W. U. L. REV. 278 (1996).

Schulhofer, Stephen J., *Reconsidering* Miranda, 54 U.CHI. L. REV. 435 (1987).

Schulhofer, Stephen J., Miranda*'s Practical Effect: Substantial Benefits and Vanishingly Small Social Costs*, 90 N.W. U. L. REV. 500 (1996).

Schwartz, Bernard. THE BILL OF RIGHTS: A DOCUMENTARY HISTORY (1971).

Schwartz, Bernard. THE GREAT RIGHTS OF MANKIND: A HISTORY OF THE AMERICAN BILL OF RIGHTS (1977).

Schwartz, Helene E., *Demythologizing the Historic Role of the Grand Jury*, 10 AM. CRIM. L. REV. 701 (1972).

Sigler, Jay A. DOUBLE JEOPARDY: THE DEVELOPMENT OF A LEGAL AND SOCIAL POLICY (1969).

Simon, David. HOMICIDE: A YEAR ON THE KILLING STREETS (1991).

Skolnick, Jerome. JUSTICE WITHOUT TRIAL (2d. ed. 1975).

Steele, Walter, Jr., *Right to Counsel at the Grand Jury Stage of Criminal Proceedings*, 36 MISSOURI L. REV. 193 (1971).

Stone, Geoffrey R. *The* Miranda *Doctrine in the Burger Court*, 100 SUP. CT. REV. 99 (1977).

Strong, John W. et. al. MCCORMICK ON EVIDENCE (1992).

Thomas, George C. III, *An Elegant Theory of Double Jeopardy*, 1988 U. ILL. L. REV. 827 (1988).

Thomas, George C. III, DOUBLE JEOPARDY: THE HISTORY, THE LAW (1998).

Thomas, George C. III, *Is* Miranda *a Real World Failure? A Plea for More (and Better) Empirical Evidence*, 43 U.C.L.A. L. REV. 821 (1996).

Thomas, George C. III, *Justice O'Connor's Pragmatic View of Coerced Self-Incrimination*, 13 WOMEN'S RTS. REP. 117 (1991).

Toobin, Jeffrey. A VAST CONSPIRACY (1999).

Tribe, Laurence H. & Dorf, Michael C. ON READING THE CONSTITUTION (1991).

Uviller, Richard. TEMPERED ZEAL (1998).

Uviller, Richard. VIRTUAL JUSTICE (1996).

Walker, Samuel. THE POLICE IN AMERICA: AN INTRODUCTION (1983).

Walker, Samuel. POPULAR JUSTICE: A HISTORY OF AMERICAN CRIMINAL JUSTICE (1980).

Weisberg, Robert, *Criminal Law, Criminology, and the Small World of Legal Scholars*, 63 U. COLO. L. REV. 521 (1992).

Westen, Peter, *Confrontation and Compulsory Process: A Unified Theory of Evidence for Criminal Cases*, 91 HARVARD L. REV. 567 (1978).

Westen, Peter & Drubel, Richard, *Toward a General Theory of Double Jeopardy*, 1978 SUP. CT. REV. 81.

White, Welsh S., *What Is an Involuntary Confession Now*, 50 RUTGERS L. REV. 2001 (1998).

Wigmore, John Henry. EVIDENCE IN TRIALS AT COMMON LAW (McNaughton rev., 1960).

Wollin, David A., *Policing the Police: Should* Miranda *Violations Bear Fruit?* 53 Ohio St. L. J. 805 (1992).

Wood, Gordon S. The Creation of the American Republic, 1776–1787 (1969).

Wood, Gordon S., *Ideology and the Origins of Liberal America*, 44 William & Mary Quarterly 632 (1987).

Wood, Gordon S. The Radicalism of the American Revolution (1992).

Younger, Richard D. The People's Panel: The Grand Jury in the United States (1963).

Zeldin, Theodore. An Intimate History of Humanity (1994).

INDEX

TABLE OF CASES

About the Author

ALFREDO GARCIA is Professor of Law, St. Thomas University, School of Law. In addition to teaching criminal law and procedure, he has served as an Assistant State Attorney in Florida and as a criminal defense attorney at both the state and federal levels. He is the author of *The Sixth Amendment in Modern American Jurisprudence* (Greenwood, 1992) and has published numerous articles in the field of constitutional criminal procedure.

DATE DUE

Demco, Inc. 38-293